Also by James R. Holbrook

Potsdam Mission: Memoir of a U.S. Army Intelligence Officer in Communist East Germany

Moscow
MEMOIR

An American Military Attaché
in the USSR 1979-1981

Second Edition

JAMES R. HOLBROOK

LIEUTENANT COLONEL, U.S. ARMY (RET)

authorHOUSE

AuthorHouse™
1663 Liberty Drive
Bloomington, IN 47403
www.authorhouse.com
Phone: 1 (800) 839-8640

Maps by Dion Good, Cartographer

None of the facts or views presented here are the official views or positions of
the Defense Intelligence Agency or any other U.S. government entity.

Published by AuthorHouse 05/23/2018

ISBN: 978-1-5462-1759-6 (sc)
ISBN: 978-1-5462-1760-2 (hc)
ISBN: 978-1-5462-1758-9 (e)

Library of Congress Control Number: 2017917670

Print information available on the last page.

This book is printed on acid-free paper.

For my Moscow family:

Elaine, Yasha, Tarisa, Misha and Holly

PREFACE

This is a personal memoir. I have attempted to portray my life and work as a Russian specialist and military attaché in the Soviet Union during the Cold War. Despite the fact that most of what I write about my tour in the USSR occurred more than thirty-five years ago, there remain some classified issues I could not cover here. In my efforts to discuss as much as possible, I have pushed as hard as prudence and the law (and U.S. government review boards) allow. This statement, which suggests some of the difficulties of writing about intelligence, is a paraphrase of what Michael Hayden, former Director of both the Central Intelligence Agency and the National Security Agency, wrote in his memoir, *Playing to the Edge.*

Although the USSR dissolved more than twenty-five years ago, current conflicts between the United States and Russia remain. Some are new. I believe a serious lack of mutual understanding persists. Given the present leadership of both countries, it is unlikely real understanding will prevail. Several issues in our relations with today's Russia have taken on Cold War characteristics.

My hope is that this memoir will shed some light on the challenges facing military attachés in hostile environments, as well as some issues in U.S.-Russian relations for both the general reader and the specialist in Russian affairs.

CONTENTS

Part IV: Moscow

ACRONYMS AND ABBREVIATIONS

Acronyms and abbreviations can be difficult to keep straight. I've tried to avoid using them as much as possible. Unfortunately, repeated use of expanded versions would make any text very cumbersome.

CGSC	U.S. Army Command and General Staff College
CIA	Central Intelligence Agency
DAO	Defense Attaché Office
DIA	Defense Intelligence Agency
DOSAAF	Volunteer Society for Cooperation with the Army, Air Force and Navy *(Dobrovolnoye obshchestvo sodeistviya Armii, Aviatsii i Flotu)*
FAO	Foreign Area Officer
GSFG	Group of Soviet Forces, Germany
INTOURIST	Soviet Foreign Tourist Agency
IR	Information Report
JCS	Joint Chiefs of Staff
KOMSOMOL	Communist Youth Organization *(Kommunisticheskii soyuz molodezhi)*
MfS	Ministry for State Security *(Ministerium für Staatssicherheit)* (East German)
MOD	Ministry (Minister) of Defense (Soviet)

NKVD	People's Commissariat of Internal Affairs *(Narodnii kommisariat vnutrennikh del*—a precursor to KGB)
NSA	National Security Agency
ROTC	Reserve Officer Training Corps
SIGINT	Signals Intelligence
SIS	Secret Intelligence Service (British)
STASI	Nickname for East German Secret Police
TWIM	"This Week in Moscow"
UPDK	Directorate for Servicing the Diplomatic Corps *(Upravlenie obsluzhevaniya diplomaticheskogo korpusa)*
USAREUR	United States Army, Europe
USARI	United States Army Russian Institute
USMLM	United States Military Liaison Mission to Commander in Chief, Soviet Forces, Germany
VDNKh	Exhibition of the Economic Achievements of the National Economy *(Vystavka dostizhenii narodnogo khozyaistva)*

RUSSIANS ABOUT RUSSIA...

Two Romes have fallen, but the Third Rome, Moscow, will stand; a fourth is not to be.

Monk Filofei of Pskov, 16th century

Russia cannot be understood with the mind alone.
No ordinary yardstick can span her greatness.
She stands alone, unique.
In Russia, one can only believe.

Fyodor Tyutchev, Russian Poet, 1866

In truth, what is it that has essentially upheld Russian statehood? Not only primarily, but exclusively, the army. Who created the Russian empire, transforming the semi-Asiatic Muscovite tsardom into the most influential, most dominant, grandest European power? Only the power of the bayonet. The world bowed not to our culture, nor to our bureaucratized church, nor to our wealth and prosperity. It bowed to our might.

Sergei Witte, Prime Minister of Russia, 1903-1906

We were a military nation; 70 percent or so of the economy was, in one way or another, tied to the military. We need a powerful military... People respect us as long as we're strong, but if we become weak no "new way of thinking" will convince anyone of anything.

Unidentified high-ranking Soviet about the USSR
(Quoted by Svetlana Alexievich, *Secondhand Time*)

PART I: ARRIVAL IN MOSCOW

MY FIRST CHALLENGE

I approached a Soviet general who had just stepped into Spaso House.

"Good evening, *Gospodin* (Mister) general. I'm Major Holbrook, Assistant Army Attaché. I'll escort you through the reception line to our hosts."

One would expect that once I introduced myself, the Soviet guest would offer his name also. Not so simple. I had to ask him for it. The general mumbled his name in such a way that I had no idea what it was. Soviet officers didn't wear nametags like we did in the U.S. Armed Forces. I was afraid to ask him again.

This was my first diplomatic function as an attaché—the 1979 U.S. Armed Forces Day reception. It was being held in the ballroom at Spaso House, residence of U.S. Ambassador Malcolm Toon. Spaso House had been the official residence of all American ambassadors since U.S. recognition of the USSR in 1933. It was here in this ballroom, at the very first U.S. Embassy Christmas party in 1934, that three seals borrowed from the Moscow zoo flopped among Ambassador William Bullitt's guests. That was topped the following year during a Spaso House party when a "un-house-broken" baby bear ruined a high-ranking Red Army officer's uniform. Ambassador Bullitt's parties at Spaso became legendary. One memorable party, which the famous Russian author, Mikhail Bulgakov attended, became his inspiration for the "Grand Ball of Satan" in *Master and Margarita*. At our reception this evening, however, a much more formal and sedate atmosphere prevailed.

We American military attachés were all decked out in our dress uniforms, replete with ribbons on our chests and an elaborate braid looped around our left shoulders. Our task for the evening was to meet and escort each Soviet officer who appeared in the foyer. It seemed pretty simple and straightforward.

The Defense Attaché, U.S. Major General Richard Larkin, and Ambassador Toon stood with their wives at the end of the reception line. When the Soviet general and I approached General Larkin, I selected a name that was close to what I thought I heard. The Soviet general didn't object.

I wasn't completely surprised the Soviet military treated their names as some sort of state secret. I remembered similar instances when I was stationed in East Germany. There, on separate occasions, some officers would occasionally appear in the uniform of a different service! I admit I wasn't entirely innocent of this kind of "disinformation." Like the other U.S. Army attachés, I wore General Staff insignia on my lapel instead of Military Intelligence. (In Vietnam I had worn first Signal Corps and then Infantry brass.)

I guess I was just irritated. I had hoped our relationship with the Soviet military wouldn't be as adversarial as it was in East Germany. The Soviets and Americans were supposed to be pretending to be on friendly terms. Besides, since this was my first official function as an attaché, I wanted to think I had more control over my task for the evening. I should have known better. Dealing with the Soviet military here in the USSR was always going to be a challenge. But I couldn't help feel I wasn't doing my job right if I couldn't even get a name straight.

When the second Soviet general I escorted gave me his name, I listened very closely. But again I wasn't sure. As we approached General Larkin, I got up the courage to ask him to repeat his name, only to hear him give me what was an entirely different one.

My next turn to escort coincided with the appearance of a short, balding one-star general. He sported the usual little paunch that appeared on many Soviet officers once they reached field-grade rank. (Soviet General Ivanovsky once remarked in East Germany that American sergeants were fat, but the officers were trim. "In our army, it's just the opposite," he said.) As my new general came through the door, I stepped up, addressed him in Russian and extended my hand.

"Welcome to Spaso House, *Gospodin* General. I'm Major Holbrook, Assistant Army Attaché." The general smiled and shook my hand.

"*Ochen priyatno* (Pleased to meet you)," he said. But he didn't give me his name.

"May I have your name, sir, so I can introduce you to General Larkin?"

He stopped and looked at me with obvious surprise.

"You know who I am."

I didn't know who he was, but told myself not to panic. As we moved to catch up with the others in line, I said again, "No. I'm sorry, general, but we've never met."

He repeated, this time a little exasperated, "You know who I am."

"General, forgive me. But…but I arrived in Moscow only recently. This is my first diplomatic function."

"You know who I am," he insisted.

I stopped and looked at him very closely. All I saw was that he had a slight smile on his face.

"Leonov!" he blurted out.

Oh no! Suddenly a light bulb came on. The name I *did* recognize. Could it be? Was this the cosmonaut who in 1965 was the first man to walk in space? Was this the cosmonaut who commanded the Soyuz spaceship during the linkup with our American Apollo in 1975, only four years ago? My memory of that historic event didn't include the faces of the cosmonauts. Not even of the American astronauts. Now what do I do?

"Not… not *the* Leonov?" I sputtered.

"The very same." Now he was flashing a broad smile. What an idiot he must have taken me for. Alexei Leonov was a very famous Soviet cosmonaut, taking a back seat in celebrity only to Yuri Gagarin, the first man in space, and perhaps Valentina Tereshkova, the first woman in space. I would have recognized Gagarin or Tereshkova, but I drew a complete blank on Leonov. This little guy knew he was famous and apparently was sure an American military attaché would recognize him.

"Oh, how dumb of me, *Gospodin* General. Of course. Now I recognize you."

All this time, we had been shuffling along in the reception line toward where the Ambassador and the Defense Attaché were standing. When we reached them, I introduced my guest.

"General Larkin, allow me to present the famous cosmonaut who piloted the Apollo-Soyuz spaceship, General-Major Leonov."

"And the first man to walk in space," said General Larkin.

General Leonov glanced at me, smiled again and nodded. Then he turned to shake hands with General Larkin. I returned to the queue of attachés near the door of Spaso house. I wondered how many more famous Soviets I would have to deal with that night.

I met General Leonov several more times at Spaso House during my tour in Moscow. Each time he saw me, he would grin and ask, "You remember who I am?"

Welcome to Cold War Moscow

My heart started to beat faster the minute we landed. What kind of reception would I have here at the airport? Soviet authorities had approved my assignment to the American Embassy as a military attaché. They knew, of course, I was an intelligence officer who had served with our U.S. Military Liaison Mission (USMLM) attached to their headquarters in East Germany. They surely had a record of my earlier visits to the USSR. Even though I had a diplomatic passport, I knew the Soviets didn't always allow diplomatic protocol to interfere with their actions. For example, they often violated the diplomatic extraterritoriality of our vehicles in East Germany.

KGB border guards with AK-47 assault rifles slung over their shoulders stood at the bottom of the Pan Am 707's stairs as I descended to the tarmac of Moscow's Sheremetyevo Airport on April 25, 1979. They glared at the passengers, as if searching for someone. The expressions on their faces suggested they believed us all to be dangerous intruders.

I tried not to make eye contact with the guards. When I did sneak a peek at those armed protectors of their homeland, I couldn't be sure they were necessarily looking at me. Would they report that I had arrived? Years later I saw a fragment of my East German secret police dossier with a description of me as "freckled face, Asiatic features, lightly hooked nose and limps to the right." If the Soviet guards were looking for someone who fit that description, they would have missed me. I was a normal short Caucasian with no freckles, a nose of no particular prominence, and I didn't limp. Ears that stuck out were my only prominent feature.

I retrieved my suitcase from a stack of luggage beside the plane, then followed the rest of the passengers to a bus that shuttled us to the roundhouse-style terminal.

The airport was not yet twenty years old. The smell of cigarette smoke, the trash on the floor and the chill in the air added to the unease I felt. The airport must have been an embarrassment to Soviet authorities. I heard they were building a new one nearby (or more correctly, the Germans were building one for them) in preparation for the 1980 Moscow Summer Olympics. Here, in what would later be called Sheremetyevo I, whole banks of overhead lighting were turned off, suggesting the gloom was intentional. For me, and presumably for many others, the dreary atmosphere created a sense of foreboding. It was as if the airport was saying: "You are entering a dark country that will try to keep you guessing and on the defensive during your entire stay."

Even though I carried diplomatic credentials, I approached the passport control booth with trepidation. Would there be any kind of delay? What kind of questions could I expect? I handed over my passport and visa to a taciturn KGB guard in a military uniform with blue shoulder boards. The counter obscured the surface on which he was working, so I couldn't tell what he was doing. He stared at me for a few seconds, then down at my passport. He said nothing, asked nothing. There was no "Welcome to the Soviet Union." I stood there, trying to act nonchalant. It took several minutes before I heard the 'clack-clack' of his stamp on my passport.

As a diplomat, I passed unchecked through customs. In the public reception area a large crowd of men jostled each other, calling out fares to downtown Moscow, eighteen miles away. I remained tense until I cleared passport control and connected with my American Embassy driver. Toward the front of the mob I caught sight of a short, middle-aged Russian holding a sign with my name on it. That had to be a driver from the Embassy. When I approached him and identified myself, he smiled and welcomed me in Russian, "*Dobro pozhalovat v Moskvu*" (Welcome to Moscow)," he said. He took my suitcase and we headed for the car parked nearby. Only then did I start to relax.

We turned onto the M10 Highway and headed for the city. I began to contemplate the moment—the fact that I was finally in Russia, no longer as a visitor, as I had been twice before. I was now a diplomat, a member of the American Embassy staff. I was about to become a two-year resident. I felt a mixture of fear and excitement that I had finally come to live and work in the city and country that had occupied most of my attention for the last eighteen years. As an American military intelligence officer, an assistant military attaché, I would be participating directly in the "battles" of the Cold War, while living among the potential enemy.

I had always believed that eventually the Army would assign me as an attaché in Moscow. I almost went on very short notice in 1972. My former neighbor at West Point, then Lieutenant Colonel Bill Odom, had written me from Moscow and suggested ways I might be able to take a break from the Academy and come to Moscow to replace an assistant attaché who had departed early. That would have been great because it would have given me the opportunity to work with the legendary "General Sam"— Sam Wilson—who was the Defense Attaché at the time. That didn't pan out, but I knew my time was coming. I hoped my two years at the Army Language School, academic degrees in Russian from American and Georgetown Universities, as well as my teaching Russian at The American University, West Point and the National Security Agency (NSA) at Fort Meade, Maryland, had prepared me with the historical, cultural and linguistic background necessary to move smoothly in the Soviet milieu.

When I look back at my Army career, I think of myself as a classic Cold War veteran. I joined the Army in 1961, the year the Berlin Wall went up and retired in 1989, the year it came down. Earlier in my career, I served in a wide variety of intelligence positions. As an enlisted man in West Berlin, I monitored Soviet military conversations in East Germany. Later, while at USMLM, I traveled throughout East Germany collecting intelligence information against the twenty-some Soviet line divisions and other military units. I had experience dealing with the soldiers and officers of the Soviet Army. Working as a political-military analyst in the Pentagon and U.S. Army Europe (USAREUR) Headquarters in Heidelberg gave me an appreciation for the military's strategic role in Soviet society. In short, I spent almost all my professional life engaged with the Soviet Union on the American side of the Cold War.

As we passed the anti-tank monument in Khimki that marked the closest the Germans had advanced toward Moscow during WWII, the city skyline began to emerge in the distance. Moscow's church domes and spires, as well as the tall Ivan the Great Tower inside the Kremlin, contributed greatly to the storybook-like image of the city many Western travelers would report. But Moscow and the Kremlin also embodied the nerve center of Soviet power and culture. That some writers referred to Moscow as a "large village" appealed to me, a boy raised in rural Wisconsin. This "village," however, was the capital city of our most powerful adversary.

What would it be like for my family and me to live here? (My wife, Elaine, and our three children would arrive after the end of the school year in Virginia.) What Soviet cities and towns would I get to see? How much U.S.-Soviet history would I encounter? How would I get along with my fellow attachés and the foreign attachés in Moscow? What would the diplomatic social life be like? Would I get to know many, for that matter any, Soviet citizens? What obstacles would I run into while collecting military information during travel in the USSR and in Moscow itself? I knew that dealing with the KGB would be quite different from my experiences with the East German *Stasi* while at USMLM.

The question about how information collection would go was particularly important for me. Curtailment from the USMLM assignment in 1978 to work in a special study group in the Pentagon meant I had to leave Potsdam/Berlin just when I was getting to know my way around. I was anxious to get back to work in my primary specialty.

I was further motivated to become a successful information collector by the fact that, at the last minute, I failed to get an appointment as a permanent professor at West Point. This meant I would not become an Army scholar and that my sense of professional self-fulfillment would have to come from intelligence work.

Challenges and adventures in Moscow would come in all forms. My reactions to those challenges would tell me a little something about myself. Many of the adventures would "come with the territory" of being a military attaché in a hostile country. Others I would create myself.

THE AMERICAN EMBASSY

Microwaves bombarding the upper floors, "spy dust" possibly on our clothes and bodies, listening devices—"bugs"—in our walls and typewriters, religious refugees from Siberia living in the basement, and over 200 KGB informers working among us. Those are some of the unique aspects of the American Embassy in Moscow in 1979-1981.

Since the early 1960s, the Soviets had been beaming high levels of microwave radiation at the embassy from across the street. They were aimed at the sixth through tenth floors—the ambassador's office, and the offices where Central Intelligence Agency (CIA) officers, military attachés and NSA technicians worked. U.S. officials believed the purpose of the microwaves was either to charge the batteries of Soviet listening devices or to jam our own devices within the embassy.

Malcolm Toon, at the time director of the State Department's Soviet Desk (and now, in 1979, our ambassador), tried to get the Department to inform employees in Moscow about the microwaving. However, according to American journalist Ronald Kessler's book, *Moscow Station*, the ambassador at the time, Llewelyn Thompson, said, "Telling the employees would mean that the embassy would have to complain to the Soviets about the bombardment. He did not want to ruffle their feathers..."

I found one bizarre report in Richard Deacon's *The Israeli Secret Service*. According to him, the Rumanians reported the Russians were experimenting with microwaves used to kill frogs. Israeli experts suggested Soviet scientists were probably experimenting with the development of a system for "disorienting or disrupting the behavior of individuals, even perhaps as an aid to interrogation." These Israeli scientists wondered whether there was a possibility the Russian use of microwaves "could be so controlled and adapted to put thoughts into the human mind!" That sounded to me like something out of a science fiction novel.

By the time I arrived in Moscow, the embassy had installed wire mesh window guards on the upper floors of the building that reportedly deflected 90 percent of the microwaves.

In addition to the microwaves, at some point while I was there, the Soviets began sprinkling a chemical in the embassy, on employees, their vehicles and, reportedly, even in our apartments. According to Pete Earley's book *Confessions of a Spy*, Soviet defector Vitalii Yurchenko told our government about the spy dust in 1985. Vasilii Mitrokhin, another KGB defector, credits KGB officer Aleksandr Cherepanov for disclosing the "spy dust." Cherepanov reportedly gave the U.S. Embassy supporting documents, which for one reason or another were then turned over to the Soviet government. Cherepanov was then arrested and sentenced to death. According to Yurchenko, the spy dust was a "chemical, which the KGB squirted inside cars used by employees at the U.S. Embassy. The chemical was invisible to the naked eye, but could be seen through special glasses. The KGB looked for traces of it on the skin and clothing of Russians whom they suspected of having come in contact with CIA officers."

In a 1985 letter to the embassy's military staff, the Defense Intelligence Agency's (DIA) Director of Attaché Affairs wrote, "This activity occurred sporadically in the 1970s, was evidently discontinued after 1982, and began again in 1985." By 1985, this so-called "invisible spy dust" was apparent enough that the embassy made an official complaint to the Soviet government. U.S. Army Lieutenant Colonel Roy Peterson, a former attaché, writes in his book *American Attaché in the Moscow Maelstrom*, of having the chemical all over his car in 1985. Although it may have been used during my time in Moscow, I was unaware of it.

Whether or not the microwaves or "spy dust" caused health issues for embassy employees was problematic. Studies by Johns Hopkins

University and the Environmental Protection Agency concluded neither the microwaves nor the "spy dust" posed any real threats to the health of embassy employees. Soviet KGB General Rem Krasilnikov, responsible for targeting Americans in Moscow, declared in his memoir, *Ghosts from Chaikovsky Street,* that reports of embassy microwaving and Soviets using dangerous chemicals for the "spy dust" were "lies." He swore the KGB never did anything to harm the health of embassy employees.

The U.S. health studies and the words of a KGB general still left some of us concerned. Former ambassadors Llewellyn Thompson and Charles Bohlen died of cancer in 1972 and 1974, respectively. In the 1970s, at USMLM in Potsdam/Berlin, we wondered if the Soviets had placed dangerous intelligence-gathering equipment under the Glienicke Bridge over which we always crossed into East Germany. On the other hand, I can't imagine what they could have collected from our vehicles when we crossed the bridge. Anything of intelligence value was written or, on the return trip, stored on audiocassettes.

Years later I learned eleven former USMLM members died from cancer. At least six more were either struggling with the disease or had contracted cancer but were later cured. I was among the latter. In 2007, doctors found a non-Hodgkin's Lymphoma in my spleen. Since its removal, I've had no recurrences. Whether there was a connection between the microwaving and the cancer is uncertain. I served both at USMLM and at the Embassy during the years in question. The Veterans Administration attributed my cancer to Agent Orange, a defoliant used in Vietnam.

Around the embassy, some people actually joked about the microwaves. The Marine House Bar had t-shirts printed with "Marine House Bar: The Only Radiated [sic] Bar in the World." One compliment for women working at the embassy was "You look positively radiant." Kessler recounts in *Moscow Station* that Ambassador Toon "kept a cartoon in his den showing his family having dinner. The chef comes in and says 'I've got good news and bad news. The good news is that they've turned off the radiation. The bad news is I had the roast in the window.'"

The Soviets managed another major penetration of embassy security with electromagnetic bugs placed in our IBM typewriters. The U.S. discovered this only in 1984, but the operation had been going on since 1976. These bugs transmitted the contents of documents typed at the embassy to microphones operated by the KGB. Whether any of my reports were among the Soviet harvest of routine and highly classified documents, I'll never know. (See Sharon Maneki, *Learning from the Enemy: The Gunman Project.*)

Listening devices were nothing new at the embassy. In addition to the famous bug in the American eagle carving that was presented to Ambassador Averell Harriman by Soviet school children in 1946, both our old and new embassies were bugged.

The embassy I worked in had been previously an office and apartment building. During the process of preparing it for American occupancy in 1952, the Soviets installed listening devices in the walls. In 1979, the cornerstone for a new embassy was laid, but bugs in the walls made from pre-cast concrete manufactured in Soviet factories once again provoked protests from the U.S. government. This led to millions of dollars spent on deconstructing parts of the new embassy and rebuilding it with American workers and materials. To counter this Soviet surreptitious surveillance, the U.S. built a couple of what we called "Bubble" rooms—specially designed containers inside embassy rooms that were believed to be bug-proof. For classified or particularly sensitive discussions, embassy personnel, including families with domestic conflicts, used these Bubble rooms.

Soviet defector, Yuri Nosenko, a former KGB officer who worked in the Second Directorate responsible for recruiting Americans, identified the locations of 44 microphones in the old embassy walls. Much later, during the first years of the Russian government after the demise of the USSR, the new KGB Chairman, Vadim Bakatin, gave the U.S. the blueprints of all the bugs the Soviets had placed in the new embassy building.

In the interests of fairness, I should point out that such spying shenanigans were a two-way street. A few years after my tour of duty at the American Embassy, the U.S. Government reportedly built a tunnel under the new Soviet Embassy in Washington. Its purpose was to eavesdrop on internal embassy communications. FBI traitor Robert Hanssen divulged the existence of that tunnel to the Soviets.

During my Moscow years, "The Siberian Seven"—Pentecostal refugees—lived in the embassy basement. In June 1978, seven members of two Siberian families entered the embassy. When they heard that the Soviets stopped another member of their group at the embassy entrance and beat him, they requested asylum. The U.S. granted their request. They lived in the embassy until July 1983, at which time the Soviet government allowed them to leave the USSR.

Another feature of our embassy was the hiring of local Soviet employees. Given the circumstances of the Cold War and KGB efforts to gather information on embassy personnel, this was particularly unsettling for us. At one point there were 206 Soviet employees working for the U.S. Embassy in Moscow, while the number of American staff was only 191. According to Kessler, our Leningrad Consulate had 34 Soviet workers and 26 Americans.

Hiring of local nationals, however, was not unique to our embassy in Moscow. According to the *New York Times*, at one point there were 15,327 foreign nationals at our embassies around the world, working for 10,766 Americans. For example, in Japan there were 407 local employees and 269 Americans and in France 583 local employees for 291 Americans. In Poland there were 119 locals and 52 Americans. American posts in China employed 336 locals and 155 Americans. There were no fulltime U.S. local employees at the Soviet embassy in Washington, DC.

The KGB-controlled UPDK (*Upravlenie obsluzhivaniya diplomaticheskogo korpusa*-Directorate for Service to the Diplomatic Corps) provided the embassy with Soviet employees as maintenance and administrative personnel, as well as maids in American apartments. Soviets serviced and chauffeured our embassy vehicles, typed our correspondence with Soviet entities, made transportation and accommodation arrangements for us when we traveled, reserved seats and acquired tickets for us to attend cultural events around the city, made reservations at restaurants, and even operated our embassy telephone switchboard. In addition to the Soviets working in the embassy and our homes, the KGB used thousands of cooperative informers around the city: hotel registration clerks, restaurant managers, taxi drivers, (most) Intourist guides, and, of course, the police (militiamen), who guarded the embassies and private residences. This is why Harry Rositzke wrote in his *The KGB: The Eyes of Russia* that "The KGB virtually own[ed] Moscow."

Four Soviet women worked in the embassy administrative office. Several writers have referred to one as being a KGB colonel. These four women were privy to all embassy travel, official correspondence with Soviet entities. They knew who went to which restaurants and cultural events. The U.S. Marine Security Guard detachment believed they had a KGB colonel as their cook. In my view, it made no difference what KGB ranks the Soviet employees held. They were all informers and probably gathered some important information for their sponsors. Nonetheless, I agreed with most Moscow diplomats who believed that, unsettling or not, we would have been severely hampered without those Soviet employees. Soviet society was a connection-and status-based society. Even Soviet citizens could barely get anything done without paying bribes or knowing someone who had "*blat*" (pull). Since our Soviet employees worked also for the KGB, they had the access and connections to all Moscow entities and could get things done. It appears having Soviets work for us was a necessary evil.

The United States didn't give formal diplomatic recognition to the Soviet regime until 1933. Our embassy in Imperial Russia had been in Petrograd (named St. Petersburg until WWI, renamed Petrograd during that war, renamed Leningrad since 1924, the year of Lenin's death, and, finally, returned to its original name—St. Petersburg—after the collapse of the USSR in 1991). In 1918, Lenin moved the Soviet capital back to Moscow. After U.S. recognition of the Soviet Union, our first embassy operations were conducted from various buildings near the center of the city, occasionally including Spaso House, the ambassador's residence. In 1941, due to the German attack on the USSR and the threat to Moscow, our embassy moved temporarily south to an old schoolhouse in the city of Kuibyshev.

Our current embassy building, into which the Americans moved in 1953, was a 10-story mustard-colored building on the Chaikovsky Street portion of the Garden Ring Road. The Ring Road was, and remains, a major thoroughfare that intersects the radials emanating from the Kremlin. (Chaikovsky Street is now Novinsky Bulvar. I have no idea why they changed the street's name. Chaikovsky had nothing to do with the Communists.)

The Defense Attaché Office (DAO) was one among several sections of the embassy staff. Others included Political, Economic Affairs, Public Affairs, Consular Services and Cultural Affairs. Several other federal agencies had representation at the embassy. In fact, of all the U.S. employees at the embassy, only about one-third were from the State Department.

According to the Vienna Convention on Diplomatic Relations of 18 April 1961, military attachés became bonafide members of U.S. embassy staffs and enjoyed, together with their families, full diplomatic immunity.

In 1853, Neill Brown, the American Minister to Russia expressed his view that a minister [ambassador] to Russia "ought to be a military man because the government of Russia is a military government. The military is the predominant taste of all, from the emperor to the peasant." He believed the education and accomplishments of Russian officers rendered them "an interesting society" whose "acquaintance would be valuable." As the reader will see, such "acquaintances" were not to be for us.

During the early part of, and immediately after, the Second World War, the U.S. sent three professional military men to Moscow as ambassadors: Admiral William Standley (1942-1943), General Walter Bedell Smith (1946-1948), and Admiral Alan Kirk (1949-1951). Standley oversaw massive amounts of military equipment sent during Lend-Lease (Major General John Deane's Military Mission led this effort). During General Smith's term as ambassador, things went poorly, as Soviet-backed governments became solidified in Eastern Europe. (Smith went on to become Director of the CIA.) Events became even more dramatic during Admiral Kirk's tour as ambassador. In addition to the start of the Korean War, the Soviets blockaded Berlin.

During my tour of duty, we had two ambassadors. Malcom Toon became the American ambassador in 1976 and was still serving when I arrived. Thomas Watson, Jr. later replaced him. Toon was an "old Russian hand" who had served at the embassy earlier. Watson was the son of IBM founder Thomas Watson and a close friend of President Carter. As a captain in the Army Air Corps, Ambassador Watson had ferried Lend-Lease aircraft from Alaska to Siberia during WWII. The appointment of professional diplomats versus political friends of the President has always caused some controversy. Although it's true that professionals know their host countries better than political appointees, what the host country usually wants as an ambassador is someone who has the ear of the American President.

Ambassador Watson departed Moscow just ahead of me. In his place, Jack Matlock presided as Charge d'Affairs. He later returned to Moscow as ambassador (1987-91) and was present during the turbulent, historic *perestroika* and *glasnost* years—the last years of the Soviet Union.

MILITARY ATTACHÉS

It is impossible to conceive a more difficult assignment than that of a Military or Naval Attaché in Russia, nor one that promises less chance of success. The easiest way for Soviet officials to avoid giving our attachés information was to avoid seeing them.

Major General John Deane, *The Strange Alliance*

How in the world could the Soviets have known what I was doing in the Pentagon several months earlier? Or was it just a coincidence that during my first official meeting at the Ministry of Defense, they would bring up the subject of senior officer exchanges between our countries' militaries? A year earlier, I had been the Army action officer for a trip to the USSR by some U.S. generals.

Two days after my arrival, I made my introductory attaché accreditation visit, together with my boss, the Army Attaché, to the Ministry's Foreign Liaison Office. Although the Armed Forces Day reception at Spaso House described earlier was the first social function for me, my first official encounter with the Soviet military in Moscow was this visit. Shortly after the formal pleasantries, the Navy captain who received us sprang an issue on us that had nothing to do with my accreditation. He began to talk about the failure of the U.S. military to send a delegation of senior officers on a visit to the USSR.

"The relationship between the Soviet and U.S. militaries has cooled considerably," he said. "The reason has been U.S. refusal to accept the Soviet invitation for senior U.S. Army officers to visit the USSR. The Soviet Union is waiting for the U.S. response to this invitation." At this point the captain switched to English and said, "As you Americans would say, the ball is in your court."

As the new kid on the block I felt I should be "seen and not heard." It became obvious to me that my colonel had no idea whatsoever about my involvement in Washington with the senior officer exchange. He probably had no idea at all that the exchange was being considered. I don't remember the details of what he wrote about the meeting. If I remember correctly, what he said at the end, however, was, "It appears obvious that according to the Soviets, the best way to improve relationships is to agree to a senior officers' exchange."

Two years earlier, in 1977, I was very involved in a visit to USAREUR by the Soviet CINC of Soviet Forces in East Germany, General of the Army Evgenii Ivanovsky. During preparations for this visit, I briefed and advised our CINC, General George Blanchard, and was in charge of interpreter support.

Based partly on that experience, in the summer of 1978 (almost a year before this meeting at the Ministry), I was selected to be the Department of the Army action officer in preparing for several U.S. generals to make a visit to the Soviet Union. The planned visit was called off when Anatoly Shcharansky, whom the Soviets arrested in 1977 on charges of spying for the United States, was brought to trial in July 1978 in Moscow.

During research for this memoir, I found a formerly secret memorandum, dated 10 July 1978, from Zbigniew Brzezinski to President Carter. In it Brzezinski recommends actions to take in response to the Shcharansky trial. He writes:

> Presently we are exchanging proposals with the Soviets on military visits, which could lead to six American Army general officers traveling to the USSR this summer. You could direct that these efforts be stopped or put in abeyance for the present. State and Defense prefer to proceed… However, <u>at this time</u>, [underscore is Brzezinski's] to go ahead (and some visits would

start within a few weeks), would involve the wrong symbolism here and abroad.

In short, Shcharansky's trial in Moscow torpedoed the projected visits. I was relieved of that task in the Pentagon and began preparing for the Armed Forces Staff College.

I wasn't surprised the Soviet captain brought up a topic unrelated to my accreditation. I had learned at USMLM the Soviets were always trying to catch us off guard. When we went to official meetings, I would almost always see an unopened folder on the Soviet host's desk. When the planned business was completed, the Soviet officer would open the folder and bring up a new subject. (Later, whenever I prepped our new Defense Attaché for meetings with the Soviets at MOD, I reminded him the Soviets would likely bring up a topic that might be "off the wall.")

Even though I had been forewarned, I was in for a shock about what we had to face as attachés in the USSR. Compared to the freedom of movement and operations at USMLM, the information collection environment in the Soviet Union was very discouraging. At USMLM we had dealt with the Soviet military up close, traveled about East Germany, socialized with Soviet officers and observed Soviet units in training. We photographed almost all their combat equipment. Except for some permanent restricted areas, we traveled anywhere we wanted in East Germany without seeking Soviet Army permission.

At USMLM, we conducted our operations without concern for East German authorities. The 1947 Huebner-Malinin agreement with the USSR to exchange military liaison missions was one between two WWII victors. We were considered part of the post-war Occupation Forces in a Germany that had lost the war. When we so chose, we could ignore or "shake" surveillance by the East German Secret Police (*Ministerium für Staatssicherheit* (MfS), commonly known as the *Stasi*). As a result of this aggressive collection, we almost always returned to our operational headquarters in West Berlin with something of significance, be it Soviet documents, pieces of abandoned equipment, or photos of Soviet hardware and of their units in training.

As I indicated, the severely restricted collection environment in the USSR was not a complete surprise. I had talked to former attachés and, on my way to Moscow, I stopped at West Point to visit Colonel Bill Odom who had been my neighbor when I taught there. Colonel Odom had served both at USMLM and at the Embassy in Moscow. He warned that after serving at USMLM, an officer might have a tendency to get reckless in the USSR. If so, he would most certainly run afoul of the KGB and the Soviet Ministry of Defense (MOD). This could lead to being declared *persona non grata*—'not-acceptable'—and forced to leave the USSR. He reminded me, that attachés were on Soviet territory and almost completely under "their" control. "Unlike the USMLM attitude of disregard for the East German *Stasi*," he cautioned, "attachés should not play games with KGB surveillance."

In 1979-81, the Moscow DAO was the largest in any U.S. Embassy in the world and the largest among other foreign embassies in the Soviet capital. In Moscow, among the 141 accredited military attachés representing 50 countries, the largest contingents were: 14 American, 12 Indian, 8 Iraqi, 7 each French and British. All other countries had five or less; nine countries had only one. General officers or their equivalents represented the United States, Poland, Hungary, Peoples Republic of China, Great Britain, France and Germany. Our senior American attaché position—Defense Attaché —rotated among the Air Force, Army and Navy.

The DAO included personnel from all four military services. There were three levels of officers. A flag or general officer headed the office as the Defense Attaché. The Defense Attachés during my time were Major General Richard Larkin and Rear Admiral William Sizemore. The next level consisted of three "principal" attachés —an Army and Air Force full colonel and a Navy captain. The rest of the officers were "assistant attachés" —lieutenant colonels, majors and captains from the Army and Air Force, lieutenant commanders and lieutenants from the Navy, and one U.S. Marine lieutenant colonel. Additionally, we had one Army chief warrant officer, some civilians, and several enlisted men from all the military services.

I, like the other Army attachés in the DAO, was a Foreign Area

Officer (FAO). The Russian FAO program evolved after WWII—first as Det[achment] R, then FAST (Foreign Area Specialty Training) and, finally, FAO.

Our Army FAOs came from all branches, for example, infantry, armor, artillery, and military intelligence. Each had specialized foreign language and regional training needed to perform security assistance to foreign countries, strategic and operational planning at various Army levels, and as military attachés at American embassies.

The Army developed similar programs for other geographic areas of the world. The role of the FAO, especially in U.S. Ground Forces, has become more critical as the nature of warfare has evolved into more political and civil operations in those countries where our forces find themselves today. For example, the Army now trains FAOs for the Middle East and Southwest Asia on how to interact with local populations and powerful regional leaders. According to news reports, these FAOs have made significant contributions to the missions of our diplomats and commanders in Iraq and Afghanistan. The concept of interaction with local leaders and populations in the Soviet Union during the Cold War, however, was both alien and irrelevant. Soviet and Eastern European FAOs were trained primarily as subject-matter experts in military affairs. Today a special exhibit of FAO history and accomplishments is displayed in a corridor of the Pentagon.

As part of FAO training, officers traveled for a year in their target country. Since, for the most part, travel was not possible in the Soviet Union, Russian FAOs attended a special course at the U.S. Army Russian Institute (USARI) in Garmisch, Germany. After language training and civilian graduate school in subjects similar to Russian Area Studies, officers attended USARI for a two-year course in language, economics, and culture of the Soviet Union. The Institute taught all courses in Russian. The school was originally in Oberammergau, then Regensburg, then back to Oberammergau, Germany. Its location during my years in the Army was Garmisch-Partenkirchen in Bavaria.

Foreign area programs in the other U.S. military services are much younger; the Air Force, Navy and Marine Corps have now developed this career field for selected officers. In fact, since 2009, the Office of the Secretary of Defense manages a joint FAO program.

I became a FAO shortly after I received a direct commission to first-lieutenant as a military intelligence officer. Since I already had a master's degree in Russian, six years experience as an enlisted signals intelligence (SIGINT) collector/transcriber, spoke Russian, and had traveled in the USSR twice as a tourist, the Army saw no need for me to study further in Garmisch.

Lieutenant Colonel Tom Spencer (a USARI graduate) and I arrived in Moscow as assistant army attachés in the spring of 1979. Both of us had served at USMLM, one after the other. We underwent attaché training together in the Washington, DC, area just prior to departing for the Soviet Union.

Language proficiency in the DAO was uneven, especially among some of the non-Army attachés. The U.S. has too often placed people— both civilian and military—with little or no language proficiency in positions that required language fluency. For example, when a soldier from the Soviet Army fighting in Afghanistan walked into our Kabul embassy in 1980, there was no one there proficient in Russian. Our Moscow Embassy sent a civilian Russian speaker to Kabul to talk with the soldier.

There was even a time when foreign language proficiency for attachés was viewed as having doubtful value. In 1923, Brigadier General Naylor, Chief of Army Intelligence, told an Army War College class that whether an attaché should be able to speak the language of his host-country was "open to question." The general feared an attaché fluent in his host-country's language "risked losing his objectivity." In my view, without fluency in the host country's language, it is very difficult to move around or be objective about events one witnesses.

In more recent years, the U.S. Government has publicly emphasized the need for foreign language proficiency. Unfortunately, although it has conducted study after study (I was involved in one) and initiated program after program, the civilian and military organizations have failed to implement many of these study recommendations. We are still far from filling the need for qualified foreign language speakers in critical positions abroad. One of the reasons is the immense amount of time and money needed to do the job right. Another reason is that knowledge of foreign languages is not a crucial element of American culture and it's tempting to adopt the attitude that "most of the world speaks English so why should we waste time and money learning a foreign language?"

Our military attaché program in Russia dates back to 1889—the first time the U.S. sent military attachés to any country. That year the U.S. government appointed five military and naval attachés—one each to Berlin, Vienna, Paris, London and St. Petersburg, Russia. Before that, there had been instances where U.S. military officers observed and reported on Russian military operations as "observers." Russia permitted U.S. Army First Lieutenant F.V. Greene to personally observe operations in the Russo-Turkish War in 1877-1888.

From then until the end of WWI, military attachés often had excellent access to the Russian government, although nothing to equal that of British Military Attaché, Brigadier General W. H-H. Waters in 1917. He was a favorite of Tsar Nicholas II and his wife Alexandra. Because of his Russian language skills, they often conducted a wide range of official discussions directly with him. British Military Attaché Colonel Frederick Wellesley, who served during the reign of Alexander II, writes: "foreign military attachés in St. Petersburg always have the greatest hospitality extended to them at court.... they are received as personal guests of the Emperor."

According to S.J. Lewis, files of the Military Intelligence Division in the National Archives reveal that in 1914, American Army Lieutenant Sherman Miles observed and reported from the WWI Russian Front in Poland. He toured the battlefield dressed in a Russian officer's cap and overcoat, carried a Russian sabre [!] and was "permitted to see practically anything he desired."

The turmoil that followed the abdication of the Tsar in March 1917 found some American military attachés quite involved in Russian political and military events. U.S. Army Lieutenant E. Francis Riggs provided important contact between the American embassy and the

Russian Provisional Government during the first weeks of the new regime's existence.

After the Bolshevik coup in November 1917, the new military attaché Lieutenant Colonel Vorhees Judson maintained contact with Lenin's Bolshevik Headquarters at Smolny Institute. (I use the word 'coup' here because, in fact, no actual revolution brought the Bolsheviks to power. 'Coup' is not even the most appropriate word as, according to Stephen Kotkin, "Red guards... had never actually "stormed" the Winter Palace: they had just climbed unopposed through unlocked doors and windows, many going for the storied wine cellars... Members of the Provisional Government either fled or gave up.")

When the U.S. refused to recognize the Bolshevik regime in 1917, Leon Trotsky, Lenin's closest confidant, chose to deal with our military attachés. Colonel Judson met often with the Bolsheviks and on December 1, 1917, had a 40-minute meeting with Trotsky. Colonel James Ruggles, the new American military attaché in February 1918, negotiated with Trotsky from March to May 1918 about a reorganization of the Russian Army with the help of Allied military missions, instructors and materiel.

The U.S. Government finally recognized Bolshevik Russia in 1933, when Franklin Roosevelt took office. Although from the very first, American attitudes toward the Bolsheviks were negative, most historians believe it was the growing Japanese threat in the Far East and the desire to find new markets for U.S. goods that finally led to U.S. recognition. (We had, however, dealt with Russia on a humanitarian level. According to Stephen Kotkin, during the severe food shortages of the first years of Bolshevik rule, the American Relief Administration sent 300 field agents, set up 19,000 field kitchens... and fed 11 million people daily.)

Initially, there was great hope for Soviet-American military cooperation. The first American ambassador to Soviet Russia, William Bullitt, reported that Soviet War Commissar Klement Voroshilov made it clear that "if your government desires, your military and naval men can have a relationship of the utmost intimacy with the military authorities of the Soviet Government." That attitude, however, was short-lived due to the restrictions placed on our attachés by Maksim Litvinov, Commissar of Foreign Affairs. The U.S. was so irritated by these new restrictions that in early 1935, it recalled most of our military attachés. By the time I served in Moscow, the U.S. Government accepted all Soviet restrictions. In turn, our government imposed some of its own on Soviet military attachés in Washington.

It was during the 1930s that one American military attaché left his mark, unequalled by any other Moscow-based military attaché in the Twentieth Century. U.S. Army Colonel Raymond Faymonville, the first military attaché to the USSR, remained behind when Washington pulled the others out in 1935. He was fluent in Russian and soon developed a close relationship with Red Army officials (the Red Army was renamed Soviet Army in 1941). Although his reports on the military's situation and its potential usually differed from reports coming from others at our embassy, he usually turned out to be right.

The anti-Communist bias of U.S. officials and the lack of objective information from other sources on the Red Army caused Faymonville's positive assessments to be interpreted by some as too pro-Soviet. On the other hand, Mary Glantz, writing in *Military History Journal*, characterized Faymonville's performance as a "model for subsequent attachés, providing dispassionate, accurate assessment of the Red Army's military worth." Alfred Vagts, whose *The Military Attaché* is probably the definitive book on attachés, also described Faymonville as a "model attaché."

In 1939, Washington recalled Faymonville. Vagts writes that he was "recalled for his too favorable opinions of Russia's military strength; actually his views proved truer in the end than many other judgments submitted to Washington." In September 1941, Faymonville returned to Moscow with the U.S.-British Harriman-Beaverbook Commission and remained behind as a coordinator of Lend-Lease. His military attaché successors, Colonel Ivan Yeaton (1939-41) and Brigadier General Joseph Michela (1941-1943) were strongly anti-communist and assessed the Red Army as ill prepared to face the German Wehrmacht. According to them, the Soviets "didn't stand a chance."

At the time, this was a reasonable conclusion on the surface, since Stalin had destroyed the leadership and nearly one-half of the officer corps during his purges of 1937-1941. During those purges, Stalin executed three of his five marshals. He also purged 13 of 15 army commanders, 8 of 9 admirals, 50 of 57 army corps commanders, 154 of 186 division commanders, all 16 army commissars, and 25 of 28 army corps commissars.

The Germans attacked the USSR in June 1941. Back in Moscow, Faymonville reported to the President that the Soviet Army would regain its battle-worthiness after the disastrous defeats that summer. The Soviet Army subsequently stopped the German Wehrmacht at Moscow in December 1941—the furthest German advance is marked by the very Khimki anti-tank monument I passed on my way from Sheremetyevo Airport. They defended Stalingrad in 1942, won the Battle of Kursk in 1943, and became a vital anti-German ally to the U.S., British and other Allies fighting in the West.

In 1943, the U.S. abolished the Moscow Office of Military Attachés, recalled Faymonville again, and set up the U.S. Military Mission headed by U.S. Army Major General John Deane. Deane's Mission handled both Lend-Lease and attaché liaison work until the end of the war. General Deane had been instructed by General George Marshall not to seek military information from or about the Soviets. The sole purpose of the Mission was to foster closer U.S.-Soviet military cooperation. Despite the massive Lend-Lease aid the U.S. was providing the Soviets, they refused to work closely with the American military. General Deane wrote: "Russians were inclined to treat the mission with the same aloofness with which they had treated the attachés, convinced that only a change in name had been effected and that our objectives remained the same." Kemp Tolley, a U.S. Navy Commander and one of the attachés who lost their jobs to the new Military Mission, suggests in his *Caviar and Commissars* one of the reasons the Soviets weren't cooperative is that they believed military aid coming to the USSR might also mask "some devilish scheme to the detriment of Mother Russia. Their sharp recollections of the 1918-1919 Allied Intervention told them it wouldn't be the first time..." (More on this in the chapter about my trip to Murmansk.)

The Defense Intelligence Agency (DIA) was formed in 1961 as the intelligence arm of the Department of Defense. In 1965, DIA assumed control of all U.S. military attachés. One of the goals of the new DIA was to coordinate and disseminate intelligence from all the armed services. Those of us working in joint assignments, such as the DAO, became what we called "purple-suiters"; we were to no longer think of ourselves as purely green- or blue-suiters. Although the services maintained their intelligence staffs, we no longer reported directly to the Army, Navy and Air Force, but sent all our reports first to DIA.

From the end of WWII to the end of the Cold War (which occurred about ten years after I left my attaché assignment in Moscow), many qualified and highly motivated officers served as military attachés. However, conditions never again were such that these attachés could collect military information similar to that of Miles, Riggs, Ruggles or Faymonville. The only possible exception to this was the tour as Defense Attaché of General Sam Wilson in the early 1970s. He apparently had good access to the Soviet military leadership. But then he was the first general officer in modern times to serve in the DAO and he himself was a famous combat veteran who had served with Merrill's Marauders during WWII.

Although in principle, attachés were supposed to provide the ambassador and his staff with analysis and advice on Soviet military and political-military affairs, in actuality we had little significant information to offer. Even though an officer from the DAO often participated in meetings with the embassy's political section, he had very little if anything to report. His overall knowledge and understanding of the USSR, however, did contribute to embassy assessment of the political-military situation.

This lack of significant military information was due to the restrictions the Soviet government placed on all foreigners, especially military attachés. The Soviet government and Ministry of Defense tied our hands and feet with rules and travel restrictions. Throughout this book, the reader will find many specific instances of ways the Soviets tried (with frequent success) to thwart our collection efforts.

In general, there were both official rules of conduct for foreign attachés and countless forms of psychological and physical harassment. The official rules for foreign attachés included:

-No contact with the Soviet military except with prior permission from the MOD;

-No photography of government buildings, rail stations, airports, military installations, highways or bridges;

-Official restricted areas throughout the Soviet Union. (Some estimate that these areas—added to areas where there was no transportation available—approximated 90 percent of the USSR);

-Restriction to a 25-mile radius of Moscow unless a prior request was approved by the MOD; and

-Detailed requests for travel by air, rail or auto to any open city in the USSR.

The Soviets divided tourists into Soviet and foreign. A government agency "Intourist" handled foreign tourists. "Intourist" is an acronym for the Russian *'inostrannyj turist'* (foreign tourist). It was known to have close ties to the KGB; several former Intourist workers admitted this later. When we traveled, an Intourist guide would often meet us upon arrival in a city and insist on escorting us around town.

It was not unusual to find KGB surveillants assigned to share our train compartments even after we had paid premium prices to reserve the entire compartment. Foot and vehicular surveillance, usually quite obvious, was with us around the clock outside Moscow. Flat tires or stolen windshield wipers could slow us down, as we would have to spend extra hours finding replacements or getting repairs. On a couple occasions, the KGB rigged our car so it wouldn't start and, consequently, we couldn't leave a city on schedule.

Former air attaché in Moscow, Thomas Wolfe, writes in his "Obstacle Course for Attachés" (*Inside CIA's Private World*):

> Cars which had passed a searching inspection before the start of a trip sometimes used to develop peculiar ailments after having been parked overnight in the courtyard of a Soviet hotel. I had a brand new

automobile, mileage still under 3000, break down with burned-out engine bearings on a trip in southern Russia. Kerosene in the crankcase—hardly the work of a mere prankster—turned out to be the cause.

Two of my attaché colleagues, Jim Hinds and Ed Baisden, once had their vehicles' sparkplug wires crossed. While traveling with our DATT, General Larkin, Jim once had to hotwire their car and wedge a screwdriver into the steering lock in order to get their vehicle running again. On a trip with his wife, Jim found the KGB had pulled all the wiring of the ignition switch and once again he had to resort to hotwire.

Obviously, the conditions for attaché operations varied from country to country and depended on the international situation and on various unique circumstances. Here the reader can see the glaring contrast between some of the working conditions for attachés in Moscow and in one friendly country:

Friendly Country	USSR
Contact with all levels of military officers	No contact except with special permission, which was never granted
Host any of them for lunch	Unheard of!
Invited to their homes	Unheard of!
Contact with all attachés in country	Contact only with friendly or neutral country attachés
Media contacts wide open	Unheard of except for official social events
No travel restrictions whatsoever	Oppressive restrictions
Visit military installation after request	Unheard of!
VIP pass to MOD in host country capital	Unheard of!

Friendly Country	USSR
Open press for identifying issues; then a chance to talk to host-country experts	Open press was all we got
MOD wives' club to which wives were invited	Our wives had absolutely no contact with the Soviet wives

During a visit to the USSR in 1947, John Steinbeck wrote in his *A Russian Journal*, "[Military attachés] do not live very happy lives, for they even more than the others are restricted in their movements, and they must live the most circumspect of lives… In front of their house stands a permanent militia man in uniform, and every time they leave their house they are accompanied by invisible followers." The situation had not changed in that regard by 1979. We assumed the militiamen were in fact KGB.

One thing military attachés in Moscow were not: spies who recruited and ran espionage networks. The Soviets, however, viewed us as "spies above all spies." A Soviet general at the MOD who dealt with Moscow attachés told one of them: "Every foreign service attaché, no matter how he conducted his life in Moscow, was regarded as a spy by the Soviet authorities." According to Soviet General Sergei Sokolov, attaché activities in the USSR should be restricted to "touring the country, sampling the climate, and visiting museums and centers of culture."

One possible reason for this suspicion may have been that at one time, attachés under control of the Military Intelligence Division of the old Army General Staff, did get involved in espionage. Bruce Bidwell, in his *History of the Military Intelligence Division, Department of the Army General Staff: 1775-1941*, states: "[U.S.] Colonel Edward Davis in Holland organized and maintained what was unquestionably one of the most amazing espionage and counterespionage nets of the entire [WWI] wartime period." According to Soviet General Victor Cherkashin, a CIA officer once worked under cover of the DAO as a naval attaché. Another reason for Soviet suspicion may have been their mirror imaging. That occurs when one side assumes the other side is doing the same thing as the first side. Almost every Soviet military attaché abroad actively recruited people for Soviet intelligence. As an attaché, Lieutenant Colonel Odom was able to smuggle a good part of Alexander Solzhenitsyn's personal archive out of the USSR, but this can hardly been characterized as espionage.

To be sure, spying operations were going on in Moscow during my tour there. Some CIA officers I knew were actively working with perhaps the most important Soviet spy the United States ever had: Adolf Tolkachev. (See David E. Hoffman's *The Six Billion Dollar Spy*.) But I knew nothing of this operation at the time and none of us military attachés used our position as cover for clandestine work with the CIA.

In short, military attachés should be the eyes and ears on the ground for reporting military developments. As "liaison officers" we did this at USMLM in East Germany, but not in Moscow. The Moscow-based military attaché had little hope of seeing or hearing anything new, despite the fact that he was in a country where military might was the foundation of the state.

PART II: LIFE IN MOSCOW

LIVING CONDITIONS

The reality of our living conditions in Moscow began to set in when my wife, Elaine, started to prepare for her and the children to join me in Moscow. The Army allowed us an extra 4,000 pounds weight limit for shipping household goods to Moscow in order to bring many essential items that were not available in Moscow stores.

Elaine spent several weeks compiling vitamins, toilet articles, American family basic groceries (spaghetti, lasagna noodles, canned tomatoes, corn, beans, flour, sugar and coffee), paper products, toothpaste, lotions, soap, all feminine hygiene items, laundry supplies and cleaning products. Other families did the same so that when we surveyed what we and others had brought, we ended up trading some of these food delicacies with each other. All in all, we needed enough hard-to-get items to last a family of six (including our nanny) for two years. Additionally, Elaine shopped for cold weather clothing, cross country skis and ice skates. In the winter, the children could put on skates in the house, take the elevator down, and walk only a few yards to skating area.

We had an inkling of what our living conditions would be like in Moscow from the advice of several people who had or were still living there. In 1974, during a short visit to Moscow, Elaine and I visited my Naval Academy classmate, Lieutenant Commander Dick Life and his wife, Sandra. Dick was an assistant naval attaché at the time.

The Defense Attaché and the three Principal Attachés lived in apartments in the Embassy. All the other attachés and many staff members were housed in leased Soviet apartments in various diplomatic ghettos around the city. Our apartment was on the second floor of a 4-story building at Leninsky Prospekt 45. It consisted of two standard Soviet apartments with the interior wall taken out, thus giving us four bedrooms—one for us, one for the two boys, one for our daughter and one for our nanny.

The Embassy outfitted our apartments with American furniture. The major appliances, converted to Soviet electrical current, were also American, although we had to use transformers to convert 220-volt Soviet electricity to accommodate our 120-volt hair dryers and other small electric devices. The embassy also provided a stand-up freezer so we could order and store some items from Berlin, Denmark and Finland. Compared to the standard of housing we were used to in the States, it was a bit primitive, but by Soviet standards, we were living quite comfortably.

One of the convenient innovations of the American-leased apartments was the storage area built into the corridor. The embassy converted half of what had been a rather wide hallway into a storage area with built-in cupboards and drawers to accommodate the extra things we brought with us. One inconvenience was that for several weeks each summer, the city authorities turned off the hot water so it could clean the pipes. Since only certain sections of Moscow were affected at one time, we could visit friends in other parts of the city in order to take showers. At home, we heated water on the stove so the children could take baths. That reminded me of my childhood baths in a large tub heated on our wood-burning stove (my family had no running water in DeSoto).

We were convinced that surveillance existed within the apartments by the use of listening devices in the walls. Who knows, perhaps also cameras? It became somewhat of a joke in the family that when we wanted to vent against the Soviet government or something the Soviets had done to upset us, we discussed it at the dinner table. We addressed our remarks to "Boris," a name we assigned to all our KGB microphones. For private and personal discussions, Elaine and I would go for a walk or discuss matters during official receptions, where the noise level was high.

As John Steinbeck pointed out, a guard shack occupied by a policeman 24 hours a day stood immediately opposite our American stairwell. (Soviet police were called *militsionery*, from the Russian word *militsiya* (militia). Our slang for them was "milimen.") We assumed our miliman-guard was a KGB agent, or at least a link in the KGB surveillance network. Every time one of us would depart or arrive home, the miliman went straight to his telephone. In the event we invited a Soviet citizen to our apartment, the miliman would be there to challenge our guest. The only way a Soviet guest could get into our apartment was by our escorting him or her and explaining to the miliman that all was well and our guest was, indeed, invited for a visit. What happened to the guest after he or she left, we never knew.

On one occasion we were glad to have a miliman outside our apartment. Elaine and I were coming home one night after dinner at a fellow attaché's apartment. We saw a Soviet car hit a man who was trying to dash across the street. The car didn't slow down so we decided to follow it to see if we could get the license number. We were able to do that and I gave that number to the miliman at our building. A few weeks later, a letter of commendation came down through channels to the Embassy from the Moscow Chief of Police thanking me for my effort.

Proof of listening devices came from an incident involving our youngest son, Misha. He and a friend often played with their Matchbox cars on the top floor of the stairwell because the apartments there were locked and the children didn't have to contend with people going up and down the stairs. One day Misha came running into our apartment. "Papa, you should see the tape recorders in the apartments upstairs. They're much bigger than yours." A man had come out of one of the rooms and Misha was able to peek in.

Our building complex was rectangular and surrounded an interior street, which in turn circumscribed a playground. The entrance to our stairwell faced the interior quadrangle. Other foreigners and some Soviet families lived in the other wings of the complex. Our stairwell contained only American Embassy staff.

The playground inside the quadrangle contained swings, a slide, and a small merry-go-round. It was a typical Moscow residential playground—large enough to hold a fenced-in basketball court that doubled as a soccer field in the summer and a hockey rink in the winter. Benches and tables dotted the edges of the area. In the daytime, old women sat around chatting while they watched their wards. At night, the benches and tables provided a gathering place for teenagers and drunks who threw their bottles on the ground. It's well known that alcoholism was a serious problem in the Soviet Union. Although not everyone in the USSR was an alcoholic, it was not unusual to see all ages, both male and female, drinking openly. I don't know if there were age-limits for buying liquor, but there apparently weren't any for consuming it. Consequently, there was often trash, including broken glass, lying around.

At one point, I decided we needed a cleanup session in the playground. We needed a *subbotnik*. Every spring since 1919, and for special occasions, the Moscow Communist Party called out the citizenry to help clean up the city. Since these events took place on Saturdays, people named them after the Russian word for Saturday—*subbota*. I made up a sign in both Russian and English and posted it in the nearby stairwells. Not long thereafter, I heard a knock on our door. When I opened it, I saw two Soviet maintenance men.

"*Gospodin* (Mr.) Holbrook, we understand you're organizing a *subbotnik*."

"Yes. That's correct. We need to clean up the playground. There's broken glass out there."

"Cleaning the buildings and the courtyard is our responsibility. Your so-called *subbotnik* is inappropriate."

"That's silly. You know the playground's in terrible condition. Someone has to clean it up."

"Excuse me. Are you suggesting we don't do our job properly?"

"I'm just saying the playground's dangerous."

"We can take care of it."

"Fine. I'll check again in a couple of days."

The two men turned and shuffled down the stairs, grumbling to themselves. Within a couple of days, they had picked up the broken glass in the playground area.

Despite the need to bring so many items from home we felt were necessary and unavailable in Soviet stores, food was not really a serious issue for us. We had a small embassy commissary that was supplied twice a year from our military commissary in Berlin. My two oldest children, Yasha and Tarisa, worked part-time in the commissary. Whenever the run to Berlin was about to take place, embassy personnel placed private orders for food to be brought in at the same time. When the trucks carrying the Berlin Commissary goods arrived, we all pitched in, unloaded the food in the embassy courtyard and organized the embassy commissary items. Our personal boxes of food had our names on them. Additionally, we received weekly shipments of dairy products from Helsinki and were able to order meat from Denmark and Finland.

Produce, however, was scarce. The embassy published a weekly newsletter, the TWIM (This Week In Moscow). It provided local embassy news and administrative announcements, as well as the Soviet TV schedule. Occasionally, a parody of the TWIM would appear. It was called the TWIT. Here is one item from a TWIT that highlights the lack of green vegetables:

> LETTUCE ANONYMOUS. If you or anyone you know secretly chews leaves of houseplants or digs through snow at night to eat blades of grass, call Lettuce Anonymous via Finnair at 200-4027 or Clemente at 199-8246.

Finally, there was a special Soviet grocery store not too far from the embassy—*Gastronom* No. 1—where we could buy some basic foods. Only diplomats and accredited correspondents had access to this store. For money we used D-Coupons there and in the Beryozka stores. Beryozkas were shops scattered throughout the city that sold Western and hard-to-find Russian goods, some of them luxury items. They were accessible only to foreigners with hard currency or D-Coupons. The coupons were a form of currency created in the 1960s to be used in these special stores by the Moscow diplomatic community and journalists. (After the demise of the Soviet Union, the D-coupons gradually gave way to dollars and other hard currency.)

And, of course, we could always try to buy food in the regular Soviet stores for rubles. Delicious Russian bread was pretty much available all the time. Butter and cheese were another matter. We could tell when a supply of dairy products came in because there were long lines in the stores, often extending out onto the sidewalk.

An anecdote about buying butter illustrates the complexity of shopping for such a product in a regular Soviet store. One day, I asked Yasha, our oldest son, to go down to get some butter at the Soviet store around the corner of our apartment. He'd done it before, but apparently had had a bad experience the last time. Yasha spoke Russian and generally enjoyed getting out and mixing with the Muscovites.

"Papa, please don't make me go this time," he pleaded. "You don't know what it's like."

"Well, I think I do know. I've done some shopping here myself. I'm not entirely new to Soviet stores, you know."

I understood it wasn't an easy task to shop in Soviet stores. They seemed to have lines for everything. The first time I shopped in town, culture shock temporarily set in. In the States we simply walked up, selected a product and took it to a cashier. Not in Moscow. Not in 1979.

"Papa, how about you come with me?"

"OK. Let's see what's going on."

We walked down from our second-floor apartment. It was a rule of thumb for all of us to use Soviet elevators only when necessary. By walking down, we believed the elevators would last longer and be operating when we needed them to carry up groceries or suitcases.

The noise of Russian chatter and the smell of bodies greeted us as we edged our way through the crowd into the store. This market sold only butter and cheese—and then, of course, only when they had it in stock. Apparently, today was one of those days.

We headed for our first line. From here we were able to peer over the shoulders or between the bodies into the display case to find out prices. From there we went to our second line that led to the cashier.

When we got there, we told the woman how much we had to pay for the butter—50 kopecks—and handed her a one-ruble note. As if this was a major mathematical problem for her, she went to work on her abacus and then returned 50 kopecks, together with a receipt for 50 kopecks. (Sometimes the change was in the form of candies.) Now off to our third line to pick up our butter.

This was the longest line and many Russians were complaining about it. From time to time someone would try to jump the line, which always brought loud calls and some colorful Russian profanity. This was turning out to be an interesting cultural event for both of us. And Yasha was right. The number of people in this store made buying butter a little more hectic than I had experienced in other stores. Just trying to figure out what lines to be in was a challenge.

We could see Russian "team-shopping" in action. How this worked is that a family of two or three would enter the store. Each member would take up a position in a different line. The first member would determine how much they needed a receipt for. He or she would then tell the second member who was already in line at the cashier. When that member got the receipt, the first one would carry it to the third member, who was already in line to pick up his or her product. It still took some time to get in and out of the store, but it was faster than the way we were doing it.

I was getting impatient at having to wait in such a long line.

"Yashenka, let's see what happens when they find out we're Americans."

"Pardon me," I asked the woman ahead of me. (Almost all the people in the store were women.) "Pardon me, but could you explain what's going on here? You see, I'm an American and have never witnessed anything like this in my country."

"You're an American?"

"Yes, I'm an American diplomat. This is my son, Yasha."

Suddenly, the woman stepped out of line and went directly to the front. She said something to the people at the head of the line and everyone turned to look at us. Then they began exclaiming, "They're Americans. Let them to the head of the line."

"No, no," I said. "We want to do things the Russian way. This is all part of our learning experience."

Now a chorus: "You must go to the head of the line."

"That's OK. That's not necessary."

The Soviet women up and down the line motioned us to the head of the line. I was a little embarrassed, but we followed their directions.

"Thank you all. You Russians are so polite," I said as Yasha and I advanced to pick up our butter. I thanked them again and we left the store.

"Wow," I said to my son. "I see what you mean. Next time you come here, don't hesitate to tell them at the outset you're an American."

Living in Moscow as an American diplomat was a rush. Despite the hardships of Soviet life that lowered our overall standard of living, we always felt special. And special we were. We represented the most powerful nation on earth, with an economy and moral standing that— at the time—almost everyone around the world envied. There was no doubt the Russian man or woman on the street was fascinated by Americans and their consumer goods, as well as the political traditions personified for them in such American presidents as Abraham Lincoln, Franklin Roosevelt and John F. Kennedy. Soviet citizens were eager to get to know us. Given the Soviet taboos about associating with foreigners, it seemed that many citizens threw caution to the wind just to be able to talk with us.

THE FAMILY

Elaine's eyes lit up. "I've died and gone to heaven!"

We had just entered the icon exhibits in the Tretyakov Gallery. It, together with the Hermitage in Leningrad, may be Russia's answer to Paris's Louvre. Elaine was staring at two of the most famous and revered icons in Russian history: *The Virgin of Vladimir* and *The Old Testament Trinity*. Displayed in a section of the Tretyakov labeled "Ancient Russian Art," these and several other icons were just too much of a Russian treasure for the Communists to destroy or hide, despite the fact that they were religious artifacts. Very religious, indeed. Russian Orthodox believers don't view icons as "pictures," but rather as sacred images. They are Bible stories in paintings. Icons have always been a very important part of Russian culture.

The scene above took place in 1974. I had just finished my tour of teaching Russian at West Point. Elaine and I had escorted eight cadets to the U.S. Army Russian Institute in Garmisch, Germany, and then went to Moscow for four days. It was her first time in Russia. The visit to the Tretyakov was high on our list of priorities. Elaine's excitement derived from the fact that she herself had made a study of Russian icons and had been crafting reproductions of the more famous ones for several years.

One of my personal rewards with this assignment in Moscow was that I was able to provide my family with an opportunity to experience Russian culture first-hand. Elaine had been with me from the beginning of my study of the language in Monterey. At night I sometimes went to sleep with earphones on, listening to language lessons. She began to learn Russian bit by bit at the same time. In Monterey we lived next door to a Russian Orthodox priest so we were both able to practice our new language with him.

Elaine's interest in icons, however, came a few years later when I was teaching Russian at West Point. She had been doing découpage, a craft of gluing cutout pictures to wood and then varnishing them several times until the cutout looked like it was painted on the original surface. I asked her to découpage a picture of *The Virgin of Vladimir*. I explained that the picture before her was one of the two most famous icons in Russia. The fact that this was a Russian picture, and our whole family had long been involved in Russian culture, led her to try to make the picture resemble the original. So, while still at West Point, Elaine became a serious student of icons. Now, in 1979, we were in the land where the original icons were displayed.

The *Virgin of Vladimir* was not painted by a Russian, but was a gift in 1131 from the Greek Patriarch to the Grand Prince of Kiev, Yurii Dolgoruky. Although the author of the icon was an unknown Greek, some Russian Orthodox believers maintain St. Luke himself painted it. It became known as the *Virgin of Vladimir* after Andrei Bogolyubsky took it to the city of Vladimir. Legend has it the horses transporting the icon stopped near Vladimir and refused to go further. People interpreted this as a sign that the *Virgin* wanted to stay there.

The *Virgin of Vladimir* has many interesting legends surrounding it. For example, in 1395, when Tamerlane was threatening Moscow, Vasilii I had the icon brought from Vladimir. Tamerlane's armies retreated. The icon is credited with saving Moscow from two additional Tatar attacks in 1451 and 1480. Before the Revolution, Russians used the icon for coronations, patriarch elections and other important ceremonies. Russian troops sought its miraculous powers again during WWI, as did Soviet troops during WWII. According to one report, Stalin had the icon taken up in an airplane and flown around Moscow during the Battle of Moscow. A few days later, the German army retreated.

The Moscow diplomatic community learned Elaine was an icon expert and before long she was lecturing and conducting tours of the icon exhibits in the Tretyakov. She was like an unpaid docent at the art gallery. She went there so often the *dezhurnayas*—women who stood guard on the exhibits—came to know her. They would let her and her little band of foreign ladies take short cuts through the gallery to the icon displays. The last time she visited there she went alone with a Canon camera. Although the Gallery didn't allow picture taking, she convinced the *dezhurnayas* to allow her to photograph the icons so long as she didn't use flash.

Elaine's icon reproductions were in great demand in the Moscow diplomatic community. It was very difficult to purchase authentic icons and ship them home because the Soviet government considered them to be national treasures. As a result, Elaine's authentic-looking icon reproductions substituted for the real things. At an art show within the embassy, she sold all her stock.

She continued to produce icon reproductions even after leaving Moscow. Before she stopped her icon work, she had placed her pieces in galleries, churches and homes around the world. Some were blessed in Orthodox churches in both Moscow and Washington, DC, making them official artifacts of the church. The National Cathedral in Washington purchased many outright for resale in its gift shop. One of the more interesting sales she made came toward the end of her icon work. At the LaJolla Museum of Art in San Diego, she sold two large reproductions to Theodor (Dr. Seuss) and Audrey Geisel. When Audrey asked which one of the two to buy, Dr. Seuss said, "Buy them both."

The family joined me in May after school was out in Virginia. Our sons, Yasha and Misha, were 14- and 9-years old; our daughter, Tarisa, was 13. Elaine would be involved on the diplomatic social circuit and would also occasionally travel with me when I left Moscow. Therefore, as with most of the other families from the embassy, we needed a nanny. For that we hired a remarkable young lady, Holly Vorhies, the daughter of an Army colonel I worked with in Washington. When we entertained other diplomats in our apartment, Holly helped out.

The children now got a taste of living in this strange country their father had been involved with for so many years. I spoke only Russian with my first two children—from the time Yasha came home from the hospital in 1964 and Tarisa in 1966, until I went off to Vietnam in 1967. Elaine spoke only English with them, so they became fluent in both languages at an early age. While I was in Vietnam, the family lived in my little village, DeSoto, Wisconsin. By the time I got commissioned and returned from Vietnam, they had forgotten much of their Russian. I decided to speak to them in English. Their early experience with Russian had been natural for them. I didn't want them to have to approach the language as something purely academic. They also learned German in an almost natural way. In the mid-1970s, they attended German schools in Heidelberg and Berlin and we spoke some German at home.

Now, in Moscow, we had to decide whether to send the children to a Soviet or to the Anglo-American school. They had been in American school only two years between my Potsdam/Berlin USMLM and my Moscow assignments. We all felt it was best for them to return to an American-style school. It would have been complicated to get them into a Soviet school and I didn't want them to be subjected to any pressures there just because their father was, according to the Soviet official view, an "American spy."

The Anglo-American School was open to all foreign embassy employees and children of non-government Americans in Moscow who could pass an English test. Altogether, there were about 40 different nationalities among the students, which resulted in a culturally rich environment for our children.

The American, British, Australian and Canadian embassies sponsored the school, which was located up the street from our apartment. Most of the American students rode there in a yellow American school bus. Founded in 1949, the school's faculty consisted of certified teachers from the four Anglophone countries. (Two teachers—a married couple—had been evacuated from Teheran just before the hostage crisis.)

The school had a gym where young and old both could play basketball. The Japanese school was on the top floor. Outside was a playground that was converted to an ice rink in winter. Students followed an international curriculum, which provided a solid grounding in English; language arts; mathematics; science and social studies; Russian, French or Spanish languages; art and music. The school had only first through ninth grades, however. So in the fall of 1980, we sent Yasha to a boarding school at High Wycombe Air Force base in England.

In the summer of 1980, the school sponsored a field trip for the upper grades to the Transcaucasus. They flew to Tbilisi, Georgia, trained to Yerevan, Armenia and Baku, Azerbaijan and then flew back to Moscow from there. These were destinations I would travel to during my tour at the Embassy. (In recent years, Yasha became a Caspian Sea expert and dealt with these Transcaucasus countries as a Department of Defense civilian. In 2015-16, he worked for a year at the American Embassy in Tbilisi, Georgia.)

It was at the Anglo-American School that Tarisa had one of her most memorable experiences—a humorous exchange with Bob Hope. During his 1980 visit to Moscow as guest of Ambassador Watson, Hope visited the Anglo-American School. With all the faculty and students gathered in the small auditorium, he began telling jokes and talking about his career. Then he took questions from the children. One student asked him how old he was and he replied, "Thirty-nine, the same as Jack Benny." Another student asked him how long he had been in show business. His answer: "Over 45 years."

At that point, Tarisa piped up from the back of the room.

"But you said you were only 39 years old."

Everyone, including Hope, laughed. When they stopped, he said to Tarisa, "Look, young lady. I'm the one who's supposed to be telling jokes here."

As I wrote earlier, one of the rewarding aspects of my being a military attaché in Moscow was that my family would have the chance to experience Soviet culture. After having lived all their lives with a father who was a Russian scholar, the children would now get to see a little bit of what Russia was all about. I might never know all the escapades they got involved in, but after we left the Soviet Union, Yasha told me the following story.

He and his friend, the son of the Norwegian ambassador, climbed nervously into a taxi.

"Where we going?" Yasha asked.

One of the two Russians with them said, "To the store, of course. These hats are not for sale in a regular *voentorg* (military store)."

The story began a few weeks earlier when the boys decided to acquire some Soviet military insignia—patches, branch markings, etc. They began by visiting the *voentorgs*—what we would call post exchanges in the U.S. military. Although the general public is permitted to buy some things in a *voentorg*, certain uniform items were for Soviet military only.

What the boys were especially interested in were the leather belts with the brass buckles that depicted a Red Army star with a hammer and sickle in the middle. They gave them to their friends as souvenirs. Initially they had trouble because the sales ladies refused to sell them anything. Yasha wasn't sure whether it was because they were civilians or obviously non-Soviets. They decided to try a new tactic, one that most Soviet sales personnel understood.

They began to offer the sales ladies Western nail polish, lipstick and other women's items. Yasha doesn't remember where they got the gifts, but he admits he and his friend might have "borrowed" a few items from their mothers, sisters and nannies. The fact that the boys had to conduct their business surreptitiously only heightened their fun.

The one item they couldn't cajole the ladies into selling them was the Soviet Army cap. When they saw some civilian young men buying caps, they decided to try to talk them into helping out. With some cigarettes and a little cash they were successful. The young men were perhaps members of DOSAAF (Volunteer Society for Cooperation with the Army, Air Force and Navy)—the Soviet pre-military training organization. Almost all youth belonged to DOSAAF, as all Komsomol members were required to do. (The Komsomol—the Communist youth organization—was a first step to getting a higher education and advancing professionally in society.)

The day this latest adventure started, two men came into the *voentorg* wearing white caps. The boys decided to try to get a couple. When offered cigarettes and money, the Soviet men agreed to buy the caps.

"Sure," one of the men said, "we can get them. No problem. Just come with us."

That's when things got dicey. Now here they were in a cab, going who knows where with two strange Soviets. When they pulled up to a corner store, they saw several men wearing the same white caps. Their new Soviet friends told the taxi to wait. Inside the store, the Soviets asked the shopkeeper to fit the boys for the white caps. Now sporting their new headgear, the boys handed over cigarettes and money and were about to leave. But the men put their arms around them and said, "No, no. Let's get back into the cab. We're not done."

The boys assumed at this point they were going for some different uniform items. They soon noticed they were in a part of Moscow they didn't recognize.

"Where exactly are we heading?" Yasha asked.

One of the Soviets looked back and made the finger-thump-to-his-throat signal for drinking some vodka. The taxi pulled up at a train station. The Soviets paid the taxi driver and led the boys into the station. They noticed several young men wearing the nice white caps and soon realized that the symbol on their new caps denoted railway troops. When they approached one of the offices in the station, Yasha saw it was a room full of new recruits/conscripts. Just as the Soviet men let go of their shoulders, the two boys looked at each other, turned and raced out of the station, carrying their new caps under their arms like footballs. They ran and ran, looking over their shoulders, not saying anything, but sticking close to each other. They ran until they found a bus stop where a bus was just arriving. They jumped on, anxiously scanning in the direction of the station for their possible pursuers. They rode until they came to familiar territory.

Tarisa was involved in a couple of dramas—celebrating her friend's birthday drinking with Russian boys and an unauthorized trip out of

Moscow to Zagorsk. She also related an experience with some Soviet children who were playing in our apartment complex courtyard. She had stopped there on her way home from school and still had her schoolbooks with her. The Soviet children wanted to look at them. When they opened her history book to a section on the Second World War, they saw a picture of Adolf Hitler.

"Oh, Hitler," one child exclaimed, "American friend."

"You gotta be kidding," Tarisa said. "He was the enemy. You should know that. Both the Soviet Union and America were teamed up against him."

The Soviet children looked a little perplexed, but doubtless they thought they were getting American propaganda from Tarisa.

Elaine, Holly and I put together an ad hoc American Cub Scout pack. It wasn't official, but we were trying to keep the scouting traditions alive. In Virginia, my youngest son, Misha, had been a Cub Scout.

During the 20th century, scouting became an international phenomenon. Russia itself had a scout organization dating back to 1909. By 1916, there were an estimated 50,000 scouts throughout Russia. One was young Aleksei Romanov, son of Tsar Nicholas II.

After the Bolsheviks took control of Russia, however, scouting was either banned or, like every other Russian institution, coopted. It evolved into the Communist Young Pioneers. Soviet organizations for children were intended primarily to teach veneration of Lenin and the glory of the Communist Party. Between ages seven and nine, Soviet children became "Oktobrists" and wore a small star with a likeness of little Vova Lenin and the motto "*Vsegda gotov*" (Always prepared). Starting in the third grade, they became Pioneers. At age fifteen an overwhelming majority of young Soviets became members of the Komsomol. Later, if they were deemed worthy enough, they could become full-fledged Communists.

All together, our "Cub Pack" consisted of six young boys. We took our Cubs to various sightseeing venues in the city.

"Bundle up, it's cold outside," Holly told four Cub Scouts one day in our apartment. "We're going skiing in Lenin Hills."

Lenin Hills (earlier and today, once again, named "Sparrow Hills") by Moscow University was about the only place in the city where there was enough elevation to make downhill skiing possible. There were also trails along the bottom of the hills where we could cross-country ski. My most vivid recollection of the area, however, is the ski jump the Soviets used year-round. In the summer, they put sawdust on the ramp to give the illusion and effect of snow. I had grown up in ski-jump country in Wisconsin where a neighboring town, Westby, was the site of an annual international ski-jump festival. As kids, we built small ski jumps by piling up snow.

We all climbed into our car for the short ride. Four boys, two adults and six sets of skis gave our car the appearance of the Beverly Hillbillies transporting all their worldly goods to California.

It was cold. When we got out of the car, we were too busy getting skis put on to notice that there was no one else around. It was a sunny day and as such one usually could expect to see many Muscovites out there. Before we could set out on a ski run, one of the boys began to complain about the cold. Holly and I looked around.

"I wonder why no one else is here," she said.

"I think I know why," I answered. "It's too cold. And if it's too cold for Russians, then I suggest it's too cold for us crazy Americans. It must be 30 degrees below zero."

"Should we go back home?"

"Yes. OK boys, off with the skis and back into the car. We're going home for some hot chocolate."

One summer day, a large black Cadillac pulled up outside our apartment building. I'm sure the miliman was flustered and wasn't sure what to do. It was Ambassador Watson's official car, with his grandson inside. We had made arrangements for Misha to go over to Spaso and spend some playtime with him.

In July and August, all the children of Embassy staff attended seven weeks of a day camp at the American Embassy dacha. They called it "Camp Wocsom," which was "Moscow" spelled backwards. They went back and forth through the rural Russian countryside in the yellow

American school bus. In addition to normal summer Camp Wocsom activities, in 1979, the camp counselors and their charges gave a party for a nearby Soviet Young Pioneer camp. The program included songs, dances, skits, sporting events, Coca-Cola and potato chips.

Each year at Christmas time, the embassy sponsored a special party for its Soviet employees and their children. In December 1980, it included Christmas carols by the American children and our son Yasha dressed as Santa Claus. This program was entirely American in its makeup. Looking back now, I imagine the Soviet children thought it was a bit weird. I wish I had interviewed some of them afterwards to see what they thought of it all. Even Christmas was an unusual concept for the Soviet children.

Although Santa Claus was a vaguely familiar personage to them, he differed significantly from their own *Ded Moroz* (Grandfather Frost). For one thing, the Soviet children probably wondered where *Snegurochka* (Snow Maiden) was. She was *Ded Moroz's* granddaughter and his constant companion. I found an excellent translation of "The Night Before Christmas" in the U.S. Information Agency magazine *Amerika*, sent to the USSR each month. Those familiar with the poem—virtually every American present—would have understood the flow of the poem when read properly—even if one didn't understand Russian. Its rhythms paralleled those of the English original. (Later, back in the U.S., I read the poem several times at the National Cryptologic School and, finally, had a video program of my reading produced at NSA to be used in later years for training at Christmas time.)

As familiar as *Ded Moroz* was to the young children, none of them knew (or cared) about the struggle for him to take his place in Soviet culture. Little did they know that *Ded Moroz*, who by the end of the 19th century had become a national Russian symbol of Christmas and gift giving, almost didn't survive the Soviet regime.

After the Bolshevik Coup in 1917, the Communists first discouraged, then forbade Christmas celebrations, the Christmas tree and *Ded Moroz* himself. In 1928, *Ded Moroz* was declared "an ally of the priest and kulak." (The priest represented religion to the atheist Communist government, while the kulak represented the well-to-do peasants who resisted Stalin's collectivization of agriculture.) By the late 1920s, Christmas was declared an ordinary workday and special patrols roamed the streets at that time, looking into windows to see if there was any Christmas merriment going on.

In 1935, a leading Communist, Pavel Postyshev, wrote in *Pravda* that some of the Christmas traditions should be resurrected, since the origins of the holiday were "pre-Christian" and the holiday could bring many benefits to Soviet children. In 1937, a man dressed as *Ded Moroz* appeared for the first time at the Moscow House of Unions. By his side appeared *Snegurochka*, a fairy-tale personage who had no connection to the religious aspects of Christmas. Just to make sure he would not be mistaken for the Western Santa Claus, Stalin ordered all *Ded Morozes* to wear blue costumes. Additionally, he ordered that the celebrations were to take place at New Years, not Christmas. (Today, in post-Soviet Russia, Ded Moroz looks a lot like our Santa Claus—even wearing a red suit—although he still has Snegurochka at his side.)

I doubt the young Russian children, or any of their parents, really appreciated our "Night Before Christmas." There are so many topics and references in the poem that don't track with the Soviet image of *Ded Moroz* and New Year festivities. For example, instead of reindeer, *Ded Moroz* rides in a sleigh with a troika (three horses). Secondly, *Ded Moroz* would never even think of coming down a chimney. In the multi-level apartment complexes in which most Soviets lived, he would get all confused and entangled in the ductwork.

ENTERTAINMENT

"We would like a table for two," I told the *maître d'* at the Sport Hotel restaurant.

"Not possible. All the tables are reserved," he answered.

"How can that be? I see many empty tables and they don't have reserved signs on them."

"But they're still reserved," he said.

"I would like to see your administrator."

"Why?"

"Just go get him or her."

Soon a middle-aged woman appeared.

"What can I do for you?" she asked.

"We would like a table for two, but your *maître d'* says they're all reserved."

"If he says so, then that must be so."

"Listen," I said, "My wife and I are here to celebrate the signing of the treaty today in Vienna by our two leaders, President Carter and General Secretary Brezhnev. Surely, you can find room for us in your restaurant."

"Just a minute," she said. She left and entered what looked to be an office. She soon returned.

"We will make a special exception for you tonight in view of the events in Vienna. Follow me."

Of all the world events that directly influenced my tour at the Embassy in Moscow, one—a high point—came soon after I arrived. The signing of the Strategic Arms Limitations Treaty (SALT II) in

Vienna on 18 June 1979 promised to usher in a period of U.S.-Soviet cooperation. (I had been in Moscow less than two months.) Brezhnev himself told visiting Senator Robert Byrd in July that the agreement between him and President Carter "promised pretty good potential" for our further cooperation.

Elaine and I decided to test in our own way whether the spirit of Vienna had reached everyday Moscow. We planned to try to have dinner in one of the close-by Soviet hotel restaurants. Although there were some stand-alone restaurants in the city—the "Arbat," "Aragvi," "Praga" and "Natsional" being the most popular—they were downtown where tourists congregated and usually required reservations. On the other hand, if one could get by a doorman in the hotels downtown that catered to tourists, one could take advantage of the restaurants inside. Around the city one could visit a *stolovaya*, a proletarian version of a buffet, but the food there was meager and of poor quality—soups, boiled chicken, etc. They were hardly places where we would think we were "dining out." On the high end, a trip to the new Sheremetyevo Airport was worth the hour drive, but that would have to come later, as the new airport was not yet finished in mid-1979. We found that making reference to the SALT II signing at the Sport Hotel gave us a little edge in overcoming hostile service personnel.

SALT talks referred to two rounds of bilateral talks and corresponding treaties involving the United States and the Soviet Union on the issue of arms control—SALT I and SALT II. SALT II was the first nuclear arms treaty which provided for real reductions in strategic forces of all categories of missiles and launchers on both sides.

Six months after the SALT II signing, however, the Soviet Union invaded Afghanistan and earlier, in September of the same year, the U.S. discovered a Soviet combat brigade deployed to Cuba. On January 3, 1980, President Carter requested the Senate majority leader delay consideration of the SALT II. In light of these developments, the U.S. Senate never formally ratified the treaty. The atmosphere in Moscow went downhill.

It wasn't long before busy schedules, traveling and demands of the diplomatic social circuit limited our dining out in Soviet venues. The same goes for taking advantage of the many cultural activities that Moscow offered. There were approximately 70 theaters in the city and many concert halls. The Bolshoi Theater, Palace of Congresses in the Kremlin, Chaikovsky Concert Hall, the Light Opera Theater and Mosssoviet Theater offered world-class shows and concerts.

In May 1979, before we became too busy with the Moscow attaché social network, we managed to squeeze in the opera "Rigoletto" at the Kremlin Palace of Congresses, my favorite stage play/movie, "My Fair Lady" (*Moya prekrasnaya ledi*), at the Moscow Operetta Theater and my favorite play, "*Revizor*" (The Inspector General), at the Moscow Theater of Satire. We also accepted a special invitation to a movie at the Soviet Ministry of Foreign Affairs. In June, we saw the opera "Prince Igor" at Moscow's Theater of Opera and Ballet and then my favorite operetta "Die Fledermaus" (The Bat, *Letuchaya mysh* in Russian) at the Moscow Operetta Theater. The early summer was topped off by a ride on the Moscow River hydrofoil with a farewell party for General Larkin on the cruise ship "Maxim Gorky."

During the rest of my tour, we were sometimes able to get to the Bolshoi Theater and Chaikovsky Concert Hall. Getting a ticket to the Bolshoi was a special event. I believe each foreign embassy had a quota of 2-4 tickets per night. The only way we could get one was to apply through the embassy, which usually meant going on a waiting list. I also went to several jazz concerts that were performed in various auditoriums of professional organizations—The House of Writers, The House of Doctors, The House of the Music Union, etc. The Moscow Jazz community warmly welcomed the American jazzmen of the Preservation Hall Jazz Band in October 1979.

Then there was the famous Moscow Circus. Actually there were two prominent circuses in Moscow and many lesser ones around the Soviet Union. In Moscow there was the "Circus Nikulin" on Tvetnoi Boulevard that was most often referred to as the "Old Circus," and featured animal acts. I went a couple of times to the "New Circus" on Vernadsky Prospekt. There we saw trapeze and acrobatic acts. There were excellent clowns at both circuses and the New Circus had the traditional dancing bears. The Moscow circuses were quite different from those I had seen in the States. Their emphasis was on various aspects of Russian culture. As one Russian historian wrote, "Since the reign of Catherine the Great, the circus has played an important role in the rich cultural traditions of Russia. In Russia, the circus is regarded as an art form on par with the ballet or opera, a showcase for highly skilled and creative artists."

The museums and art galleries were another source of cultural entertainment. When one thinks of art museums in Russia, the first name that usually comes to mind is the Hermitage in Leningrad/St. Petersburg. I visited the Hermitage a couple of times, but found its emphasis on Western art was not particularly to my liking. A mini-Hermitage, if you will, was the Pushkin museum in Moscow. It featured Western art (some of it by Van Gogh, Gauguin, Picasso, Dufrénoy, Derain and Matisse) that was transferred from the Leningrad/St. Petersburg Hermitage. The Pushkin also included several paintings confiscated by the Soviet Army in Germany after the end of WWII.

My tastes, however, ran very much toward Russian themes and Russian artists. Although the Russian Museum in Leningrad/St. Petersburg had a fine collection of Russian icons and Russian classics, no gallery in the world can compare to the Tretyakov Art Gallery in Moscow for Russian fine art. (Russians refer to it as the "Tretyakovka".) The gallery was named after Pavel Tretyakov who, in 1892, donated his collection of nearly 2,000 works (1,362 paintings, 526 drawings, and 9 sculptures) to the city of Moscow. His brother Sergei donated his own collection of Western art to the Pushkin Museum.

One of my first visits to the Tretyakovka was to see Ivan Serov's "Girl with Peaches." I had seen pictures of her in art books and wanted to see her up close. During that visit, however, I was struck by the tantalizing portrait of another girl on the gallery's wall. When I entered the room, I sensed her eyes were looking straight at me and when I moved around, her eyes continued to follow me. This was the portrait of Maria Lopukhina, painted by Vladimir Borovikovsky. Masha, as I came to call her, was born in 1779 and would have been 18 at the time of the portrait. If she were still alive, in 1979, she would have been 200 years old. To me she is the Russian Mona Lisa. I visited her several times.

The Army Air Force Exchange System (AAFES) sent us first-run movies, which provided entertainment for us at home and, occasionally, for our fellow foreign attachés and their families during functions in the diplomatic community. On one occasion, Tom and Dot Spencer went together with Elaine and me to sponsor a showing of the Muppet Movie in the embassy snack bar. We invited several foreign attachés to attend with their families. Both the movie and the popcorn were a hit. The American movies were an especially big event for children of embassy staff. It was a touchstone with American culture; some young people recorded the movie audio and memorized some of the dialogue.

AAFES sent the movies to our DAO because we were an isolated military unit. When the movies arrived in Moscow once a week, military attachés and their families got first dibs on the sign-up list. After that, all other Embassy employees were permitted to sign up. In addition to the AAFES movies, the Marine Security Guard showed videotapes of Thursday-night football at their bar in the embassy.

A highlight for all of us in Moscow was the visit of Bob and Dolores Hope. In March 1980, Ambassador Watson wrote to Hope, inviting him to visit Moscow as his guest and to "put on a couple of your famous shows to raise both the American and the Allied morale." The ambassador told him it was a particularly difficult time for his embassy staff. The Soviet invasion of Afghanistan less than three months earlier, combined with the American reaction to this and the turmoil caused by the U.S. threatening to boycott the Olympics that summer in Moscow had resulted in what Watson thought was a dip in American morale. "This is a very isolated post," the ambassador wrote, "and with the present situation pertaining between us and the Russians, it is exceedingly difficult... I think that a trip here from a morale point of view would be a tremendous thing just as your trips to our armed forces abroad have been for so many years." (Bob Hope had led 57 tours to war zones since his first USO show in 1942.)

Hope responded that he would be happy to come to Moscow. In September, Bob and his wife Dolores arrived as guests of the Watsons and stayed at Spaso. The American community was very excited to find out the Hopes would be putting on a show for them. In fact, both

Bob and Dolores entertained us one evening at Spaso House, singing and dancing and, of course, cracking jokes like only Bob Hope could. (This was not the first time Bob Hope had been at Spaso. In 1958, he took a crew to Moscow to film a program for television, part of which was conducted at Spaso.) This night with us he demonstrated his ad lib humor when all of a sudden the lights in Spaso went out. "The Soviets are playing with me, but don't let that bother you." Hope had published a book in 1963, *I Owe Russia $1,200*, in which he points out that he had never received two of the film clips the Soviets had processed for him. Hope writes, "When they do, I'll be happy to pay." (The American Seabees were the Spaso House culprits on this occasion, as they had been working on the lights.)

SPORTS

A cloud of mist hovered about two feet above my head. Through it, in the distance, I could see people walking around. They were bundled up in *shubas* (substantial overcoats) and fur hats. Understandably so, since it was 30 degrees below zero Fahrenheit. But I was warm enough in my bathing suit because I was in the heated, Moscow Outdoor Swimming Pool.

Swimming at the Moscow Swimming Pool in the center of the city was one of my sports during the winter. I would change into my swimsuit inside a warm building at the edge of the pool, jump into the water inside that building, swim to, then under, a rubber flap that was an entrance to the outside pool.

The Moscow Pool had an interesting history. It was built at the location of what was to be a Palace of Soviets, itself to be constructed at the former site of the Cathedral of Christ the Savior. In 1812, Tsar Alexander I ordered the cathedral built in Moscow in honor of the Russian victory over Napoleon. Chaikovsky's "Overture of 1812" premiered in the new cathedral.

In 1931, as part of the Communist campaign to destroy the Russian Orthodox religion and all buildings and relics associated with it, Stalin had the cathedral demolished. In 1938, the Soviets began to build a Palace of Soviets on the site. Construction was discontinued in 1941 because of the war. From the start, however, the project was in trouble. The foundation was built on ground that kept getting flooded or was always giving way. According to popular legend, this was "God's revenge" for the Communists' destruction of the cathedral. After the war, in 1958, the Soviets gave up on the Palace of Soviets and built the Moscow Swimming Pool on the site. Now, in place of the largest Russian Orthodox cathedral in the world, Moscow had the largest outdoor swimming pool in the world. In the mid-1990s, the new post-Soviet Russian government demolished the swimming pool and erected a new Cathedral of Christ the Savior, built as closely as possible to the original by using old blueprints and photos. Boris Yeltsin's body lay in state in the Cathedral in 2007.

A more personal memory of my going to the Moscow Swimming Pool is that each time I walked from the Kropotkinskaya Metro Station to the pool, I passed the Soviet Academy of Sciences Institute of the Russian Language and Literature. Inside that building worked several linguists to whom I owed a great debt. Headed by Professor Elena Zemskaya, a group of Soviet linguists had been working on Colloquial Russian. Their findings began to be published in 1967, the 50th anniversary of the so-called "Great October Revolution." When I began to research the topic "Colloquial Russian" for my doctoral dissertation, I found there was absolutely no material on the subject in the United States, not even at the Library of Congress. I found a citation in a Soviet journal to a book published by Saratov University on Colloquial Russian. I sent five letters requesting that book—to the Soviet Embassy in Washington, Saratov University, the Soviet UN delegation in New York, Moscow University and the Soviet Academy of Sciences.

After a long wait, I received an autographed copy of the Saratov book, together with a monograph by Zemskaya, and several other books on the subject. These Soviet materials became the crucial sources for my dissertation. Even by the time I defended my dissertation at Georgetown (1974), there were no references on the subject in the States. My examining board seemed more curious about the subject than in interrogating me about my knowledge. This was the first time any of them had seen work on Colloquial Russian.

I found it difficult to bypass the Institute. But I felt it would have been unwise and inconsiderate of me to go inside to personally thank the linguists who had been so helpful. Being a military attaché, I was afraid my association with them would put them on the spot with the KGB.

The second sport we participated in was platform tennis. It resembles tennis and racquetball on a badminton-or pickleball-size court. The court is enclosed in a cage made of taut chicken wire so, like racquetball, the ball can be played off the walls. The playing surface is a metal deck covered with a paint that has grit mixed into it for good traction. The surface is elevated and has small holes so snow and water can quickly dissipate. This makes the court playable year-round.

Most of us in Moscow had never heard of the sport. I didn't find out until much later that in 1979 (the very year I arrived at the embassy) Howard Cosell narrated NBC TV coverage of a platform tennis national championship. There were several tennis, ping-pong and racquetball players among us at the embassy and we welcomed the chance to "whack" a ball with a racquet/paddle. (I now play pickleball.) Our embassy platform tennis court was on the grounds of the ambassador's residence. Next to the court was a small shack in which we could warm ourselves or cool down after a vigorous match. With only one court for the entire embassy, we had to reserve it ahead of time. My whole family, including Holly, played whenever we got a chance.

Holly was most active in another sport: broomball. It is similar to field hockey, but played on ice—in tennis shoes, not skates. In 1979-1980, the sticks were short Russian brooms with the straw soaked in water, frozen, then bent to resemble a hockey stick. The ball was six inches in diameter. (Later, as the game developed around the world, new, standardized equipment became the norm.) Tennis courts or playgrounds could be flooded and the Moscow temperatures took care of ensuring there was ice all winter.

Broomball originated in Canada in the early 20th century where streetcar workers used a small soccer ball and regular brooms. As the Moscow broomball website explains: "Broomball is a contact sport— with opponents and with the ice. Goalkeepers remain on their knees at all times, do not have sticks and can catch the ball with their hands, other than that, rules are negotiable."

A Foreign Community Sports Association coordinated softball, tennis, broomball, basketball and other intramural sports. Only expats (short for "expatriates," a term given to Americans living and working abroad) were permitted to participate.

The Swedish embassy property had the only golf course in Moscow. I played one round of golf during a tournament there. Cross-country skiing rounded out our sports life. Breaking trails through the snow-laden Beryoza (Birch trees) in the pristine Moscow countryside gave us much-needed respite from the ice and slush in the city.

The sports highlight of the year 1980 for all Americans, however, took place far from Moscow—Lake Placid. That was what became known as the "Miracle on Ice." I had gone back to Wisconsin on emergency leave. On 22 February, at a bar in my hometown, I watched the American hockey team beat the Soviets. When I returned to Moscow, I was a little surprised that many Soviets came up and congratulated me on our victory.

PHOTOS AND DOCUMENTS I

Spaso House: American Ambassador's residence

Author escorting an "unidentifiable" Soviet general

Soviet Cosmonaut Alexei Leonov

Fragments of Stasi/KGB dossier on author

Office Memorandum • UNITED STATES GOVERNMENT

TO: CPT Holbrook   DATE: 16 Dec 72
FROM: LTC ODOM
SUBJECT: MOSCOW   Maj Jimmie Tucker
    ☎ 8-2231283
    or 2231343

1. I'm glad that you could use the charts.

2. I put your name to the DATT here in moscow, Brig Gen S.V. Wilson, as an excellent candidate for an east attaché assignment. He wrote BG Bowden, in ACSI, who mentioned you to MI branch but only received a formalistic response. The matter lies there now — no more movement that I know of.

3. I tried to get you forcibly removed from USMA straight to MOSCOW by next Jul-Aug (i.e approx mid 73) and a promise made to return you from moscow to USMA for 2 yrs after ~~tour~~ more in Russian Dept. No luck — Wilson probably would do so if he had the power — he doesn't.

4. As far as I know — & my information is limited — there are at this time NO - repeat, NO, nominees for two Army posts coming vacant in moscow in mid 73, i.e. next Summer. Minimum of 5 months preparatory time is needed — i.e. DIS course & briefings — but could be condensed to two-three months if the "will" is there.

OVER

Note to author from Lieutenant Colonel Odom

American Embassy, Moscow, 1980

Army Attachés, 1979. L to R: Operations coordinator, Chief Warrant Officer Jerry Wessels; Major Ed Baisden; Colonel Ron Ayotte; Lieutenant Colonel Tom Spencer; Author; Lieutenant Colonel Jim Hinds. Lieutenant Colonels Don Siebenaler and Jeff Barrie replaced Hinds and Baisden when the latter rotated back to the U.S.

Diplomatic and calling cards

Author's residence at Leninsky Prospekt 45

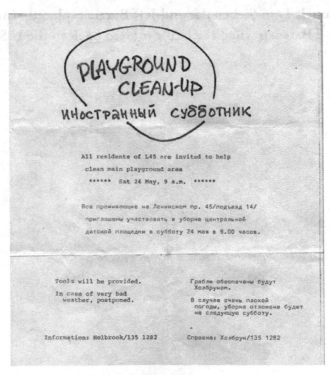

Subbotnik poster

Sorting and picking up Berlin Commissary items

Elaine in front of St. Basil's Cathedral

Elaine's reproduction of *The Virgin of Vladimir*

Misha, Tarisa, Holly and Yasha

President Carter and Leonid Brezhnev sign SALT II

Maria Lopukhina by Vladimir Borovikovsky, 1797

Moscow Outdoor Swimming Pool, 1980

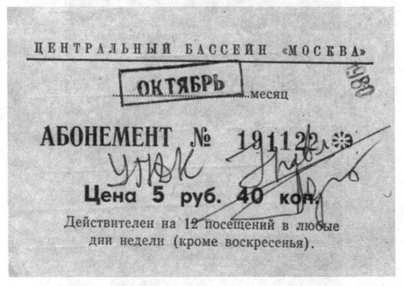

Author's October 1980 pass to Moscow Swimming Pool

American women's broomball team with Coach Tom Spencer
Holly's in the front row, fourth from left

WELCOME TO
THE FIRST GOLF COURSE
IN RUSSIA

Ulitsa Dovzhenko, 1
119590 Moscow, Russia
phone: 147 83 30 Reception
147 95 10 Pro Shop
fax: 147 62 52

Score card for Moscow Golf Club

PART III: TRAVELING IN THE USSR

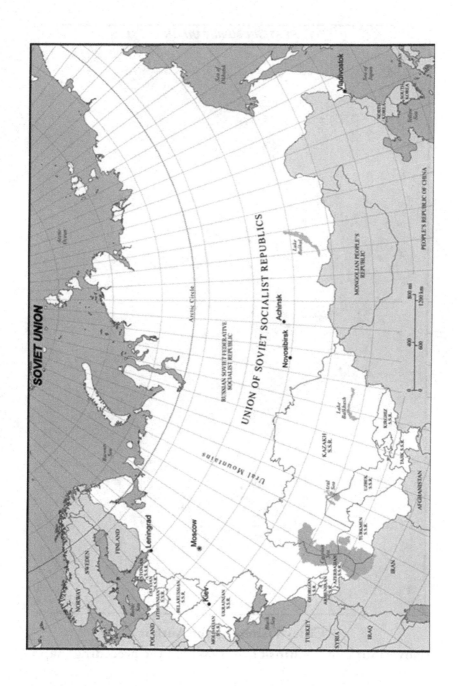

Cities Visited by the Author
(Novosibirsk and Achinsk are shown on the preceding map.)

THE SOVIET UNION (1922-1991)

At the time of this writing (2018), more than a quarter of a century has passed since the collapse of the USSR. Readers under age 40 are unlikely to have any memories of that country. Before sharing some of my experiences traveling around the Soviet Union, I will summarize some of its more salient features.

The Soviet Union was not Russia. It was a Russian-dominated conglomerate of fifteen distinct nations, called Soviet Socialist Republics, all ruled by the Soviet Communist Party. Only two Republics—Belorussia and Ukraine—were closely related linguistically and culturally to the largest Soviet Republic, Russia. Russians made up only 51 percent of the total Soviet population. Besides Russians, Belorussians and Ukrainians, there were 82 national/ethnic groups in the USSR, speaking more than 100 languages. Among these groups were about 55 million Muslims.

Several of these nations and ethnic groups were part of the pre-revolutionary Russian Empire. According to Stephen Kotkin's book, *Stalin*, the 1897 census of Russian Eurasia listed 104 nationalities speaking 146 languages. When the Soviet Union was officially formed in 1922—after the abdication of Tsar Nicholas II, the Bolshevik Coup and the Russian Civil War—it comprised only six Republics. During the 1920s, the Bolsheviks had to re-conquer some of the countries that had been a part of the Russian Empire. By 1936, there were twelve Soviet Republics. It was not until 1940, as a result of the Nazi-Soviet Pact of 1939 (Molotov-Ribbentrop), that the Baltic countries—Lithuania, Latvia and Estonia—were incorporated into the Union, bringing the total to fifteen Republics. The Baltic States always maintained they were still independent countries occupied by the Soviet Union. The European Union, the European Court of Human Rights, the United Nations Human Rights Council and the United States supported the Baltic States' assertion.

The USSR, like the Russian Empire, was Eurasian; it encompassed a part of both Europe and Asia. The Ural Mountains formed a natural geographic border between these two continents. (On one occasion in 1994, I was able to stand at a monument outside Sverdlovsk with one foot in Europe and the other in Asia.) Approximately 75 percent of the Soviet population lived in the European part of the Union.

The Soviet Union was the world's largest state, about the size of North America. It covered one-sixth of the Earth's land surface and had eleven time zones. In the northeast, in the Bering Strait, Soviet Big Diomede Island was only 2.4 miles from American Little Diomede. The USSR also bordered Norway, Finland, Poland, Czechoslovakia, Hungary, Rumania, North Korea, China, Mongolia, Afghanistan, Iran and Turkey.

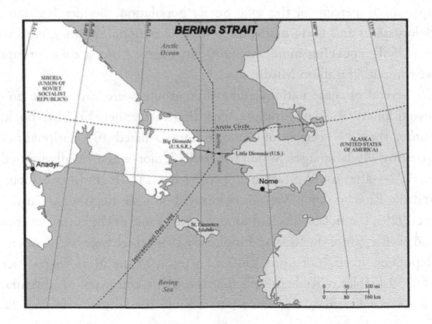

Many areas in sparsely populated and harsh Siberia were and are almost inaccessible to humans. Temperatures in the winter there often reach minus 70 degrees F., not to mention the unimaginable wind-chill factors along the northern coasts. At those times, the few air and rail transportation networks that do exist in Siberia often shut down. As an example of the weather diversity in the Soviet Union, however, the Central Asian regions below Siberia were approximately ten percent desert. The temperature in Ashkhabad, Turkmenistan has reached 114 degrees F.

Since the demise of the USSR, Central Asia now has five independent states: Kazakhstan, Turkmenistan, Kirghizia, Tadzhikistan and Uzbekistan.

Moscow is located at the same latitude as Copenhagen, Denmark; Glasgow, Scotland; and Juneau, Alaska. The highest temperatures during my time in Moscow were in the mid-80s (84 in May 1979 and 82 in June 1980). In the winter, our lows were usually in the teens, although we could get stretches where the temperatures remained below minus 30 degrees F. for several weeks. The lowest temperature ever recorded was minus 44 degrees F. in January 1940, but that was rare. In the two winters I spent in Moscow, at least a light snow fell almost every night.

The cold weather didn't bother me as much as one might expect, since I had experienced similarly low temperatures as a boy in Wisconsin. In fact, I shared the Muscovites' view regarding the temperature in winter: better to have it below freezing than to have it hover just above freezing. At warmer temperatures the snow and ice turned to slush on the streets and sidewalks, which made it hazardous for both drivers and pedestrians. Boris Pasternak wrote:

> It's February. Grab the ink and weep!
> Sob and write of February
> As you watch the thunderous muck
> Burn black with spring.

Elena Gorokhova, in her *Russian Tattoo,* described the slush thus: "[The] snow turns into porridge and walking becomes wading."

Although the Soviet Union was a multinational state with a total population of 286 million, it never became a "melting pot" in a way that we characterize the United States because the various ethnic and national groups mostly lived separately in their native regions. The exception to this—and a large part of the reason the Soviet Union was often thought of and referred to as Russia—is that millions of Russians populated much of the non-Russian part of the USSR. Ethnic Russians often held key political and economic positions in each of the other republics. "Russification" of the empire had begun well before the 1917 Bolshevik Coup, but continued at a faster pace during the Soviet era.

During my attaché years, about ten years before the collapse of the USSR, Russians made up the following percentages of the Union Republic populations:

Union Republic	Percentage	Union Republic	Percentage
Kazakhstan	41	Belorussia	12
Latvia	33	Uzbekistan	11
Estonia	28	Tadzhikistan	10
Kirghizia	26	Lithuania	9
Ukraine	21	Azerbaijan	8
Turkmenistan	13	Armenia	8
Moldavia	13	Georgia	7

For example, there were nearly 11,000,000 Russians in the Ukraine and 2,200,000 in Uzbekistan. In Kazakhstan, there were more Russians than Kazakhs—6,800,000 Russians to 5,900,000 Kazakhs. In a 2005 speech to Russians, President Vladimir Putin pointed out that with the breakup of the USSR, "Tens of millions of our co-citizens and compatriots found themselves outside Russian territory." In fact, once the Soviet Union disintegrated, over 25 million Russians lived outside the Russian Republic. One can easily see here the seeds of future turmoil.

Another reason the Soviet Union was thought of as "Russia" is because the official language of the USSR was Russian. The illiteracy problem the Bolsheviks inherited from the Tsarist regime is characterized by Isaiah Berlin thus: "The gap between illiterate peasants and those who could read and write was wider in Russia than in any other European state in so far as Russia could be called European at the time." At the beginning of the Soviet era, literacy rates were near 40 percent for men and a little over 12 percent for women. The Party's literacy campaign, begun in 1919, was motivated by the need to promote Party ideology. Lenin declared, "Without literacy there can be no politics. There can be only rumors, gossip and prejudice." The result of the Communist campaign was that by the 1950s, the Soviet Union could be considered to have reached nearly 100 percent literacy, although I did meet an occasional older person who couldn't read or write Russian.

Some schools in the 1920s and 1930s were allowed to teach in their native, non-Russian languages, but Russian was a required second language. From 1938, many non-Russian languages began to use the Cyrillic alphabet. In 1975, Communist Party leader, Leonid Brezhnev, said, "Together with one's own mother tongue one will speak fluent Russian, which the Soviet people have voluntarily accepted as a common historical heritage and which contributes to a further stabilization of the political, economic and spiritual unity of the Soviet people." This Russianization of the Soviet school system is what made it possible for me to travel throughout the USSR and speak Russian with all nationalities and ethnic groups. It also makes it possible for me now to speak Russian with almost all immigrants from the USSR who are 35-years old or older, no matter their ethnic background.

I traveled to twenty-six cities in Russia, Lithuania, Belorussia, Ukraine, Georgia, Azerbaijan, Armenia and Turkmenistan. Most of my travel took place in the European part of the Soviet Union. I had one trip to Siberia—also a part of the Russian Republic.

No book about travel in Russia is complete without the inclusion of some reference to the Marquis de Custine. He wrote what is likely the most famous travelogue on Russia: his 1839 *Journey for Our Time*. Almost every personal account of life in Russia written by diplomats, correspondents and others who have lived or traveled there extensively, are sprinkled with citations from de Custine. The reason is clear: so many of de Custine's travel experiences are nearly identical to those others encountered over the ensuing 150-odd years. Due to his aristocratic connections, de Custine traveled about Russia with the authorization of Tsar-Emperor, Nicholas I. De Custine writes: "To let me know he would not be displeased to have me travel in his country, the Tsar did me the favor of telling me I should go at least as far as Moscow and Nizhni to get a fair idea of the country. 'Petersburg is Russian,' he added, 'but not Russia.'"

Readers of Westerners' accounts know little about the French traveler. Therefore, I believe a few words about de Custine are appropriate. I strongly recommend that those interested in Russia's future role in the community of nations read one of the several editions of his book. They will find many of his opinions remain provocative even now in the 21st century.

Astolphe de Custine was born into wealth in 1790 and grew up during the excesses of the French Revolution of 1789. Looking for evidence that republican government was a travesty, he decided to make a three-month trip to a famous monarchy: Russia. He writes "I went to Russia in search of arguments against representative government." De Custine's fame among democratically inclined readers, and especially anti-Soviet Cold War Warriors, was secured by his next sentence: "I returned from Russia a partisan of constitutions.... To the extent that I have come to know the terrifying and extraordinary government formalized, if not founded, by Peter the Great, I have better understood the importance of the mission that fell to my lot."

Journey for our Time was first published four years after de Custine's return from Russia. New editions, including a revised version, were published in 1844 and 1846. A few citations from his *Journey* will show why his book was so popular during the Cold War:

"The political system of Russia could not withstand twenty years of free communication with Western Europe."

"Do you know what it is to travel in Russia? .... two nations: Russia as it is and Russia as it would like to show itself to Europe."

"If freedom of the press were accorded to Russia for twenty-four hours, what you would see would make you recoil with horror. Silence is indispensable to oppression."

And perhaps the most famous passage of all—on the final pages of his *Journey*:

"When your son is discontented in France, use my formula; say to him: 'Go to Russia.' It is a journey that would be beneficial to every foreigner; for whoever has really seen Russia will find himself content to live anywhere else."

A few years later, another Frenchman, Alexander Dumas (of *The Count of Monte Cristo* and *Three Musketeers* fame), also traveled and wrote about his experiences in Russia. Although his reports contain some criticism, he traveled primarily with Russian noblemen and enjoyed many of their privileges.

As the reader will see, in addition to general travel difficulties in the USSR, the Soviet KGB and Ministry of Defense made it next to impossible for military attachés to gather much of real military significance. In some ways, like de Custine and Dumas, we had to have the "Tsar's permission" to travel outside Moscow. Soviet officials required us to follow a strict procedure. First, we requested transportation and lodging through our embassy administrative office, run by the four Soviet women employees. They made arrangements for us through Intourist. At the same time, we filed a request with the MOD to travel. In our application, we were required to indicate the dates of travel, our flight or train number, or license plate number if we were driving an embassy car. Then we had to list the hotels where we would stay and stipulate how many days we would be in a particular city.

Once the application had been filed, we waited. The Ministry usually signaled its rejection of our application by simply not responding. If they approved our travel, we found out shortly before we were scheduled to depart. We were not permitted to deviate from our approved itinerary. The most serious consequence of violating the itinerary was to be declared *persona non grata*, which meant our assignments in Moscow were terminated and we would return to the U.S.

KGB AND GRU

The letters KGB came from the Russian name of the organization, *Komitet gosudarstvennoy bezopasnosti* (Committee for State Security). This was a large and powerful agency that spread its tentacles throughout the world—recruiting spies and collecting information. It was also deeply embedded in almost every domestic Soviet organization. With the exception of the embedding, in many ways, the KGB could be described as a rough equivalent of our CIA, FBI, NSA and the U.S. Secret Service all wrapped into one.

Most readers have read or heard about the KGB's campaign against dissidents in the USSR or about their spies in the West. None of this, however, was directly affected attachés. Our main KGB dealings were with its Seventh Main Directorate and, to a limited extent, with the Second Main Directorate. The Seventh Main Directorate of the KGB was responsible for surveillance of foreigners, especially those foreign embassy personnel who were suspected of conducting espionage against the USSR. Surveillance of military attachés was almost fulltime everywhere in the Soviet Union, with a few exceptions in Moscow. Most of my references to the KGB in this book pertain to officers of the Seventh Main Directorate.

The KGB's Second Main Directorate focused on combating foreign intelligence services in the USSR and targeting foreigners for recruitment. In 1979, Soviet General-Major Rem Krasilnikov became Chief of the department responsible for countering U.S. and British intelligence agencies and for recruiting English-speaking personnel. Krasilnikov's people borrowed surveillants from the Seventh Main Directorate to assist in this mission. I did come in contact with personnel of his Directorate, as you will see toward the end of this book. I believe there's a good chance that Krasilnikov's department orchestrated many of the KGB shenanigans I encountered during my travels and in Moscow.

Most Westerners, and for that matter, most Soviet citizens, were unaware there was (and still is) an even larger Soviet organization conducting intelligence operations around the world: the GRU.

The GRU (*Glavnoe razvedovatel'noe upravlenie*-Main Intelligence Directorate of the Soviet General Staff) reportedly had six times as many operatives in foreign countries as the KGB. Almost all its activities were conducted outside the USSR, just as our CIA works outside the U.S. The exception here is that elements of the GRU also provided normal military intelligence for Soviet combat units.

Over the years, the GRU successfully obtained technologies of the American nuclear submarine George Washington and acquired the American Red Eye missile. German-born GRU agent, Klaus Fuchs, gave the Soviets critical atomic secrets from his position on the Manhattan Project. Americans Alger Hiss, Whittaker Chambers and the most recent FBI traitor, Robert Hanssen, worked at one time for the GRU. (On the other hand, Oleg Penkovsky, a GRU colonel, worked for us.)

Although attachés had nothing to do with the GRU, I present this little sketch of that organization because it provides some background for the encounter I had with a GRU colonel later in the USSR. In my case, I believe the KGB was using the colonel to approach me because we had known each other from my days at USMLM in East Germany.

Historically, competition between the GRU and the Cheka (the original name of the secret police that eventually became the KGB) was on occasion fierce, even deadly. In July 1918, the Cheka shot the entire military intelligence staff of the Eastern Front, together with the Front commander and his staff. Earlier, in May 1918, the Cheka did the same to the intelligence staff of the Soviet 7th Army. In November 1920, the Cheka was permitted to "purge" the GRU, resulting in hundreds of GRU officers being shot.

For a time after WWII and immediately after Stalin's death in 1953, the GRU was able to exact some revenge. They presented the Politburo with documents detrimental to what remained of the Cheka/KGB. Its Head, Victor Abakumov, was shot and a purge of the state security organization ensued. Many of its leaders were shot after being tortured in GRU cellars on Gogol Boulevard. This was the same building where I went to present my attaché credentials to the Soviet Ministry of Defense in 1979.

As a result of this history, there has always been a question of the relationship between the two spy agencies. KGB General Oleg Kalugin, a former Head of KGB Foreign Intelligence who defected to the U.S. in 1980, wrote: "The inescapable fact was that we were the dominant agency; the KGB even had a counterintelligence unit that operated clandestinely inside the GRU, recruiting officers and soldiers to work for us. During my time, one of the Soviet Union's top admirals—a commander of one of our four fleets—worked for the KGB." The example I discuss later of my meeting with a GRU colonel, however, suggests the two agencies could work together, or the KGB could enlist the cooperation of the GRU when needed.

After the demise of the Soviet Union in 1991, the new Russian government disbanded the KGB and formed two organizations from it: the Federal Security Service (FSB) and the Foreign Intelligence Service (SVR). The GRU, however, remained intact within the Russian General Staff.

MURMANSK
FIRST VENTURE INTO THE
SOVIET HINTERLAND

Moscow intrigued me, but Moscow was no more a good portrayal of the Soviet Union than New York City is of the United States. Finally, after little over a month in the capital, I was going out into the "hinterland"—north to Murmansk. (See map of cities visited by the author.) I'd never been to this region of the USSR—one that held historic significance for me, a few American soldiers and sailors, and almost all Soviet citizens. My first trip out of Moscow was going to bring me to a site of an early and very little-known U.S.-Soviet conflict. American troops had actually fought the Bolsheviks on Soviet soil.

The city of Murmansk, located on the Kola Peninsula close to the Norwegian and Finnish borders, was a strategically important seaport and industrial city, but one foreigners could visit. I believe it remains the largest city in the world north of the Arctic Circle. In 1979, its population was just under 500,000. Murmansk was the only ice-free port in the Soviet Arctic, which led to its playing an important role as a supply route in support of the Eastern Front during WWI and for Lend-Lease convoys in WWII. In 1979, it was a center of Soviet submarine and icebreaker activity. The nearby city and naval base of Severomorsk was the headquarters of the Soviet Northern Fleet.

German forces launched an attack against Murmansk on 29 June 1941—one week after the general offensive against the USSR. Fierce Soviet resistance in the tundra and several Soviet counter-attacks made a Nazi breakthrough impossible. The Germans discontinued their attacks in late October 1941, having failed to take Murmansk or to cut off the Karelian railway line. In 1985, Murmansk was awarded the title Hero City, an honor similar in many respects to our Congressional Medal of Honor.

We were scheduled to fly up and take a train back. Most Soviet cities and regions with major military facilities were officially off limits to foreigners. (The U.S. government placed a similar restriction on Soviet diplomats in our country.) Hundreds of other Soviet cities were *de facto* off limits because of the lack of transportation. Even those towns that were ostensibly accessible to foreigners could be visited only with special permission from the Soviet government. This included Murmansk.

The excitement about going on a first information collection trip was tempered somewhat by my fellow assistants' warnings and friendly kidding about the fact that I'd be traveling with our principal Army Attaché. It turned out there was a great reluctance to travel with the colonel. He had a reputation of being a man with strange habits. The rumor was that his main diet was baby food. Apparently, as the junior attaché in the office, I drew the short straw. I had met the colonel two years earlier during a luncheon at the Potsdam House in East Germany. So here we were together again; this time he would be my boss for the next few months.

Intourist provided an attractive female guide who met us at the airport in Murmansk and showed us around town. Being under her wing most of the time, we saw very little of military significance. A naval attaché may have been able to glean something from the ships in the port, but it meant little to us ground-pounders.

The colonel was particularly interested in one facility we visited: a swimming school. (He had lettered in swimming at West Point.) The most remarkable aspect of this school was that many of the children were toddlers, some even infants. The Soviet government placed a high premium on identifying potential champion athletes as early as possible. Olympic competition was one of the highest priorities for the USSR, as it was seen as a way to prove to the world the superiority of the Soviet system. (A similar attitude toward Olympics existed in Nazi Germany.)

At that time (and to some extent also today in Russia), athletes who performed well in the Olympics enjoyed privileges shared by very few in the USSR. A Soviet athlete who failed to medal at an event during the games, however, could be punished when he or she returned home.

The school appeared to be a testing ground where instructors placed each child in a swimming tank in order to determine whether he or she had any natural talent for staying afloat. School officials selected those who displayed "talent" (or a keen sense of survival) for further training. Those who failed the tests were apparently rescued, but sent back to their families. I couldn't help but think about the origins of Russian ballet in the 18th century, when some say authorities forcibly took young children from their families if they showed any talent for dancing.

Later in the day, Intourist allowed us to walk about the city on our own. I felt a rush of adrenalin the instant I spotted a plaque dedicated to Red Army soldiers who had fallen during the "Allied Intervention." This is a little-known but important episode of both American and Soviet history. American soldiers and sailors actually fought here against Bolshevik forces during the Soviet Civil War of 1918-1920.

Now, some sixty years later, I was walking the same streets traversed by those forgotten Americans. Being here now made me feel connected to that historical event. The Intervention had interested me since I began to study Russian at the Army Language School. It was there, in 1962, that I read E. M. Halliday's *The Ignorant Armies*. In fact, the first short story I wrote in Russian—*"Poslednee nastuplenie"* (The Last Offensive)—was centered on the departure from this very same Murmansk of an American soldier who had befriended a Russian orphan.

Although there are a few books on the subject, none has gained widespread reading by the American public. In fact, two former U.S. presidents displayed their ignorance of this important historical event. In 1972, President Nixon went on Soviet TV and told the Russians, "Most important of all, we have never fought one another in war." The Russians knew this was wrong. In 1984, while talking of America and Russia during his State of the Union speech, President Reagan said, "Our sons and daughters have never fought each other in war." Probably no one in the House of Representatives Chamber at the time knew this wasn't true.

Unfortunately for future American generations, the resulting ignorance at our government's highest levels of this historic episode may have contributed to the folly of our later military interventions undertaken without clearly defined objectives in countries whose populaces did not support us.

The original rationale behind the Intervention in Russia in 1918 was that the Allies wanted to protect enormous stores of equipment and goods shipped to Murmansk, nearby Archangelsk and Vladivostok in the Far East for use by the Russian Army in WWI. Those considerations soon faded once the Bolsheviks pulled out of WWI after their October 1917 Coup. The Western Allies, especially the British, decided to support the "White" anti-Bolshevik factions (of which there were many) in their struggle to overthrow Lenin and Trotsky and the "Reds." Against the advice of the U.S. General Staff Chief, General Peyton March and General John "Black Jack" Pershing himself, State Department officials convinced President Woodrow Wilson to intervene in North and Far East Russia.

Ironically, one of the most notable battles by Americans, Canadians and Scots against the Bolsheviks began on 11 November 1918—the day WWI ended in Europe. American military units didn't leave North Russia until June 1919. By the time we pulled out, nearly 5000 Americans, many from my home state, Wisconsin, and from Michigan had deployed to North Russia.

The Allied Intervention is an intriguing and extremely complex story. Soviet citizens were well aware of this period in their history; the Intervention was widely taught in Soviet schools as part of anti-Western propaganda and became ingrained in the Soviet consciousness.

By the end of the American participation in the North Russian Intervention, 244 American soldiers and sailors had died— 109 killed in direct combat; 35 died later of wounds received in combat; and 100 from drowning, accidental death or disease. In addition to the dead, 305 were wounded. From actions in the Far East and Siberia, 179 American soldiers died and 52 were wounded. (See Appendix D for a more detailed look at three battles.) (The Veterans of Foreign Wars magazine *VFW* identified in its November-December 2015 issue the passing of the last surviving veterans in 2003 and 2005 of the North Russia and Siberia Expeditions, respectively.

All the warring sides were upset with us. The Bolsheviks/Reds obviously didn't like our fighting against them. The Russian White armies didn't think we were doing enough to help them. Great Britain and other allies likewise felt we weren't helping the effort enough. The Japanese thought we were causing problems for their own ambitions in Russia. U.S. Major General William Graves, the commander of U.S. troops in Siberia stated, "I must admit, I do not know what the United States was trying to accomplish by military intervention."

All in all, it was a giant fiasco, the consequences of which linger today. G.J.A. O'Toole writes in his *Honorable Treachery*, "One thing emerges clearly, however: the entire episode was the result of a monumental intelligence failure by the Wilson Administration." George Kennan, U.S. Ambassador to the USSR for a short period in 1952 and one of the most highly regarded experts on Russia, has suggested the Cold War may have begun, not after WWII, but as the aftermath of this Allied Intervention. The Cold War was a major factor behind my being in Moscow as a military attaché. (Many years later, during the Korean "police action," the Cold War almost became WWIII when Soviet and American pilots fought each other. These skirmishes are almost entirely ignored by most historians but are noted in an NSA booklet: *The History of Traffic Analysis: World War I - Vietnam.)*

For our return to Moscow, the Army Attaché and I left Murmansk at 9:45 in the evening on 30 May. Our train—No. 15, the *"Arktika"*— would take us to Moscow via Petrozavodsk and Leningrad. I liked trains. I grew up along the Burlington route on the Mississippi River; my step-dad worked on the tracks there. I was looking forward to this, my first extended ride on a Soviet train. The trip was scheduled to take two days.

As always, the girls in the embassy office back in Moscow had reserved an entire first-class sleeper for us. Since there were no two-person sleepers on this train, we were issued tickets for all four berths in one compartment. Unfortunately, the tickets meant nothing to the Soviets. They put two KGB agents in with us. One told us he was a researcher in the shipbuilding industry. The other's story was that he worked in railway production. Since the sun didn't set in the far north at this time of year, the trip would take place in daylight. The two KGB agents, assisted by their trusty helper, the car attendant, kept us under complete observation through the night.

The next morning, just north of Petrozavodsk, in the small village of Lizhma, our train pulled off on a siding and came to a stop. The car attendant offered no explanation for the delay. We later learned from the train engineer there had been a derailment further south on the track and our passenger train had to pull onto the siding so military trains had a clear passage on the otherwise clogged rail lines.

We all got off the train and wandered into the village. The local inhabitants came out to see what was going on. Stopping in this village presented a rare opportunity for us to see a piece of rural Russia. The Soviet government didn't permit attachés to travel into the countryside. If we were using one of our embassy cars to travel somewhere, we could not stop in any village along the way for lunch, as one was able to do in Western Europe. As much as we wanted to, our Soviet surveillants wouldn't allow us to take pictures of Lizhma. One of them told my colonel the reason for this prohibition was that it was next to a rail line.

We approached two soldiers who turned out to be from the Estonian Republic. It was clear they weren't too keen about being in the Soviet Army. (I never met a Soviet soldier in East Germany who wanted to be in military service). But NATO was very interested in Baltic States' soldiers—from Lithuania, Latvia and Estonia. NATO planners wondered how loyal they would be to their Russian masters in the event of a military conflict in Europe. As I noted earlier, the Soviet Union seized these countries as part of a secret deal with Nazi Germany in 1939.

In a short while, the colonel told me he was going jogging. That bothered me, as attachés were supposed to stick together when they traveled, since we knew we were under KGB surveillance. In fact, I was a little paranoid on this, my first attaché trip. I recalled how, on my first trip to the USSR in 1971, I had (somewhat comically, in retrospect) inched my way around the hotel my first morning in Moscow, expecting to encounter the dreaded KGB each time I turned a corner. Although there may have been times in Moscow during my attaché years when surveillance was lax or non-existent, during our travel outside the capital, KGB agents were always with us. Sometimes they might be hard to identify. Other times, they would be quite obvious as we drove or walked around town. Who and where they were at this point in our trip, except for our berth-mates, I wasn't sure, but I knew they were there. I admit I was a little nervous. Still, the colonel felt the need to go off jogging, leaving me alone in the village. Where he went, I don't know.

In the meantime, I noticed many of the Soviet passengers had rushed to the small village store. Soviet train food was notoriously poor or scarce. In fact, whenever a train stopped along the way, peasants often appeared along the track with food. Passengers passed money through the train windows to the locals for potatoes, beets, onions, tomatoes and sometimes *kvas*, a fermented Russian drink. Here in the village, however, we had a real food store.

When I saw train passengers coming out of the store with bread, cheese, vodka and wine, I decided to go in and see how it was stocked. Here was a chance to gather some economic data to pass on to our people at the embassy. Food stores in Moscow were infamous for their lack of produce and other food items. (As I wrote earlier, diplomats and other foreigners used special stores in Moscow where we could buy necessities for hard currency—D-coupons, dollars, pounds, Deutsche Mark, etc.) I was curious about what it was like here in the provinces.

I entered the store and saw there was nothing on the shelves. The only person left in the store was the shopkeeper. She looked at me, saw the astonishment on my face, and threw her hands in the air.

"Nothing. Nothing," she exclaimed. "They bought everything I had. We just received a delivery. I don't know when we'll get more goods. What will our villagers do?"

"I understand," I said and made a quick exit.

I started back toward the train. All of a sudden, I heard a shout and turned to see an old man running up the hill.

"Vanya!"

"Sasha! Is it you?"

Vanya was carrying an empty gunnysack and had come from a nearby field to see what all the commotion was in the village. Sasha was a train passenger. He obviously had been to the store and was carrying a bottle of vodka and a loaf of bread.

"*Ne mozhet byt!* (It can't be!)," exclaimed both men at the same time. They dropped what they were carrying, ran to each other and embraced. Then they stepped back and looked at each other. Both had tears in their eyes.

"How long has it been, Sash?" asked Vanya.

"Since '43. That's... that's 36 years!"

Amidst a steady stream of exclamations, Sasha quickly recovered his vodka and bread. Vanya spread his sack out on the ground. Sasha opened the vodka. Both men took long gulps from the bottle and sat down together.

Everyone loves reunion stories and here I was witnessing one. From what I could gather, they had been close friends in the same Red Army unit during WWII. They became separated in 1943 and were never able to reestablish contact after the war. Now they were reunited by the freak circumstance of our train having to lay up at the siding. The vodka bottle was rapidly losing it contents, the loaf of bread was in pieces and the tears returned from time to time. This was surely one example of the fact that Russians are people like all of us. I had goose bumps as I returned to the crowd milling around our train.

I considered engaging one of the villagers in conversation, but was afraid it might get me in trouble—a mistake on my part, I believe in retrospect. Maybe I was concerned about whether my surveillants would intervene. I don't remember. I don't recall how long the colonel was gone, but after he returned we boarded the train again. Soon we were on our way back to Moscow.

One of the revelations for me from this trip was how little military information we had acquired. From my experience at USMLM in East

Germany, I was accustomed to bringing back at least some pictures of installations, if not some military objects we picked up in a training area. With Intourist and the KGB on us all the time in Murmansk, however, I don't know that we could have done any better.

No Room at the Inn

No room at the inn? The desk clerk insisted the hotel in Mogilyov was full. I knew that not to be the case, because Soviet hotels always held back some room in the event a high Party official or some other muckety-muck showed up at the last minute.

"Listen, we're American diplomats traveling with permission of the Ministry of Defense. Your hotel was put on our itinerary, so we must stay here tonight."

"Like I said," the desk clerk insisted, "We simply have no more available rooms."

"Let me talk to the hotel manager."

"As you wish."

In about ten minutes a woman appeared, stating she was the hotel manager. "What can I do for you?"

"We're American diplomats and need a room for the night," I said. "It's already getting dark."

She glanced at a couple of books, shuffled some papers on the counter and then looked up at me.

"I'm sorry. We have no available rooms."

"That can't be."

"That's the way it is."

At that moment she reminded me of the arrogant and rude clerks in most Soviet stores. But I could see I wasn't going to get anywhere pleading with her. I looked around for a policeman. For the first time in my experience traveling in the USSR, however, there was none in sight.

I turned to my wife. "Lyena, have you seen a policeman?"

"No," she replied. "But I've been focused on watching our luggage."

"I'm not sure what to do, " I said. "We have to have a place to sleep tonight."

I wandered around the lobby and looked outside. No policemen. Returning to the hotel desk, I asked for the phone number of the police. As soon as the police desk sergeant found out we were diplomats, he wanted nothing to do with us. When I identified myself further as a military attaché, he recommended I contact the city's military commandant.

"I'm not allowed to do that. The Ministry of Defense forbids us from approaching any military personnel without its express permission."

"Then, maybe you should contact the Committee," he said.

"What committee?" I asked, although I knew what he meant. "Committee" was a way of referring to the KGB—Committee for State Security.

"Committee for Security," he replied.

"Let me have their number."

I then called the local KGB office and talked to the officer on duty. I knew the KGB could force the hotel to give us a room. The KGB could do anything. When I explained my situation, he asked, "Who am I talking to?"

"Major Holbrook, American Assistant Army Attaché."

"You're kidding."

"No I'm not. I have Ministry permission to be here in Mogilyov. My wife and I need a hotel room."

"I had no idea you were in town."

"That's hard to believe. We filed all necessary paperwork at the Ministry of Defense."

"Let me talk to the hotel desk." I handed the phone to the manager. My smile said, *Now you'll see who's running the show.* She took the phone and stepped away. I couldn't make out what she was saying. After a few minutes, she returned the phone to me and the KGB duty officer told me there was nothing he could do. The hotel was, he said, indeed full.

The KGB was my option of last resort. So Elaine and I took a taxi to the train station where we commandeered a bench in the waiting hall.

After we put our heavy luggage in a locker, Elaine got settled in on a bench. It was cool—about 50 degrees Fahrenheit—so I covered her coat with my jacket and then tried to stand watch. Sometime in the middle of the night, I sat down on the bench beside her, with my camera strap wrapped around my wrist, and dozed.

The next morning we ate an early breakfast at the station and then learned we couldn't get confirmation for our tickets to Smolensk until 10 a.m. We decided to walk around town and try to ascertain whether there was any unusual military activity. That was, after all, our purpose for being there. We saw nothing of any significance—a military vehicle here, a couple of soldiers there. When we returned to the station just before 10, the woman at the ticket counter told us we had to wait until noon to get our new tickets.

During our walk around town we had seen a large meadow near the rail station. Since it had warmed up considerably, we headed straight back there and spread our coats on the ground. There were no trees within 50 yards and we had a clear 360-degree field of vision. Not completely secure, but the best we could do. I placed my hat on top of my camera and used it for a pillow. No sooner had I slumped to the ground than I was asleep. I knew I wouldn't sleep too soundly, given the circumstances, but I needed some shut-eye. Elaine did her best to stay awake and guard against any intruders.

Backing up a couple of days… Elaine (I called her Lyena in Russian) and I had planned on a late-May visit to Bryansk in western Russia, then on to Gomel and Mogilyov in the Belorussian Republic. Finally, we would visit the Russian city of Smolensk before returning to Moscow.

I should have known before we left Moscow that this trip was going to be a challenge. First, Intourist would not provide train tickets for the entire journey and would not guarantee us hotel accommodations in Mogilyov. Add to this the fact that the MOD restrictions on our travel itinerary required that we take certain trains between destinations and stay at designated hotels. Not only were we going to have to arrange our own tickets, but they also had to be on specific trains. So we started the trip with a lot of unknowns. I'm sure the Soviets hoped the lack of prior confirmed arrangements would discourage us from traveling.

Second, I was traveling outside Moscow with my wife for the first time. Occasionally, DIA allowed attaché wives to travel with their husbands. They were not involved in information collection as some of the CIA wives were. Soviet KGB General Krasilnikov points to these CIA wives a few times in his book. He does not, however, accuse the attaché wives of the same intelligence activities. Of course our wives were aware that we took some pictures, but why we would photograph an antenna was beyond them. We didn't discuss the intelligence value of such photos.

I believe, however, information collection for the attaché was degraded when wives traveled. In my case, at least, there was a keen sense of danger, given the need to protect my wife from any unpleasant incidents. We talked it over and decided to accept the challenge. After all, we both spoke Russian and had diplomatic status. We hoped to present the appearance of a normal foreign couple.

So two days earlier, we had left Moscow on a night train and arrived in Bryansk the next morning. We spent the first four hours there haggling with the woman at the ticket counter to get a ticket to Gomel. Our diplomatic cards and passports didn't impress her. What finally worked was when I showed her our official itinerary from the MOD—in Russian and English. She saw the Ministry required that we travel on a specific train. By now, though, we had little time to reconnoiter Bryansk.

We arrived in Gomel in the late evening and went straight to our hotel. The next day, after spending three hours arranging train tickets to Mogilyov, we walked about town looking for something significant to photograph or make notes on. Perhaps a military convoy with some interesting artillery pieces or missiles. Or maybe some new conscripts, identifiable by their freshly shaved heads, who were involved in Troop Rotation—the Soviet semiannual call-up and demobilization. No luck.

Andrei Gromyko, the long-time Soviet Minister of Foreign Affairs and former ambassador to the United States was born in Gomel. So also were the parents of Kirk Douglas and the grandparents of Wayne Gretsky.

When we boarded our train to Mogilyov, we found a young woman in our compartment. She was partially undressed, under the covers and reading a book. Food and sour milk on the compartment table suggested she had been on the train for some time. Before the train departed, a young man, dressed stylishly in a suede leather jacket, entered our compartment. This, of course, was unwelcome, but not unprecedented. Once again, just as on the trip back from Murmansk to Moscow, the Soviets took our money and then put other travelers in with us. We assumed our fellow travelers were KGB, but allowed that sometimes they might just be ordinary Soviets.

We initially ignored both Soviets and they didn't talk to each other. The woman read her book; the man read a newspaper. I stepped out into the corridor for a smoke and when I came back, Elaine was teaching them a card game. She had pulled out a deck of cards to play Solitaire, she told me, and when the Soviets expressed an interest in playing, she decided to teach them Crazy-Eights. At that time, we all introduced ourselves. I identified myself to Soviets as an American "diplomat," but not as a "military attaché." If the Soviets had asked what my position at the embassy was, I would have revealed I was a military attaché. The man said he was going to Mogilyov on a business trip. The woman said she was continuing to another city.

The rest of that train trip passed uneventfully, with the final Crazy-Eight score ending up: Americans 5, Soviets 1. When we arrived in Mogilyov, the man left the train and disappeared into the station. The woman remained on the train. It seemed to us to be just another benign encounter with a KGB surveillant and an innocent traveler. Some eighteen hours later, however, we saw them both again—this time as a couple, sitting on a bench outside the train station. I wondered if they had spent the night with us somewhere in the train station.

After the night in hell we spent in Mogilyov, we were anxious to get on to Smolensk, where we had a hotel reservation. We both napped on the train ride there. It was after midnight when we arrived at our hotel. Outside it was quite nippy, but the hotel lobby was warm. It didn't take long, however, before the atmosphere turned cool. The hotel desk clerk told us our room reservation had been canceled.

"I don't understand," I said. "A reservation is a reservation."

"We're sorry. We sent a cable to Intourist in Moscow telling them the reservation was no longer valid. We're having a music festival in honor of Glinka and we need all the rooms for attendees."

Mikhail Glinka (died 1857), a native of Smolensk, was the first prominent Russian composer of secular music. His music highly influenced many subsequent composers, especially Modest Mussorgsky, Nikolai Rimsky-Korsakov and Alexander Borodin. Glinka's most famous work is the opera "A Life for the Tsar" (renamed during the Soviet era as "Ivan Susanin").

Whether or not Intourist notified our embassy about these reservation cancellations was irrelevant. Once we were on the road, there was no way the embassy could communicate with us. Those were the days before cell phones.

"How long have you known there was to be a Glinka festival?" I asked.

"Well, we have one every year. We shouldn't have confirmed your reservation in the first place."

"What do we do, then? We've just come from Mogilyov, where we were also unable to get a hotel room. Don't you have a room where we can at least clean up?"

"I'm sorry."

I turned to Elaine. "This is too much. We're not going to spend another night in a train station."

We just looked at each other. I felt doubly embarrassed. First of all, I had failed twice to get a hotel room. My wife and I were both exhausted. Second, it seemed information collection was completely out of the question. I had to do something. Although we were pretty much at the mercy of the KGB, there had to be a way we could take some control over our situation. I decided we were not leaving the hotel.

"If you have no room for us, we'll just camp out here in the lobby," I told the desk clerk.

"You can't do that."

"We can and we will. At least it's warm here and, presumably, safe. If you won't give us a room, after having already confirmed one before we left Moscow, we will stay right here. You can call the police if you want and explain to them what your hotel has done to us."

With that, Elaine and I stacked our luggage at the end of a bench in the lobby and settled ourselves in for the rest of the night. The hotel clerk disappeared into a back room. At that late hour there was no one else in the lobby—not even any apparent surveillance—and we both quickly fell asleep.

We awoke to loud voices. It was 6:30 a.m. and about 50 people surrounded us. They turned out to be musicians, members of the Moscow Philharmonic Orchestra, who had just arrived to participate in the Glinka Festival. We again asked for a room, if only for a short time, so we could clean up. Not possible, we were told. According to the desk clerk, even high-ranking officials and some famous musicians were being turned away.

"Our train to Moscow doesn't leave until this evening. At least, can you guard our luggage until then?"

"Yes, we can do that. Bring it to the storage room."

Somewhat rested now, we had breakfast at the hotel and then went into town where we walked about, examining the stores which held very little goods. We bought a couple of *piroshki* (small meat pies) for lunch. At the southwest corner of Glinka Park, I took some photos of a TV tower that had several interesting antennas attached to it. Some probably had military uses. The photos might be interesting to NSA. That was the extent of my potentially useful "information collection" for this entire trip.

We boarded our train back to Moscow about 10:00 p.m. As if being rewarded for our troubles on the trip, we found ourselves in a two-person, first-class compartment. We even had a private bathroom in which we were able to clean up a little before falling into our bunks and deep slumber.

From an information collection standpoint, it was an unsatisfactory trip. But we had gained some interesting experience. I wondered how our surveillants viewed our behavior and how they would report on us during this trip. What was in store for us the next time Elaine and I took a trip out of Moscow?

LENINGRAD

The Soviet officer who was to lead us up to the monument insisted on teaching us the Soviet version of the goose step.

"No, no," I said. "That's not the way we march."

"But this is a Soviet ceremony, you need to use the 'ceremonial step,'" he argued.

"No, this isn't a Soviet ceremony," I said. "It's an American ceremony to honor Soviet citizens who fell in the Siege of Leningrad. The presenter here is a United States Senator."

"But, but…"

"And furthermore, we're American officers and we march the American way."

Since there was little time left to argue, the Soviet officer gave in and we proceeded to the monument with him doing his "ceremonial" goose step and our shuffling along the American way. (The first time I saw Soviet soldiers goose-stepping, I was shocked. I associated that step with the Nazis. But it turns out the step entered Russia from Prussia long before the Soviets came to power.)

We were at the Piskaryov Cemetery in Leningrad, assisting Robert Byrd, the U.S. Senate Majority Leader, in a wreath-laying ceremony.

One of the ways our military attachés supported the Moscow embassy was to make arrangements for visits to the USSR of high-ranking U.S. government officials. Since flights carrying these dignitaries were always on U.S. Air Force planes from the Presidential Fleet, our air attachés were the primary coordinators of these visits. Occasionally, one of us other attachés would be called upon to assist.

In July 1979, shortly after the SALT II signing in Vienna, Senator Byrd visited the USSR at the invitation of the Soviet Parliament (Supreme Soviet). His first stop was Leningrad. Air Force Captain Mike Hritsik and I went to Leningrad to coordinate the landing of Byrd's aircraft there. We worked with officials at Leningrad's Pulkovo airport. Senator Byrd arrived in a Boeing 707, former President Lyndon Johnson's Air Force One.

Most of our time in Leningrad was spent with the Air Force crew, either on their aircraft or with them at the hotel. While on the plane, an Air Force sergeant asked me when I had last spoken to my mother.

"It's been a few months. I don't call from Moscow but I do write frequently," I said.

"Would you like to talk to her now?"

"How do you mean?"

"We have a communications system aboard from which you can call anywhere in the world. Remember this is an old Air Force One."

"You mean I could call her from here?"

One can imagine how surprised my mother was back in Wisconsin when I told her I was calling from President Johnson's plane and that I was in Leningrad.

The other formal duty we had in Leningrad was to carry the wreath for Senator Byrd at the Piskaryov Memorial Cemetery. The cemetery on the northern edge of Leningrad is one proof of the sacrifice Leningraders made during the war. Piskaryov has 186 mass graves containing approximately 420,000 civilians and 50,000 soldiers of the Leningrad Front who perished (many from hunger) during the 872-day siege of the city.

On a wall near the entrance to the cemetery an inscription summarizes the tragedy. It reads: "From 8 September 1941 to 22 January 1944, 107,158 bombs and 148, 478 artillery shells bombarded the city, killing 16,744, wounding 33,782 people. A total of 641,803 Leningraders died of hunger." In 1971, during an earlier tourist trip, I had talked in my hotel lobby with an older woman who survived the Siege. She confirmed that it was a horrible time for all Leningraders, but she refused to go into detail.

In the adjacent museum one can see the diary of 11-year old Tanya Savicheva that reads like the one left by Anne Frank. She records the deaths of her grandmother, then uncle, then mother, then brother. The last sentence says, "Only Tanya is left." The dead Tanya's diary was shown at the Nuremberg trials.

It was one of the longest and most destructive sieges in history and overwhelmingly the most costly in terms of casualties. Leningraders refused to surrender. But even if they had wished to, the Germans were instructed not to accept surrender. The Nazi plan was to destroy the city completely. One of the German orders reads: "Early next year we enter the city ... lead those still alive into inner Russia or into captivity, wipe Leningrad from the face of the earth through demolitions, and hand the area north of the Neva River to the Finns." In October, Hitler sent a further directive signed by Alfred Jodl reminding Army Group North not to accept capitulation.

Economic destruction and human losses in Leningrad on both sides exceeded those of the Battle of Stalingrad, the Battle of Moscow, or the atomic bombings of Hiroshima and Nagasaki, combined. For more details on this event, I recommend Harrison Salisbury's *The 900 Days: The Siege of Leningrad*. To me the Siege had current military significance in that it was a warning to anyone planning to invade the Soviet Union. The Leningraders' refusal to capitulate illustrated the sacrifices Russians would endure in the defense of their homeland. On the other hand, I once met a Russian guide in Leningrad who had not included a visit to Piskaryov Cemetery for his foreign tour group. I said to him, "You ought to be ashamed of yourself. Have you no respect for what your fellow Leningraders did during the siege?" He didn't reply.

We returned to Moscow, together with Senator Byrd and his party, aboard the former Air Force One.

Leningrad was a Navy town. The only collection trips I made to that city were with our naval attachés. Upon our return, they wrote the reports. Since DIA sent me only reports I had authored, I have none on Leningrad in my file.

Although Leningrad was the second largest city in the USSR and had an important role in the history of Russia, I had no warm feelings for it. In the first place, it was, as so many travelers have called it, a "European city." I was more interested in Old Russia, the Russia of Kievan Rus and Old Muscovy influence. Perhaps even more relevant for me personally was the fact that the first trip I ever made to Leningrad (in 1971) left me with negative memories. That year a fellow Russian scholar, Dex Dickinson, and I took a two-week tourist trip to the Soviet Union. We were in Leningrad at the end of April and the beginning of May. The weather was terrible—overcast, rain and snow. Weather has always affected my disposition.

Although I visited Piskaryov also on that earlier trip, one of the highlights in 1971 was a visit to the Aleksandr Nevsky Lavra, a particularly special cemetery. Many of Russia's cultural notables are buried there. I went to the grave of one of my favorite writers, Fyodor Dostoevsky, and found the caretaker of his grave was working that day. We sat down and discussed Dostoevsky, which pleased the caretaker, who was also a devoted fan of the writer. I had several pictures taken of us together, as well as some of the grave monument, atop of which was a bust of Dostoevsky. I was using a Kodak Brownie and upon return to the States, I discovered my pictures didn't turn out because of the dark skies over Leningrad.

KIEV
HISTORIC CRADLE OF
THE RUSSIAN STATE

Sometimes KGB surveillance bordered on the comical. On a warm August day in 1979, a fellow attaché and I were walking along the street in Kiev. A taxi pulled up beside us. In it a KGB photographer began taking video of us while he sat astride the window of the vehicle's right, front door—one leg in the taxi, one on the running board, with a video camera on his shoulder. At the time we weren't near any known military installations. We continued walking and the taxi followed us for an entire block.

Surveillance in Kiev often stood out as original and obvious. It was always heavy, both by foot and vehicle. One couple followed us around town, passing us, going some distance, then turning around and coming towards us on the sidewalk. This happened so many times, there is no way they could think we hadn't noticed them. That was a form of obvious surveillance meant to let us know we were under observation and had best do nothing wrong.

KGB surveillance, as well as other encounters with Soviet citizens often provided the main lasting memories of a trip. This was partly due to the fact that we seldom saw anything of real military value during attaché travel outside Moscow. For example, during a trip to Kiev in May 1980, as the city was preparing to serve as one of the 1980 Olympic venues, not only did we not see any significant military activity, we observed nothing at all special in the city. Admittedly, Kiev needed to do little for the Olympics since the only events it would host were the early rounds of the soccer games.

Kiev is a very special city. First of all, it's the birthplace of Russia. Kievan Rus was the center of ancient Russian politics, economy and culture. Kievan Grand Prince Vladimir brought Christianity to Russia in 988. Kiev's "Golden Age" was in the 11th - 13th centuries. At the time, it was considered the largest city in the world and was a European commercial, educational and cultural center, while Moscow was still a backwoods minor principality. Despite these historic origins, Russians have for decades referred to themselves as "Great Russians" and to Ukrainians as "Little Russians." For centuries Ukraine's fertile lands were known as the "breadbasket of Russia." Ukrainian grains not only fed the Russian/Soviet Empire, but also were exported around the world.

Kiev's preeminence as the center of Ancient Russia came to an abrupt and violent end, however, in 1240 when the Mongols—the Golden Horde—invaded and destroyed the city. It never fully recovered its prominence. In fact, from that time forward Ukraine (for which Kiev is now the capital) was divided and ruled by a multitude of powers until its eastern lands became a unit of the USSR as the Ukrainian Soviet Socialist Republic in 1922. Other areas of ancient Ukraine had been parts of Poland or Lithuania. Since the establishment of the Soviet Ukrainian Republic, significant tension has existed between those who were primarily Roman Catholic in the western parts of the Republic and those in the east who were Russian Orthodox.

When the United Nations was established, the organization allowed Ukraine and Belorussia to have national status in the General Assembly, giving the USSR three votes instead of the one held by the U.S., Great Britain and other countries. Except for a brief chaotic interlude after the First World War, however, when several groups claimed to be the Ukrainian government, that country was never really an independent state until it declared its independence from the USSR in 1991.

During my 1971 tourist trip to the Soviet Union with Dex Dickinson, we flew from Leningrad to Kiev. Just as the weather in Leningrad had soured me somewhat on that city, the sun, warmth and green of Kiev had the opposite effect. First impressions remain for a long time. Since that 1971 trip, I've always had positive feelings for Kiev.

In August 1979, I made my first attaché trip to the city. No longer was I focused on tourist sites and cultural activities. We had military information to collect. One of our tasks was to verify the location of a radio research institute. Why we were tasked to do this I don't know. In my report of that trip, I noted that an earlier IR (February 1979) "provided detailed description of this facility."

Another task was to take pictures of Ukrainian ministries. These included the Ministry of Energy and Electrification, the Central Post Office, the Ministries of Meat and Dairy Industries, Agriculture, Procurement, Culture, Lumber and Wood Processing, Trade, Building Materials, Justice, Education, Communications, Finance, Chemistry, as well as the building housing the Council of Ministers. I didn't think much about it at the time, but in retrospect that was probably also a waste of time. I'm sure other attachés had photographed and described all the government buildings along the main street—Khreshchatik—several times in the past. At the end of a long report where we described the exterior of the major government buildings, I wrote in my report:

> Before [we] attempt to collect against future targets of this nature, it would be very helpful to get further guidance on what is considered essential, satisfactory coverage... Would it be better to cover as many targets as possible or to zero in on one or two each time a republic capital is visited?

I never received a response.

Coincidentally, one of our tasks did take us to a tourist location—Babi Yar. Babi Yar is the site of several Nazi massacres during World War II. In September 1941, the Germans killed 33,771 Jews here and buried them in the Babi Yar ravine. This was the single largest massacre during the Holocaust. By the end of the war, in addition to the Jews, the Nazis killed and buried in Babi Yar also thousands of Soviet prisoners of war, Communists, Gypsies, Ukrainian nationalists and civilian hostages. Scholars estimate that between 100,000 and 150,000 persons were killed at this site.

With all the people in the area taking pictures, we were not conspicuous when we took pictures of the TV tower nearby. We focused on TV towers during virtually every trip out of Moscow. The importance of this activity was not the towers themselves, but the several attached radio-relay antennas.

SIBERIA
WARM WEATHER AND
WARM RECEPTION

Upon seeing me exit the aircraft, the head of the welcoming delegation broke into laughter. They had been waiting on the tarmac as our plane taxied up to the small terminal at Tolmachova Airfield in Novosibirsk.

"Will you look at Nanook of the North there?" The head of the delegation called up to me. "Friend, do you think you're in Siberia or something?"

We *were* in Siberia. We were in Novosibirsk, the largest city in Siberia. It was late September and had already started getting cold in Moscow. *What would it be like in Siberia?* I had thought. In Moscow I bought a heavy Soviet overcoat—a *shuba*—with a nice warm lamb-fleece collar. I wore that and a Russian fur hat—*shapka*—when we arrived in Novosibirsk. The city greeted us, however, with a temperature of 70 degrees Fahrenheit.

Yes, I did look a little strange. I grinned sheepishly.

"We *are* in Siberia," I said. "What's with this warm weather? Are you having a heat wave?"

"Not really. It's often nice this time of year. Indian Summer, you know. But don't feel bad. This happens a lot with first-time travelers to Novosibirsk in September. Stick around for a month and then you'll really need that *shuba* and *shapka*."

My traveling companion, the new Army Attaché, was dressed more modestly. If we had had Google back in those days, I would probably have checked and found that average September temperatures were not that bad in Novosibirsk—low 60s. I should also have realized that Novosibirsk is only one location in a massive continental expanse. At over 5 million square miles, Siberia takes up more than three-fourths of Russia. Perhaps the best way to convey the size of Siberia is to compare it to Canada, a country more familiar to American readers. Canada's land mass is less than 80 percent of Siberia's.

I was in the Russian "Wild East" frontier. In contrast to the European part of the USSR, Siberia has several mountain ranges. And its rivers run from south to north! I agree with those experts who believe Siberia holds the key to Russia's economic growth. It contains, after all, extensive and untapped oil and natural gas deposits and holds in its depths almost all valuable metals: nickel, gold, lead, diamonds, silver and zinc. It has some of the world's largest deposits of coal and boasts the world's largest forests.

In Novosibirsk, we did the usual things. In our pursuit of military information we photographed a TV tower and an installation suspected of being an air defense headquarters, just down the street from the Military District headquarters. But we saw no unusual military activity anywhere in the city. Since we seldom observed anything of military importance on our travels about the Soviet Union, we always tried to see some of the more memorable features of the towns we visited. The highlight of our stay in Novosibirsk was a visit to Akademgorodok—literally, "Academic Town."

Way out in Siberia, one might say in the middle of nowhere, was a little city, twenty miles from Novosibirsk—Akademgorodok, the home and workplace for many scientific and scholarly elite. There were several smaller Akademgorodoks around the Soviet Union, for example, in Tomsk, Krasnoyarsk and Kiev. But this was the most prominent of them all.

Because of their special status and value to the Soviet state, as many as 60,000 residents—scholars and their families—lived much better than most Soviet citizens. This little city had stores, hotels, hospitals, restaurants, movie houses, clubs and libraries. All residents had access to special stores, although even here there was the class distinction so prevalent in the "classless" USSR. Scholars with a doctorate had a special source for their food and goods. The highest-ranking Soviet scholars—Academicians (full members of the USSR Academy of Sciences)—had even better services.

Akademgorodok boasted a university, a medical academy, museums and more than 30 research institutes. A flavor of the research performed here can be deduced from the names of such institutes as Thermal Physics, Inorganic Chemistry, Nuclear Physics, Mathematical Geophysics, Semiconductor Physics, Theoretical and Applied Mechanics, as well as History, Philology and Philosophy.

Foot surveillance in Novosibirsk was normal, but "not obtrusive," according to our report of that trip. Of course, since we were under the watchful eye of our Intourist guide, our visit to Akademgorodok did not require additional surveillance personnel.

Novosibirsk was only the first stop of our trip. From there we planned to go on further east to Achinsk, Kansk (the latter only a few hundred miles southeast of the famous 1908 "nuclear" explosion in the Siberian Tunguska region so convincingly explained by Baxter and Atkins in their *The Fire Came By*), and Bratsk. In Novosibirsk, however, the Soviets told us the flight to Bratsk, for which we had tickets, did not in fact go to Bratsk, but rather to Irkutsk. All other flights from Bratsk stop in Krasnoyarsk, a city closed to foreigners, so we couldn't fly on those planes. We were stuck with a couple of days in Novosibirsk, after which we took a train to Achinsk.

The train ride to Achinsk was a special experience in itself. We started out by witnessing an army major and his wife being ejected from the compartment assigned to us. It turned out, however, this was only to make room for two additional travelers who occupied our compartment—one that, once again, we had paid to have all to ourselves. Of course, we assumed they were the KGB surveillants assigned to watch over us on our train ride to Achinsk. One was an elderly gentleman who said he was going to visit his children. The other was a younger man who said he was going to Krasnoyarsk. We wrote in our report that at first we thought the elderly man was not a surveillant, but now as I look back and remember my training, I believe he too probably was KGB.

We were on Train No. 2, the so-called "Trans-Siberian Express," which traveled from Moscow to Vladivostok in the Far East. It arrived in Novosibirsk four and one-half hours late. We were supposed to have left Novosibirsk at 9:45 p.m., but instead left at 2:30 in the morning. By the time we reached Achinsk, the train was 16 hours late. Part of this was due to the many stops along sidings to let military trains pass. Some express!

Just as on our trip back to Moscow from Murmansk, whenever we stopped, peasants or collective farmers lined the tracks with the food they had grown in their private gardens and almost everyone, including us, often detrained in order to buy something to eat. At one stop, I stepped onto the platform to have a smoke (no smoking on the train) and saw the young surveillant get off and meet a man who had arrived in a black Volga. They talked for a few minutes, then the new man boarded the train car ahead of us. The young surveillant returned to our compartment.

We arrived in Achinsk at 11:30 p.m., just missing the train traveling west that we were scheduled to travel on back to Novosibirsk. A city representative met us at the station.

"Welcome to Achinsk," said the Soviet representative. "We have a full itinerary planned for you. Many people are waiting to see you, as we have very few Americans visit us." The mayor told us later the only Americans to visit Achinsk in recent years had been members of an environmental delegation.

"Thank you. But... but we've just missed our train back to Novosibirsk. We have to abide by our approved travel plan," said my colonel.

"Don't worry about that," the man said, "We've made arrangements for you to fly back to Novosibirsk tomorrow."

With that we were bundled into a black, chauffer-driven Volga and taken straight to city hall, where we met the mayor.

"I apologize for the train being so late, but we won't let that stop our festivities," he said. "First we're going to visit the aluminum plant, then go to dinner."

It was now past midnight.

We met the factory director and several of his subordinates, including one man who was the curator of the archeological museum. (*National Geographic* had once mentioned Achinsk as a site of archeological interest.) They took us on a tour of the factory, which was boring, except for the museum and the computer center that controlled the manufacturing. We saw a poster that indicated the number of employees of the plant had jumped from 700 in 1971 to more than 1400 in 1979.

Next came a full-course meal served by very pretty waitresses at a nearby resort. It was now after 1:30 in the morning. I flirted with the waitresses and joined or proposed many toasts to better understanding between our two countries, to peace and friendship.

After the meal—I have no idea what time it was—we were treated to a Russian *banya* (bathhouse*)*. Although not unique to Russia, the *banya* is a special sauna-type ritual for most Russians, especially men. Temperatures can reach 200 degrees Fahrenheit in an enclosed room where men, usually stripped down entirely, sit around until they begin to sweat. Then they leave for fresh air, cold water, or even snow banks, where they cool off until they reenter the *banya* for a second sweat or even a third. During the sweating they beat themselves or each other with birch, oak or eucalyptus branches. During the cooling off periods, they often eat, drink beer, tea or vodka and generally relax. The *banya* is believed to have many health benefits, including improving kidneys, removing excess water and salt, opening and cleaning pores, ridding the muscles of excess lactic acid—the source of pain—and increasing the flow of oxygen. There was no snow yet in Achinsk, but the cool night (or early morning) air gave us enough of a shock to gain the desired effect.

By the time the Soviets had delivered us to the factory's guesthouse, it was already 6:00 a.m. I was in pretty bad shape and the colonel, who had found a way to avoid many of the toasts, had to help me into bed. I always believed anyone who hoped to get along in Russia must be able to drink. Often not to drink with Russians was a source of great offense. On occasion, however, just to keep the KGB guessing, I would beg off from any alcohol, citing medicine or other health concerns as my excuse. I prided myself on the ability to hold my liquor. But the combination of 22 hours on the train and the all-night festivities was a little too much for me. Additionally, I felt secure with my traveling companion who was very conservative in all his behavior. When we got back to Moscow, however, the colonel did have a few words with me on my drinking in Achinsk.

Four hours after we had gone to bed, our hosts rousted us out. We set off to visit an elementary school and a kindergarten. None of the children had seen Americans before and we had a delightful time engaging them in conversation about America, Russia and the English language. At least these children were on their regular schedule and hadn't had to wait up for hours, as had the workers at the aluminum plant and the restaurant. I wondered if they were surprised at our appearance, as Americans are often portrayed in Soviet literature as fat, cigar-smoking capitalists.

We ended our visit to Achinsk shortly after noon by joining the mayor and some factory officials at a local restaurant for another full meal. We were neither hungry nor in a mood for heavy drinking, but tried to be polite and express our gratitude for the fine hospitality they had shown us. The colonel worried about our being late for our flight, but the mayor said, "The plane doesn't leave unless I say so." From the restaurant, the mayor had us driven to the airport where a small Yak-40 jet (20-25 passengers) stood waiting to take us back to Novosibirsk. After some ceremonial photos at the small airport, we boarded and waited ten minutes while the other passengers were allowed on. Then we returned to Novosibirsk.

The warm reception in Achinsk succeeded in preventing us from collecting military information, but the VIP treatment was unusual and quite enjoyable.

BREST AND MINSK

An embattled Red Army soldier had inscribed onto the wall, "I am dying but will not give up! 20/VII-41" and "Farewell, Motherland."

A fellow attaché and I were inside the Brest Fortress, site of one of the first German attacks on the USSR in WWII—22 June 1941. The Nazis crossed the Bug River from occupied Poland and thought they would take the fortress in a few minutes. As can be seen from the above inscription (20 July 1941), the fortress held out for weeks. Germans encircled the fortress, which contained 4,000 Soviet soldiers. Despite being outnumbered 10:1, running out of food, water and ammunition, the defenders fought fiercely for four weeks before losing the battle. For the Germans, Brest was a bitter first taste of the type of fierce Russian fighting they would later experience in Stalingrad and elsewhere. The battle at the fortress became a symbol of Soviet resistance throughout the war. I couldn't help but think of the parallels between the Brest Fortress and our Alamo.

In 1965, the Soviet government awarded Brest Fortress the title "Hero Fortress." It joined other Soviet "Hero" cities. After my return from the Soviet Union, Murmansk and Smolensk became "Hero" cities. The others are: Leningrad (today St. Petersburg), Stalingrad (today Volgograd), Odessa, Sevastopol, Moscow, Kiev, Novorossiysk, Kerch, Tula and Minsk. Each city has a marker behind the Moscow Kremlin, along the wall by the Soviet "Eternal Flame" Memorial to the Unknown Soldier. During my tour of duty in the USSR, I traveled to five of these Hero cities. The city I most regret not having visited was Stalingrad/Volgograd.

Brest and Minsk are both situated along the Moscow-Warsaw-Berlin highway, the main route for the German Wehrmacht advance during the first months of the war. It was also one of the main routes the Nazis took on their return to Germany as the Red Army and partisans relentlessly attacked and pursued them back out of the Soviet Union after the Battles of Stalingrad and Kursk. Brest is also situated on the main rail line connecting Berlin and Moscow. Here, at the border, Russian wide gauge ends and the European standard gauge begins. Consequently, all trains crossing the border into or from Poland must have their freight transferred from cars of one gauge to cars of another.

Understandably, most of the military units in Brest in 1979 were border guards (all border guards came under the jurisdiction of the KGB). When we approached any of the border guard installations, we were chased away by soldiers. On our way to a military storage area and motor pool, a civilian truck overtook us. A private jumped out of the back and told us we must return to the center of the city. We told him we were authorized to be here. He said, "I know, but I've been told you can't stay here."

Brest and Minsk were in what was during my tour the Belorussian Soviet Socialist Republic. After the demise of the Soviet Union it became the country Belarus. During my time in the USSR, we referred to it as Belorussia. It was one of those Soviet republics that had never really been independent. Parts of Belorussia belonged at one time or another to Lithuania or Poland. Russian Empire efforts to gain control over the region began when Ivan III (the Great) began military operations in the late 15th century, designed to reunite the lands of Ancient Kievan Rus. As with many countries in Eastern Europe, borders changed with every new alliance or war. The Belorussian area first came under Russian control in the late 18th century when Catherine the Great ruled.

During their checkered cultural and administrative attachments to one or another country over the centuries, the Belorussians developed their own language. Belorussia, Ukraine and Russia are part of the Eastern Slav peoples (other Slavs fall into the categories of Western and Southern). Although their languages are closely related, they are now more or less mutually unintelligible.

In 1979, Brest was on the Polish-Soviet border and I found pockets of Polish speakers when I was there. During the Soviet era, many Russians moved, or were moved, to non-Russian republics and the Russian language became more and more prevalent. For example, in Minsk, although Russian was declared the official language in the 19th century, Belorussian had become the major language in the 1920s and early 1930s. Since the late 1930s, however, Russian again gained dominance. This process accelerated after World War II; by the late 1970s, almost everyone in Minsk, the capital city, spoke Russian.

Statistically, Belorussia was the hardest-hit Soviet republic in World War II and remained in Nazi hands until 1944. During that time, according to Albert Axell's *Russia's Heroes, 1941–45* (cited in Wikipedia), Germany destroyed 209 out of 290 cities in the republic, 85% of the republic's industry, and more than one million buildings. Scholars estimate the casualties at between two and three million (about a quarter to one-third of the total population). The Jewish population of Belorussia was devastated during the Holocaust and never recovered. The Soviet Army liberated Brest only in July 1944.

We saw no significant military activity in Brest or Minsk, although there was a large army headquarters in the capital. We had planned to go on to Rovno and Lvov, but on the morning we were to leave Brest, we found the car wouldn't start. Intourist called in Soviet mechanics, but they hadn't shown up before we decided to return to Moscow by train. The Soviets later moved the car to a guarded lot.

THE ROAD TO KHARKOV

TULA

Driving through Tula, about 120 miles south of Moscow, we felt like we were leading a caravan. Soon after we entered the city in our DAO Zhiguli (a Soviet version of the Fiat, manufactured in Togliatti, USSR and exported as the Lada), four sedans—presumably carrying KGB surveillants—picked us up. Partly because of this heavy vehicular tail and partly because we were on our way south to Oryol, we didn't stop in the city. All our photography—of a brewery, a slaughterhouse and a grain elevator—was from our car. By the time we were ready to depart the city, several police cars had joined the line of vehicles behind us. They all followed us to the Tula city limits, then stopped and turned around.

Tula was famous for two major industries: armaments during wartime and samovars during peacetime. The samovar is a large iron urn with a spigot. It heats water for tea and is found both in Russian public places and in homes. Usually a pot of highly concentrated tea sits atop the samovar. Users put tea in their cups and then draw the hot water to dilute it to the strength desired. Most Russian samovars are quite ornate and have won many international awards. If the reader ever comes across one, he or she should look carefully at the embossed awards and the place of manufacture. It will likely be Tula (the 't' and 'a' are the same as in our alphabet; the 'u' looks like an English ''y and the 'l' is a form of the Greek lamda.)

During World War II (the Soviets called their part of the war "the

Great Patriotic War"), Tula not only made armaments for the Red Army, but combat units and citizens there also defended the southern flank in the Battle of Moscow. I consider the Battle of Moscow the most significant one during Soviet wartime operations. Stalingrad and Kursk were great victories for the Red Army in that they helped shift the strategic initiatives on the Eastern Front to the USSR. The Battle of Moscow in 1941, however, was the first time the German Wehrmacht's advance was stopped since it began its aggression against European countries in 1938. In 1976, the Soviet government awarded Tula the title of "Hero City."

Nearby, about nine miles from Tula, is Yasnaya Polyana, the estate of my favorite Russian writer, Leo Tolstoy. My family and I visited it a couple of times during unofficial "cultural" trips. Walking the grounds of historic sites was always for me almost a spiritual experience. To be in Tolstoy's home, to see his work area and to walk out to his grave in the woods is something I'll never forget.

ORYOL

The road from Moscow to Kharkov passes through several cities with military and industrial facilities. From Tula we continued on to Oryol, where we overnighted.

At USMLM in East Germany, we ignored the police—the *Volkspolizei*. I had been in the USSR a little more than two months and still hadn't fully adjusted to the need to pull over when the police signaled. But we did have to stop in Oryol when local militia/police signaled for us to pull over.

"You have deviated from your approved plan. You're not allowed to be here," the policeman said.

"What are you talking about?" I asked.

"We know you are not following your official itinerary."

I was driving, so my fellow attaché pulled out the approved itinerary and showed it to the policeman. He looked confused.

"One moment. I'll be right back. Don't go anywhere." The

policeman walked over to his car and got on the radio. In a few minutes he returned.

"You may proceed," was all that he said and walked back to his car.

Curiously, this happened a couple of times in Oryol, including once again just before we left the city on our way to Kharkov. Same story: police said we weren't supposed to be there, we showed them our authorization, they made phone calls and then let us continue on our way. There must have been some sort of communications mix-up between the local police and the KGB (probably directing them from Moscow). At one point, a policeman stopped us and told us we couldn't go down a particular street. When we argued with him and insisted we had every right to use that street, the policeman simply waved us on, muttering, "Go ahead then."

The Nazis occupied Oryol for nearly two years, so much of the city we saw had been rebuilt from the ashes of WWII. Oryol was the hometown of Felix Dzerzhinsky, first chief of the infamous Cheka, forerunner of the NKVD/KGB. On a more positive note, the famous author Ivan Turgenev also came from Oryol.

Our only military observation was of a MiG-19 as it approached the Oryol airfield. That plane seemed almost a symbolic gesture to us from the city, as Oryol was the birthplace of Artem Mikoyan, designer of the famous MiG aircraft.

On another road trip in November 1980, the KGB in Oryol apparently messed with our vehicle. We came out one morning to find our battery dead. Assistance arrived and jump-started our Zhiguli. But as soon as the engine began to turn over, the distributor cap flew off and the rotor fell into the fan. Despite Oryol being a major distribution point for Zhiguli, "no rotor or distributor cap could be found." We were forced to abort the scheduled trip to Kursk and Kharkov.

On one trip, as we proceeded from Oryol to Kharkov, we photographed six radio-relay towers along Route 4. We took the photos, of course, from our car. This probably went unnoticed from the helicopter that followed just above us for 15 miles. Throughout the drive south, we took notes and photographed various major road improvement sites, as well as three highway accidents. At one point near Belgorod, we stopped and measured the depth of the road surface, which was 13 inches.

The route from Oryol to Kharkov took us through Kursk. It is unlikely that I would ever have gotten permission to visit the actual battle site of the Battle of Kursk, primarily because the battle did not take place in the city. It occurred near the village of Prokhorovka, to the southwest of Kursk. This battle in July and August 1943 between the German Wehrmacht and the Red Army was the largest tank battle in history. After the Battle of Kursk, the Soviet counter-offensive managed to liberate Oryol, Belgorod and Kharkov. The Battle of Kursk was a decisive Soviet victory and a turning point in the war. From there the Red Army gained and maintained a strategic advantage over the Germans until the latter's defeat in 1945.

KHARKOV

Kharkov was a popular destination for attaché visits. It was a major scientific and industrial center with over 50 scientific institutes and many heavy-machine building plants. We assumed most were closely linked to the Soviet military-industrial complex. As the second largest city in the Ukraine, after Kiev, its population was over one million.

Surveillance was always heavy in this city. On one trip we identified at least four vehicles that followed us very closely, 10-12 surveillants on foot, stakeouts and briefcase cameras. Despite what might have seemed oppressive coverage, the KGB did not interfere with us directly.

Other attachés had covered most of Kharkov industrial facilities many times, but on this trip we found something a little different. The surveillance in Kharkov may have tipped us off to what was important and what was not. As we drove around some installations, the surveillance seem to drop off completely until we approached another, apparently important installation. Referring to this installation, I quote here an excerpt from my report:

If surveillance coverage is any measure of the sensitivity of an installation, this place remains the hottest location in Kharkov. Every visit made to this plant revealed stakeouts, some of which had men carrying cameras, displayed overtly or carried covertly in briefcases. On one pass, we turned east on the road along the south edge of the plant and then turned north and drove along the river on the east side. This road had been considered impassable on all previous trips, but looked in pretty good shape this time. It turned out to be easily negotiable and allowed access to an area of the plant not seen before. The extreme southeast corner of the plant is apparently a "graveyard" of old armored vehicles. Through cracks in the wooden fence, we could see junked tanks and piles of non-descript metal. This departure from our normal pattern of coverage of this plant produced near panic on the part of the surveillants. One commandeered a passing motorcycle and raced down the dirt road after our car. Another surveillant with a briefcase camera was posted at the southeast corner of the plant to photograph us as we retraced our path back to the main road.

This reminded me of counter-productive signs the Soviets often posted in East Germany. They were called Military Restriction Signs and were not part of our formal U.S.-Soviet agreement. We didn't abide by these signs. In fact, we might be driving along and see a sign posted in an area where we previously had no knowledge of a military installation or training activity. When we saw the sign, however, we often decided to go look for what it was the Soviets were trying to hide.

Kharkov was one of the few cities I visited where we were able to observe busy military activity going in and out of installations and factories. We actually photographed new construction going on in some of the plants. Such photography could not be easily accomplished when we were on foot, but it was relatively easy to take pictures from the car. When we were done in Kharkov, we left our car at a guarded lot at the hotel and returned to Moscow by train.

Returning from a subsequent trip to Kharkov in May 1980, one of the assistant air attachés and I had an interesting exchange with our compartment-mates. Although we had first-class tickets for a two-person compartment, Intourist and the train-station director refused to honor them. Our request for an entire second-class compartment (four persons) was similarly refused. Once again, they put us in a compartment with two men.

One was an older man who we felt was most likely an innocent "civilian." We had seen him arrive at the station with, as he later explained, his son, daughter-in-law and grandchild. He was traveling to Kalinin to visit relatives. The other, younger man introduced himself as Evgeny. We pegged him as KGB. When he told us to call him Zhenya or Eugene, a bell went off for us. Other attachés had reported a Zhenya KGB escort. When we asked him if he knew a certain lieutenant colonel who was a British attaché, he replied he didn't know the man was a lieutenant colonel, but yes, he did know him.

The older man, whom we addressed in the polite Russian way as Viktor Konstantinovich, had brought along a bottle of vodka and wished to share it with us to celebrate Victory Day (it was 9 May). He poured tea glasses completely full. We begged off, saying that was too much to drink at one time. Zhenya apparently decided to go macho on us and downed the entire glass without stopping for a breath.

This was a rare opportunity to engage in conversation with a supposedly ordinary citizen. He was interested in America, but was careful not to stray from the Communist Party line. He said he didn't understand why the U.S. was going to boycott the Olympics. Furthermore, he said, he didn't see why we had made such a fuss about the Soviets going to the aid of Afghanistan, a brother Communist country on its border. We attempted to explain the U.S. position on the Afghanistan invasion and the Olympics in the most diplomatic fashion we could.

SHUTTLE BOMBING

When we drove or took a train from Kharkov to Kiev, we passed through Poltava. To Russians, Poltava is remembered as the site of Peter the Great's historic defeat of Sweden's Charles XII in 1709— the crucial battle in the Great Northern War. To 1,300 WWII U.S. Army Air Force members, however, Poltava had been the site used as a sanctuary after our bombing raids in central Europe. Like the Intervention discussed in my chapter on Murmansk, this is one of those significant U.S.-Soviet episodes that very few Americans know about.

Under the code name "Operation Frantic," American aircraft conducted seven shuttle-bombing operations from bases in Great Britain and Southern Italy. The bombers then landed at three Soviet airfields—Poltava, Mirgorod and Piryatin—in the Ukraine. The operations began in June 1944 and ended in September, a few months later. On one mission, a German plane followed the Americans back to Poltava. When the German pilot reported his findings to headquarters, the Luftwaffe launched a bombing raid against the Poltava airfield and its ammunition dumps. The U.S Eighth Air Force lost 43 B-17s and 15 P-51s. The next night the Luftwaffe bombed the other shuttle airfields. The Soviets insisted their air defenses be used to protect the airfields. The Americans knew this would be inadequate, so by September the U.S. cancelled the shuttle-bombing operations. Thus ended a rare opportunity for U.S.-Soviet military collaboration against the common Nazi enemy.

THE GOLDEN RING

YAROSLAVL

"I'll see your *pyat* (five) and raise you *pyat*," said my 9-year-old son, Misha, as he put ten kopecks into the pot. Sure enough, he had the winning hand. Misha had a lot of winning hands that night in our hotel room in Yaroslavl. In fact, he pretty much wiped us out. We were playing kopeck-ante. (A kopeck was 1/100 of a ruble and worth 1 ½ cent. Because of inflation and devaluation of Russian currency, the kopeck is no longer in circulation.) Poker remains a favorite family pastime when we get together. Our children learned to count in English, Russian and German during family poker games.

There were seven of us crowded around the coffee table in our hotel room. In August 1979, I had brought my entire family and that of a sergeant in our office to this quaint and picturesque city.

Yaroslavl is an ancient city (founded in 1010) going back to the days of Kievan Rus. It is located only 155 miles northeast of Moscow at the confluence of the Volga and Kotorosl Rivers; it has many beautiful churches and a historic monastery. It was Russia's second largest city and the country's de facto capital during the Polish occupation of Moscow early in the 17th century. In 1979, it had about 500,000 inhabitants. Even with that many people, however, it just didn't feel like a big city. It reminded me of a large village in a Russian fairytale book, mainly because of the architecture.

At the outset of our trip, as we drove in two cars north from Moscow, I detected no surveillance. When we made attaché trips in the USSR, we sometimes didn't see our surveillance, but we always assumed it was there. This time, however, it was likely the KGB assumed these two families were not on a working trip.

Later, in September 1980, when another attaché and I made a trip to Yaroslavl and Vologda, surveillance was normal—cars and walkers. On that trip military activity in Yaroslavl was, as usual, very light. Nothing special. Yaroslavl had two military academies. Actually, they weren't called academies in Russian, but rather "higher military schools." The U.S. military has three main service academies, West Point, Annapolis and Colorado Springs. The Soviet Armed Forces had 140 such military schools. Ours are meant for Army, Navy/Marines and Air Force. Soviet military schools are set up for every branch within the services: infantry, artillery, tank, rocket forces, finance troops, etc. Moreover, while our academies are four-year programs, most Soviet cadets are in their higher military schools for five years.

The two higher military schools/academies in Yaroslavl were for Air Defense and Missile cadets and one for Railway Communications cadets. There was really no need to spend time observing these schools, however, since both were listed and described in a Soviet publication (the name of which was deleted by DIA from my reports).

On that trip we drove in a DAO car to Yaroslavl, and then went by train from there to Vologda.

VOLOGDA

Vologda was at one time the center of Russian trade with West European countries. Its significance decreased, however, after Peter the Great built his city—Saint Petersburg—on the Gulf of Finland.

Like so many towns to the north, east and west of Moscow, Vologda is an "open air museum" of ancient Russian architecture. Although not included in the Golden Ring of ancient cities around Moscow, it should be. The Golden Ring is a popular tourist route that takes in eight ancient Russian cities, all of which played important roles in the history of Old Muscovy. Among the other cities in this Ring are: Yaroslavl,

Kostroma, Ivanovo, Suzdal, Vladimir, Sergiev Posad, Pereslavl-Zalessky and Rostov Veliky (The Great). Each of these picturesque towns contains spectacular kremlins (fortresses), churches and monasteries. Despite being a little out of the way (318 miles from Moscow), Vologda has all the characteristics of the Golden Ring cities. First mentioned in the chronicles in 1147 (the same year as Moscow), it contains 224 monuments of history, architecture and culture.

In February 1918, out of fear the Germans would occupy St. Petersburg amidst the chaos brought on by revolution and civil war in Russia, most of the foreign embassies (led by the American ambassador) moved to Vologda.

Military activity in Vologda was not significant. For most of our stay, we were in the hands of an Intourist guide. During a taxi ride to and from the Spaso-Prilutsky Monastery, we were able to see a couple of barracks, a tank, some new construction and some soldiers inside one installation, as well as some new residential construction in the city. We found it impossible to photograph anything on that taxi trip due to the presence of our guide and the driver who was probably a KGB agent. The guide had a good command of English, had served in East Germany with the Soviet Group of Forces, and spoke fluent German.

Later, on foot, we investigated what was suspected to be a motorized rifle division headquarters. It appeared to be under construction; we photographed a couple of antennas in the compound. We also took pictures of several antennas near the city's Internal Affairs Directorate. According to our report, surveillance was "constant but not oppressive." Two of the surveillants, a man and a woman, stayed in our hotel. I overheard the woman arguing with the hotel desk clerk because they had combined her bill with that of her male colleague. As we left Vologda on a train returning to Yaroslavl, we photographed more antennas in the southern part of the city.

I've mentioned in other parts of this book some of the difficulties we encountered in our attempts to reserve whole rail compartments to ourselves. On this trip, we lucked out. The car attendant told a couple of young KGB officers who were hoping to bunk with us that they couldn't. When they objected (they couldn't openly reveal themselves as KGB in our presence), the attendant told them, "Comrades, you have places. They're all the same. Why should one or the other matter?"

ZAGORSK

Driving back to Moscow from Yaroslavl, we passed through Zagorsk. This is a truly magnificent little town. As pointed out above, it *is* among the cities of the Golden Ring. The city was originally named Sergiev Posad after the most revered saint in Russia, Sergius of Radonezh. In 1930, the Soviets renamed it Zagorsk after a Bolshevik revolutionary. In post-Soviet Russia the city regained its original name.

We detected no surveillance after we left Yaroslavl, so we spent some time photographing from our car what we suspected to be a biological warfare research, production and storage facility in Zagorsk. At least that's what we reported. In retrospect, however, I doubt it was involved in biological research. There were no guard towers around the installation and we saw no security measures that one might expect for a facility of such importance.

Zagorsk was the location of the most important monastery in Russian history: the Holy Trinity-Saint Sergius Lavra. It played an important role in the political and religious development of Muscovy. Lavras are special Orthodox monasteries that report directly to the Russian Patriarch. Three of them are now in Ukraine. Russia has two— the Aleksandr Nevsky Lavra in St. Petersburg and the one in Zagorsk/ Sergiev Posad.

RYAZAN

In late July 1980, another attaché and I traveled by train 115 miles southeast from Moscow to Ryazan, arriving much later than we had hoped because the Soviet ticket agency changed our schedule at the last minute. This had happened before with attachés traveling to Ryazan. There was no clear reason for this. Perhaps it was just harassment. Our primary objective in Ryazan was... guess what... the TV tower, which we photographed together with its antenna appendages.

Ryazan first appears in the chronicles in 1095. It was the first Russian city to be overrun by the Mongols in 1237.

To Russians, Ryazan is most prominent because of its native son, Sergei Yesenin. He was one of the most popular Russian/Soviet poets. He lived a wild life, however. He is said to have slashed his wrists and used his blood to write his "Farewell" poem. He then hanged himself, ending his life in 1925 at the age of 30. To the outside world, however, Yesenin is best known as having been a lover of the American dancer, Isadora Duncan.

When anyone knowledgeable of the Soviet Armed Forces hears the word "Ryazan," he or she immediately thinks of airborne troops. An airborne academy and a regiment of these elite soldiers were located there. According to Victor Suvorov in his *Spetsnaz: The Inside Story of the Soviet Special Forces*, this academy is where the officers of GRU's Spetsnaz (*spetsialnogo naznacheniya*-special forces) train. We were able to get a glimpse of the airborne training area with its practice jump tower. But military activity in the city was very light. We saw few soldiers, which led us to speculate the airborne units may have been in Afghanistan.

VILNIUS, LITHUANIA

I admit we looked a little strange. My wife, Elaine, and I walked down the sidewalk, each carrying two hangers of clothes and a bag of toiletries. When we stopped to wait for the light to change, I told the waiting Soviets who were staring at us that we were going over to the hotel across the street.

"The hotel "Neringa" doesn't have any hot water," I said. "They've arranged for us to go to another hotel to shower." I often had trouble getting hot water in Soviet hotels, but usually if I ran the water long enough, it would warm up.

This was August 1980 and my only trip to the capital of Lithuania. I had been looking forward to it for some time. My maternal grandfather had emigrated from there to America some seventy years earlier. He joined his sister Beatrice and older brother John in the Chicago area. My Aunt Bea told me grandpa had been smuggled out of Lithuania under the seat of a wagon. His parents had sent him to America so he would never have to soldier for the Tsar.

I hadn't given much thought to my grandfather's childhood until I visited him in 1963, in Valparaiso, Indiana, on my way to an Army assignment in Germany. When I told him I had just finished a course on the Russian language, he looked at me and got a strange smile.

"*Ty razumeesh po-russki?* (Do you understand Russian?)," he asked.

"*Da, Dedushka.*"(Yes, Grandpa.)

"I've forgotten a lot," he said.

My grandfather speaking Russian came as a shock to me. Grandpa never spoke any when I was a child. In fact, although he always spoke with an accent—a brogue we called it—I assumed it was from his Lithuanian. From a practical point of view, however, his speaking Russian came in handy for me several times later. When people got suspicious of me because of my Russian fluency, I would explain it away by saying my grandfather spoke Russian. No need to explain that I had studied at the Army Language School for nearly two years, had advanced degrees in the language, and had been using it since in Military Intelligence.

I probably had relatives in Vilnius. I figured the KGB likely knew about my grandfather and might expect me to do some looking around for Lithuanians with the name Kailus—my grandfather's last name (changed to Kail in America). Surveillance was very heavy and I attributed that to the KGB's anticipation that I would try to make contact with civilians under the guise of looking for distant relatives. Because of that and the fact that Elaine was with me, I decided not to do anything of the sort. I hoped at a later date to return to Lithuania and spend some time inquiring about possible relatives. However, I never made it back.

Lithuania was the only Baltic country I visited during my tour as a military attaché. The other two are Latvia and Estonia. The Lithuanians are a proud people with a glorious past. During the 14th century, the Grand Duchy of Lithuania was the largest country in Europe and included present-day Belorussia, Ukraine and parts of Poland and Russia. By the late 18th century, however, most of Lithuania had become part of the Russian Empire. After the First World War, it became independent again.

The Germans occupied Vilnius during the invasion of the USSR in June 1941. Later, when the Red Army drove the Nazis back toward Germany, they installed pro-Soviet governments in the Baltic countries, who then "asked" to be annexed by the USSR. Thus they became Soviet Republics.

The Soviets engaged in massive deportations of Lithuanians to Siberia, then began to impose all the Soviet forms of government and economy on the country. From 1944 to 1952 approximately 100,000 Lithuanian partisans fought a guerrilla war against the Soviet system.

The Soviet Communists killed an estimated 30,000 partisans and their supporters, arrested many more and deported them to Siberian gulags. In 1979, there were 330,000 Russians living in Lithuania (nine percent of the population).

We found nothing of significance around the military installations in Vilnius, although we confirmed that a couple of them had been demolished to make room for business and residential buildings.

We had a new experience in our collection of TV tower photos. Vilnius was building a new TV tower. Following instructions from an earlier attaché visit, we took a trolley to a point where we could photograph the new tower from a small wooded area. Construction was still going on and there were no antennas attached to the tower yet. We went from there to the sight of the old tower, which was apparently and understandably still being used. We noted it had additional antennas oriented to the north. When we later mentioned the new tower to our Intourist guide, she said it was to have been completed by summer 1980, but construction had been put on hold. The government diverted funds for the tower to Moscow for Olympic-related construction.

ASHKHABAD, TURKMENISTAN

"Don't fall," my wife said, stifling a laugh.

"Right," I said. "I have to get up here so I can get a direct 90-degree shot of the list."

"You don't look much like a sophisticated diplomat up there," she added.

"What we won't do for our country," I replied.

In late October 1979, the British Military Attaché and I, together with our wives, traveled to Ashkhabad (post-Soviet era—Ashgabat), the capital of Soviet Turkmenistan. It was the only Central Asian city I visited during my years as an attaché. Ashkhabad is almost on the Iranian border. In fact, the city was part of Persia (the early name for Iran) until 1881, when it was ceded to Russia. I was surprised we were allowed to travel there, both because it was near an international border that was always out of bounds for us, and because of the situation in Iran. Rioters had just taken U.S. hostages in an assault on the U.S. Embassy in Teheran.

Later, waiting to return to Moscow, we learned our flight had been delayed. When the KGB saw me talking to a Nigerian military officer in the regular waiting room, the Soviets put us in the *Deputatsky zal* (Deputies' Hall)—the VIP lounge normally reserved for high-ranking Party and government officials—to wait for our plane. It was empty except for a couple of chairs and a desk at the end of the room. Not much of a "lounge." Atop the desk was a large sheet of telephone numbers. I climbed up on the desk. There were no windows in the hall, a feature designed to keep outsiders from peering in. Elaine, the General and his wife stood guard at the door while I took a small Minox camera out of my pocket.

I often carried the Minox. It was easy to hide and perfect for taking clandestine pictures of documents because of its size and close-focusing lens. The camera had been around for many years; both the Allies and the Nazis used it during World War II. The OSS was particularly fond of it. It wasn't a camera in a cigarette lighter or fountain pen, but it wasn't a normal one either. To be caught with it might not have been serious, but it had a reputation as a "spy" camera. (Soviet spy, John A. Walker Jr., used it to photograph U.S. Navy documents and crypto secrets for the KGB. He was arrested in 1985. The KGB found two Minox cameras in the apartment of GRU Colonel Penkovsky, who was working for British and American intelligence.)

On the desk were three telephones. One telephone had a normal seven-digit Ashkhabad city number, but the other two numbers were only three-digits and were probably for special government or party circuits. The paper contained the names and phone numbers of Turkmenistan Communist Party and government officials.

One might wonder why obtaining telephone numbers was such a big deal. In the Soviet Union telephone numbers were treated almost as state secrets. I never saw a Moscow telephone book and doubt there ever was one. Imagine everyone in Washington DC having an unlisted number! (At a luncheon scheduled for Spaso House in late 1980, I asked Marshal Ogarkov for his number. He hesitated and then gave me the number of our MOD contact officer. When in Rovno in the Ukraine in January 1981, I asked Colonel Kanavin for his number. He gave me what he said was his office number in Lvov, but was actually a Moscow exchange. I treat both these instances later in the book.)

Turkmenistan was bordered by Afghanistan to the southeast, Iran to the south and southwest, Uzbekistan to the east and northeast, Kazakhstan to the north and northwest and the Caspian Sea to the west. In the 13th century the Turkmen suffered the same fate as other peoples along the invasion routes of the Mongols.

Russian forces began occupying Turkmen territory late in the nineteenth century. The last significant resistance in Turkmen territory ended by 1881. Shortly thereafter, Russia annexed Turkmenistan, together with adjoining Uzbek territory, into the Russian Empire. In the 1920s, Turkmen insurgents joined Kazakhs, Kyrgyz, and Uzbeks in the Basmachi Rebellion against the rule of the newly formed Communist Soviet Union. By 1924, however, the Soviets had prevailed and the Turkmen Soviet Socialist Republic became a reality.

The name "Ashkhabad" is derived from Persian, meaning "City of Love." I could find no mention anywhere of it being a sister city to our "City of Brotherly Love," Philadelphia. It is a sister city, however, of Albuquerque, New Mexico. From what I knew of both cities, I failed to see the similarities (unlike Baku and its sister city Houston, Texas). Certainly, Albuquerque didn't have 30-foot-high portraits of President Carter scattered around the town. In Ashkhabad we could hardly avoid the billboard-size portraits of government and Communist Party leader Leonid Brezhnev decked out in a marshal's uniform with a chest full of medals.

The morning we were checking out of our hotel, we discovered the city definitely didn't live up to its name as a "City of Love."

"Your bill comes to 235 rubles," said the hotel clerk.

"What? When we checked in, the rate was 18 rubles a night and we've been here only two nights," I said.

"As of last night, the rates for foreigners have gone up all around the Union," the clerk said.

Americans had to pay approximately $1.50 for one ruble. Our hotel bill had just jumped from $54 to $352.

"Do you have enough to pay your bill?" the general asked me.

"Well, yes. I do, but I don't want to pay that much."

"What else can we do?" he asked.

"Simply refuse and offer to pay at the check-in rate."

"But that'll cause a stir."

"We can't just cave in," I replied. I motioned for him to step off with me to the corner away from our wives. I was, after all, arguing with a general, although among traveling partners rank was not so important.

"Jim," he said. "I don't really want to cause any trouble. I'm scheduled to rotate back to London soon."

"It's they who are causing trouble."

"Like I said, I don't think we really have a choice."

"Why don't we just tell them to send the bill to our embassies in Moscow," I suggested.

"You do what you think is right, but I feel I have to pay at the new rate."

I gave in, but told the clerk I would report this to my embassy, which would issue a protest to the Ministry of Foreign Affairs. The clerk took my money and just looked at me without a show of any interest in what I was saying. Ironically, a few months later, in Ryazan, we were charged only 19 rubles ($27) for a room listed at 70 rubles. The hotel clerk gave no explanation and we asked for none.

One of the irritations of being an American in the Soviet Union was that we had to pay so much for the Soviet ruble. At the time, the ruble was not a convertible currency outside the USSR. It was used only within the Soviet borders. Since the Soviets had complete control over the internal exchange rates, they could charge whatever they wanted. Countries that were allies or friends of the USSR paid as little as 15 cents for a ruble. The scale went up, depending how the Soviet government viewed a particular country. Americans were forced to pay the most.

During our search for information of a military nature in Ashkhabad, we photographed some installations and some new military construction. We also observed some Hind-D helicopters at the military airfield, which was contiguous to the civilian airport. These attack/gunship helicopters were not supposed to be in Ashkhabad. At the time, we surmised they might have redeployed to Ashkhabad in connection with the American Embassy situation in Iran.

My earlier discussion with the Nigerian military officer was of some value. It turned out he was the leader of a group of military students on their way back to Nigeria. They had been training for a few months in Mary, to the east of Ashkhabad. (In the lore of the local Christian sect, Mary, mother of Jesus, was buried there.) The Nigerians were all dressed in civilian clothes, but wore Russian *shapki*. Two things stuck out from our conversation. One man, a captain of artillery, had contracted a disease in Mary that the Soviets could not diagnose and, thus, could provide no treatment. He was flying to Moscow to seek help from a British doctor. The second interesting fact was that during their training in Mary, all instruction was in Russian, which had to be translated into English for the Nigerians. The Nigerians all spoke English since, in the words of the captain, "The English were our colonial masters." The captain offered that the atmosphere in Mary was "bad, due to the fact that we were black."

TRANSCAUCASUS

The Caucasus region—so named because of the Caucasus Mountains—was one of the most interesting in the USSR, both geographically and ethnically. To get an idea of the ethnic diversity I relate a story an Azerbaijani told my son Yasha: "After God created the earth, he began sprinkling it with different peoples from a salt shaker. When he was over the Caucasus region the lid of his salt shaker fell off."

The mountains are spectacular, rivaling the Rockies and the Alps. Flying over the Caucasus Mountains in fall or winter was breathtaking. Rocky peaks jutted out from under a snow that blanketed the entire range. The range goes from the Black Sea to the Caspian and contains Europe's highest mountain: Elbrus, rising 18,600 feet above sea level. By contrast, the highest mountains in the lower 48 American portion of the Rockies are between 14,000 and 15,000 feet. Mont Blanc, the highest mountain in the Alps is 15,781 ft. The highest mountain in the Ural range that divides European from Asian Russia is Mt. Narodnaya, which is only 6,200 feet. Denali (Mt. McKinley) in Alaska is 20,237 and Mount Everest peaks at 29,029 feet.

The Transcaucasus is that landmass on the south side of the mountain range. There are 27 different ethnic groupings in this region. The full-fledged Soviet Republics were Georgia, Armenia and Azerbaijan. Georgia and Armenia were primarily Christian, while Azerbaijan was mostly Muslim. Although I traveled to the capitals of Armenia and Azerbaijan, Georgia was the only republic where I was able to visit other, outlying towns.

GEORGIA

First, a note on Iran...

Rioters in Teheran

A crowd of four or five hundred people, waving clubs and swords, had already gathered outside the embassy in Teheran. After a lull of an hour and a half, the mob appeared outside the embassy in far greater numbers than before. This time many of them carried firearms. The mullahs declared a jihad against the entire mission, which led to an attack on the gates and walls of the embassy. The crowd threw stones and fired weapons. Soon they scaled the walls, broke through the gates, and swarmed into the compound.

That is how Laurence Kelly in his *Diplomacy and Murder in Teheran* described an event that occurred in 1829.

In that year, rioters in Teheran overcame the Russian Embassy. The ambassador, Alexander Griboyedov, and 43 members of his staff died in the fighting. Six others were killed when they were caught at a neighboring embassy. The dead totaled fifty Russian Embassy employees. The Persian Shah, out of fear of Russian retaliation, sent one of his sons to St. Petersburg with an apology and a gift of a large diamond for Tsar Nicholas I.

One hundred fifty years later, in November 1979, the seizure of American hostages in Teheran took place. I was then serving in Moscow. A mob of Iranian students assaulted and occupied the American Embassy in Teheran. In retaliation, President Carter curtailed the shipment of manufactured goods, stopped importing oil from Iran and froze Iranian assets in the U.S.

The Soviet government did nothing to assist the U.S. in getting the hostages released. In fact, it seemed to me they increased their anti-American propaganda. What galled me was that I knew almost every Soviet citizen was familiar with the story of Griboyedov's fate in Teheran. (Thirty-three years later, in 2012, writing about the American hostages, Russian Dmitri Trenin, Director of the Carnegie Moscow Center in Moscow, reiterated this fact: "Russians... remembered their own embassy trauma at Iranian hands in 1829. Every schoolchild knows the fate of Alexander Griboyedov, the tsar's ambassador to Persia, who was murdered, along with his entire embassy staff, by an angry Teheran mob.")

In April 1980, I traveled to Tbilisi, the capital of Georgia, with the new British Army Attaché. I knew Griboyedov was buried there and I intended to find some way to highlight the glaring hypocrisy of the Soviet approach to our hostage situation.

The purpose of our trip was to check on general military activity. In town, as one would expect, we saw military personnel and equipment near Soviet military installations. When the opportunity presented itself, we peered into military installations if there happened to be an open gate. At one hospital we saw no one who appeared to be a casualty of the new, four-month-old Soviet war in Afghanistan. There were no military columns on the streets. In other words, we observed nothing of real military value. (I often wondered if this was a well-developed scenario whereby the MOD and KGB would allow us to travel only to towns where either nothing interesting was going on, or it had already been completed before our arrival.)

At our hotel I asked where Griboyedov was buried. A guide told me his body was in the Pantheon of Heroes—the Mtatsminda Pantheon, located in the monastery of Saint David on the slope of Mt. Mtatsminda. Griboyedov had married a young Georgian princess four months before his death. Georgians looked upon him as one of their own. He and his wife, Nino, were the first people to be buried in the pantheon.

"Let's go up there," I suggested to the brigadier. I explained to him about Griboyedov and what happened in 1829.

"Sure, why not," he answered. "Besides, it's high up on the mountain. We should get a good view of the city from there."

"First, I want to make a stop in town and get some flowers."

We hired a taxi and I had the driver take us to a flower vendor. I bought five carnations, then told the driver to take us to the Pantheon. When we approached Griboyedov's crypt, I noticed some Russian tourists standing there and several more in the vicinity. I asked the brigadier to photograph me before and after I had placed the flowers inside the steel grate protecting the site. Then I turned and addressed all the Russians who had gathered out of curiosity.

"Good afternoon, friends," I said. "I'm Major Holbrook, American Assistant Army Attaché and this is my colleague, the British Army Attaché. You may wonder what we're doing here."

I paused. The Russians stared in silence.

"I've placed five flowers on the grave of your writer and ambassador, Alexander Griboyedov, who was murdered by a mob in Teheran in 1829. In addition to honoring Griboyedov, each flower symbolizes ten American diplomats who are now, 150 years later, being held hostage in *our* embassy by a similar mob in Teheran."

Not a word. I waited for some reaction. After about a minute more of staring at us, they began to wander off to other gravesites. I heard murmuring, but had no way of knowing what was going through their minds. I was sure none of them was proud of their Soviet government's current behavior regarding our Teheran crisis.

When I returned to Moscow, I reported what I had done and gave copies of the photos to our Defense Attaché, who passed the story and photos on to the Embassy Counselor for Press and Cultural Affairs. He in turn sent the photos and a short narrative to UPI, AP and Voice of America. I hope Voice of America broadcasted it back to Georgia.

A unified Georgian state reached the peak of its political and economic strength in the 11th–12th centuries when Kutaisi was the capital. Located at the crossroads between Europe and Asia and lying along the historic Silk Road routes, Georgia and its current capital, Tbilisi, were often a point of contention between various rival powers and empires such as Persia, the Byzantine Empire, Arabia and the Turks. Since the beginning of the 19th century, however, Georgia had been part of the Russian or Soviet Empires.

When I first arrived in Tbilisi I got the impression I was visiting a Mediterranean country, not a Soviet Republic. The people were lively and appeared more cheerful than most people in other republics. The Georgian food, drink and music definitely gave a visitor the impression this was a land of hearty, happy people. Additionally, Tbilisi is one of the few places in the world where a synagogue and a mosque are located next to each other.

During an earlier trip, in November 1979, my wife and I flew to Tbilisi and picked up an embassy vehicle that had been left at the hotel by other attachés on a previous trip. The DAO often had one or two vehicles (Soviet Zhigulis) out in the provinces. Attachés would drive them from city to city, leave them in a guarded parking lot and, eventually, return them to Moscow for servicing. We were scheduled to pick up the DAO car in Tbilisi and drive to Sukhumi on the Black Sea. Once we were finished with the vehicle, we would leave it there and fly back to Moscow. Along the way to Sukhumi, we would visit Gori, the boyhood home of Joseph Vissarionovich Dzhugashvili—known to the world as Stalin. After this, we would stop overnight in Kutaisi.

Gori is 47 miles from Tbilisi so it was a relatively short drive. When we visited the town, not only was there a large statue of Stalin in front of City Hall, but on Stalin Avenue the town boasted a museum to the city's (in)famous native son. We spent a couple of hours at the museum, then resumed our trip, arriving in Kutaisi in the late afternoon. We decided to go straight to our hotel. After learning it was out toward the end of town just off the main street, we headed in that direction.

All of a sudden, we came to a sign indicating we had reached the Kutaisi city limit. We could see our hotel, the "Mir," but it was outside the city. I pulled over and stopped the car. We had a dilemma. The rules of travel laid down by the Soviet MOD did not allow us outside the city limits of any town we were visiting.

As soon as we entered Kutaisi, I had caught sight of a green Volga with two male passengers following us. When we turned, it turned. When we stopped at the city limits, it stopped a short distance behind us.

"So what do we do now?" asked Elaine.

"I'm not sure. It looks like a lose-lose situation. Our travel document says we have to stay in that hotel. If we don't, we're in violation of our official itinerary. If we leave the city limits to drive out to the hotel, we're also in violation." After a short pause, I said, "I've got an idea. I'll be right back." I got out and walked back to the KGB car.

"Hello. We're American diplomats and are scheduled to spend a night and a day here in Kutaisi. But we seem to have a problem. We have to abide by what our travel itinerary says or we'll get in trouble when we return to Moscow. According to it, we must stay at the "Mir," but we're not allowed to go beyond the city limit."

The KGB surveillants just looked at me. I took out the travel itinerary and showed it to the driver. He looked at it and then at me, but said nothing.

"Do you suppose," I suggested, "that if the itinerary says we must stay at the "Mir," our going out a short distance from the city limit would be considered following our instructions?"

The KGB men both nodded their heads enthusiastically. I returned to our car and we drove on to the hotel. We settled in with dinner at the hotel restaurant and returned to our room for the night. The following day we planned to explore the city. Although there had been reports of airborne troops in Kutaisi, we saw no soldiers or equipment associated with that branch of service.

It was about 125 miles to Sukhumi. Sukhumi is a city on the eastern shore of the Black Sea just south of the Russian city Sochi. It's the capital of an autonomous region called Abkhazia, the people of which are not too well disposed toward Georgians. (This partially explains the Russo-Georgian War in August 2008.) The city is a port, a rail junction and, like most towns along the Black Sea coast, a holiday resort.

After taking our obligatory photographs of the Sukhumi TV tower and a Soviet submarine that lay surfaced in the port, we headed for our hotel. At one point during our drive about the city, we stopped our car to read a map. The KGB surveillance car pulled up behind a bus that was some distance back. The two KGB agents got out and lit up cigarettes. When we pulled away a few minutes later, the agents apparently didn't notice. So for the next two hours, we believed we were without surveillance. All this despite driving slowly back and forth throughout the city to give them a chance to pick us up again. We didn't want the KGB to think we had intentionally evaded them. When we arrived back at our hotel, they appeared again.

Later that night, we could hear men talking in the next room. One man was on the telephone. For some reason or other, when Russians talked on the phone they seemed to always raise their voices. (I had observed this before when I was in East Germany being detained in a room next to one in which a Soviet officer was on the phone.) Here in Kutaisi, I put my ear to the hotel room wall, thinking all the time about how I used to listen to intercepted Russian conversations from my unit is Berlin in the early 1960s. The man's side of the conversation in the next room went something like this:

"Come on up to our room, Maya."

"We're KGB. Yes, KGB on a business trip to Sukhumi."

"We're both quite cultured and behave properly toward women."

When the call ended, I heard one man say "115." That was our room number. Soon our phone rang. I picked it up, but heard only the man in the next room hanging up his phone. Five minutes later, both men apparently left their room and returned about midnight. They were taking a chance by assuming we would stay in our room all night. (Once in East Germany, after the East German Stasi confirmed my driver and I were in our room, we waited half an hour and left for a successful nighttime collection operation.)

The next day was Thanksgiving and we were looking forward to getting back to Moscow for turkey dinner. We drove to the airport where we left our car in a guarded parking lot. There we learned that Moscow airports were socked in with fog so our plane was delayed several times. In fact, we didn't get out until that evening. In order to minimize our contact with citizens around the airport, we were ushered into the *Deputatsky zal*/lounge, just as had happened in Ashkhabad. No one else was allowed into the hall. For Thanksgiving dinner we walked out to a kiosk opposite the terminal and bought some warm *piroshki*—little meat pies. What the meat was, I'm not sure, but it's not likely it was turkey.

We returned to Moscow late Thursday. Because of lingering fog at Domodedovo airport, we landed at Vnukovo, an airport used often for VIP and Soviet client states. There we encountered 25 young North Vietnamese military personnel (possibly all teenagers) clad in olive-drab overcoats, Soviet military hats and plaid civilian scarves. It was 11 years since I had been in Vietnam. The war there was over, but I always took an interest in the North Vietnamese in the Soviet capital. I often wondered what they thought of the war, but I never got a chance to discuss it with any of them. The group leader, however, did speak to me in very good Russian. (His Russian didn't surprise me, as when I was in Vietnam, Army interrogators called upon me to verify the Russian capabilities of a couple of North Vietnamese officer prisoners who said they had studied in the Soviet Union. They too spoke more than passable Russian.) He told me they had just arrived from Vietnam and were on their way to Odessa. He said they were quite uncomfortable since when they left Vietnam the temperature was 86 degrees F. In Moscow it was now 32 degrees. A couple of the young men greeted me also in Russian. Unfortunately, that was the extent of my interaction with North Vietnamese in Moscow.

YEREVAN, ARMENIA

Ararat! What a sight my first morning in Yerevan, the capital of Soviet Armenia.

We had flown in at night and our ride to the hotel was under heavily overcast skies. The next morning, however, when I stepped out of the hotel for a pipe, there it was. It seemed to cover the entire western sky. It was in Turkey, of course, but presented itself to the inhabitants of Yerevan from virtually every point in the city.

Mount Ararat is a snow-capped, dormant volcano and actually has two peaks: Greater Ararat (the highest peak in Turkey with an elevation of 16,854 ft.) and Lesser Ararat (12,782 ft.). In the book of *Genesis*, Noah's ark is said to have come to rest in the "Mountains of Ararat." Armenia is believed to be the first country to adopt Christianity (in the year 301) as a state religion. The Coat of Arms of Armenia displays a picture of Ararat.

The other dramatic aspect of my visit to Armenia was the reminder of the terrible genocide perpetrated by the Ottoman Empire Turks during and immediately after World War I. It is also known as the Armenian Holocaust. In fact, the word 'genocide' was first created to refer to this tragedy. It was the first case of genocide in modern times and second in severity only to the Holocaust by the Nazis. It involved killing of all able-bodied men through massacre and forced labor, as well as the deportation of women, children and elderly on death marches. Estimates of the number of Armenians who perished during the genocide range from 1 to 1.5 million. One cannot, should not, miss a chance to visit the Tsitsernakaberd Memorial Park.

During one trip to Yerevan, a fellow attaché and I walked along the streets of the city to nose around a few military installations. We found a small hospital in one, but saw no signs of casualties from Afghanistan. We noted a couple of uniform insignia anomalies and checked out construction on the new metro. Yerevan's population had surpassed the one million mark, which in the USSR entitled the city to a subway.

I was struck by the number of older American cars I saw. It turns out the Soviets had lured several Armenian families, whose relatives had suffered from the genocide, back to the USSR. Many of them from the United States came with their American cars.

On two separate visits to Yerevan, the local KGB appeared less than professional. For example, on one trip they assigned several men to us, using foot surveillance and 2-3 cars. At one point, we took a city bus. At a stop, two surveillants got out of a white Volga and boarded our bus. We intended to ride to the city limits, observing whatever military installations we could along the way. Since we were not allowed to go outside the city, we got off the bus and jumped on another that would take us into town again. The surveillants, however, must not have noticed that we had gotten off. They continued on and we never saw them again. On our trip back into town, we got off the bus and walked all around a military installation without noting any surveillance. Although a little uneasy about the mix-up (as always, we didn't want the KGB to think we had taken evasive action to shake them), we continued into town.

We then decided to return to our hotel. It had been two hours with no apparent surveillance. As soon as we approached the hotel entrance, the KGB picked us up again and followed closely for the duration of our stay in the city. No reprisals were taken against us during the rest of our stay there and we never received any negative comments from the MOD in Moscow, so we assumed the KGB recognized they themselves were responsible for the mix-up.

On another trip, the U.S. Embassy political counselor, Ed Djerijian, of Armenia extraction, accompanied me to Yerevan. He spoke Armenian and, due to this and his position at the embassy, we were able to visit the local leaders of the Armenian Apostolic Church in the Surb Sargis Cathedral complex. The KGB surveillants had a fit because my travel companion conducted his conversation in Armenian and they apparently couldn't understand what was being said. Why hadn't the KGB prepared its agents for this? They must have known Ed spoke Armenian.

BAKU, AZERBAIJAN

We had trouble standing upright. The winds were so terrible we often had to seek shelter behind fences and buildings. This was certainly proof that Baku was appropriately named. The name is derived from Persian and means "pounded by the wind."

Baku was the capital of Soviet Azerbaijan and was located on the west coast of the Caspian Sea. From the shore, oil derricks stretched as far as we could see. This was definitely an oil town. In fact, at the beginning of the 20th century half the world's oil came from Baku. Foreign investors at that time included the Nobel brothers of Nobel Prize fame and the Rothschild family. Four years earlier, in 1976, Baku had become a sister city to Houston, Texas—another windy oil city. Just as with Yerevan in Armenia, Baku was the only city I visited in this Republic.

In late summer 1980, our office had been trying to get an attaché team to Baku for three weeks, as a Washington intelligence agency had detected unusual activity there. The MOD continually denied our requests for travel. Finally, on 6 September, we got there and looked for a deployed command post complex. We were unable, however, to find any military activity. Obviously whatever had been going on was over. When I reported this, I wrote:

> If unusual activity actually did occur during the last half of August and first week of September, it was terminated before the Soviets allowed military attachés to travel there.

In retrospect, I suspect the Washington agency that requested the trip probably already knew there was no more activity.

We walked around the city, sampled the local cuisine (the bread—*lavash*—was particularly good) and took pictures of the antenna-rich TV tower as well as the port, although we saw no naval vessels. The

Baku subway/Metro contained murals, mosaics and ornate chandeliers similar to those in the Moscow Metro.

As usual, my report read "general observation in the city revealed no significant military activity."

PHOTOS AND DOCUMENTS II

Request for travel outside Moscow submitted to Soviet Ministry of Defense. Russian at the bottom of page states: "All times for travel by auto may change, depending on weather, road conditions or damage to the vehicle."

Bolshevik prisoners with US troops in Arkhangelsk, 1918

Nap area in Mogilyov after night in the train station

«Shuffle» stepping while laying a wreath for Senator Byrd

Baby Yar Monument

Writing on wall inside Brest Fortress

Holy Trinity-Saint Sergius Lavra in Zagorsk

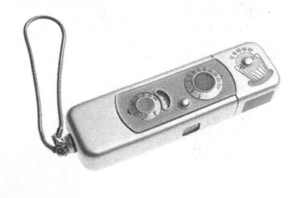

Minox camera

Author at crypt of Russian Writer Aleksander Griboyedov in Tbilisi, Georgia

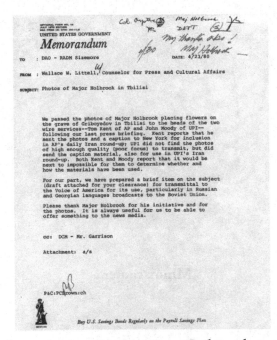

Embassy memo on my visit to Griboyedov crypt

Greater and Lesser Mount Ararat as seen
from Yerevan, the Armenian capital

PART IV: MOSCOW

THE CITY

Napoleon stood atop Sparrow Hills, the highest point in Moscow, and looked down upon the city as his Grande Armée entered. Tolstoy writes in *War and Peace* that "The view of the strange city with its peculiar architecture, such as he had never seen before, filled Napoleon with the rather envious and uneasy curiosity men feel when they see an alien form of life." When the Russians set fire to the city, Russia evacuated the Army and most of the residents, and then refused to capitulate, Napoleon wrote a letter to Tsar Alexander I, in which he referred to the city as "Beautiful, magical Moscow." He asked, "How could you consign to destruction the loveliest city in the world?" Alexander responded that the burning of Moscow "illuminated" his soul.

The greatest Russian Poet, Alexander Pushkin, wrote: "Moscow... how much there is in that sound that fills every Russian heart! So many echoes in that word!"

Moscow has long enjoyed a special place in the minds of those who have spent extended stays there. The city captivated me also. An acquaintance recently asked me why Moscow was one of my favorite cities in the world. Initially, I couldn't put my finger on it. Later, I found a quote from an English military attaché who served in Moscow in the late 19th century; it encapsulates the attraction of Moscow to all Russian scholars. He writes: "The heart of the nation beats at Moscow. Moscow is national in every sense of the term—it is more Russian than London is English, more Russian even than Paris is French."

The official founding date of the city is 1147. In 1979, the city covered 384 square miles. Its total population was over 8 million. The overwhelming majority of the population was Russian, but it included statistically significant numbers of, in descending order: Ukrainians, Jews, Tartars, Belorussians, Armenians, Mordovians, Azerbaijani, Georgians, Chuvash, Uzbeks, Kazakhs, Moldavians, Bashkir, Latvians, Lithuanians, Kirghiz, Tadzhiks, Turkmen, and Estonians—all of whom spoke their native languages as well as Russian. Forty-four percent of Muscovites were men; fifty-six percent were women. Fifty-five percent of the population was under the age of 40, which meant they had no first-hand knowledge of WWII that had taken place some thirty-plus years earlier. At best, they had only early childhood memories. I, for example, was 39 years old and remembered only the victory celebrations at the end of that war.

In 1979, there was relatively little civilian automobile traffic on Moscow streets, but the public transportation—subway, busses, trolleys, trams, trains—was very impressive. I owned a car in Moscow, but could have done without it. Pedestrians could cross the multi-lane streets— some ten lanes wide—through underpasses. The subway, known as the Moscow Metropolitan or Metro, was in fact clearly the most extensive and best in the world. There were 114 Metro stations in the city that would take you within walking distance of almost every point of interest or business. Most of the stations, especially toward the center of the city, were veritable museums with mosaics, statuary, murals and chandeliers.

A View of Moscow in 1980

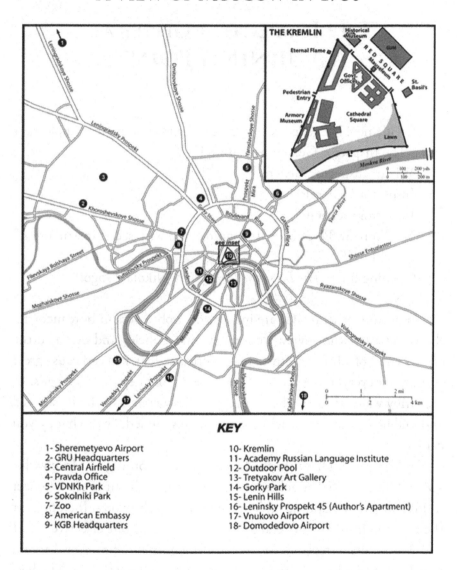

THE KREMLIN

Historical Museum
Eternal Flame
RED SQUARE
GUM
Govt. Offices
Mausoleum
St. Basil's
Pedestrian Entry
Armory Museum
Cathedral Square
Lawn
Moskva River

KEY

1- Sheremetyevo Airport
2- GRU Headquarters
3- Central Airfield
4- Pravda Office
5- VDNKh Park
6- Sokolniki Park
7- Zoo
8- American Embassy
9- KGB Headquarters
10- Kremlin
11- Academy Russian Language Institute
12- Outdoor Pool
13- Tretyakov Art Gallery
14- Gorky Park
15- Lenin Hills
16- Leninsky Prospekt 45 (Author's Apartment)
17- Vnukovo Airport
18- Domodedovo Airport

THE INSPECTOR GENERAL
A TURNING POINT

"Gentlemen! I've called you together to tell you some very unpleasant news. The Inspector General is coming!"

"What?! Inspector General?"

"Inspector General?"

"Inspector General?"

"Yes. From St. Petersburg. Incognito. And with secret instructions."

"Good Lord!"

(Opening lines, *The Inspector General* by Nikolai Gogol)

Inspectors general (IG) are independent observers in bureaucracies the world over who review documents and policies and evaluate the effectiveness of administrators. Their anticipated arrival can cause great concern for everyone, especially commanders and department heads. In the Army we used to say the two biggest lies were when the IG arrived and said he was there "to help us" and we responded, "we're happy you came."

In May 1980, DIA informed us the IG was coming to Moscow for a visit. Our principal attachés told us to go through our files and select 3-4 reports we were proud of. The Defense Attaché would then present them to the inspector general as an illustration of our effectiveness. I had written many reports. As I sifted through them, however, I found it difficult to find anything I would be proud to show the IG. The best I could come up with was: 1) the trip report on Ashkhabad, where I climbed up on a desk and photographed a roster of key officials in the

Turkmen Republic; 2) my discussion with the Chinese Naval Attaché about Sino-Soviet relations after Brezhnev; and 3) a report from a Soviet source about Communist Party discussions of Afghanistan and the Polish crisis.

I had several reports based on articles in Soviet newspapers, but I took no pride in them, as the information was second-hand. Besides, lots of people in the States could read those same newspapers.

I had traveled extensively about the Soviet Union but had not observed or reported anything of real military significance, with the possible exception of the many antennas I photographed. They may have been useful to NSA. Otherwise, I wondered what value I had contributed to U.S. intelligence. What information could I add to that captured by U.S. technical collection means (satellites)? According to Thomas Powers in *Intelligence Wars*, "CIA and DIA could pretty much find, count, and describe any piece of large-scale military hardware on or near the surface of the earth." By the 1960s, Powers writes, photo interpreters "counted tanks on flatbed railcars… with a resolution in yards, then feet, and finally inches for signs of a new bump on a tank turret, different antennae on the roof of the local KGB office…" So, I asked myself, "What were *we* doing?"

As a result of the meager results I found in my IRs, I conducted a complete reevaluation of my approach to being a military attaché in Moscow. I realized that something had to change; I couldn't go on like I had the past year. In short, I had been on the job in Moscow for a little over a year and couldn't see much return for the money my country had spent preparing me to be a Soviet/Russian FAO. I was frustrated and discouraged. I remembered something that then Lieutenant Colonel Bill Odom had written me while I was at West Point. In the note from Moscow, he wrote, "Life here is a mixture of delightful and <u>tough</u> aspects. If you come, bring very <u>low</u> expectations." (Underscore by Odom)

I concluded that my lack of accomplishing anything really significant was closely tied to my time only photographing buildings in Soviet cities where no significant military activities were discernible. At this point in my tour, I had taken no risks in the pursuit of unique information—some of which perhaps only I, because of my command of Russian, might have been capable of obtaining. It occurred to me that the primary value of being an attaché was turning out to be educational. Certainly my travels provided me with the opportunity to get to know the Soviet Union in more detail. That would help in any future assignments as an analyst or advisor on U.S.-Soviet affairs. But I was contributing very little at present.

It is well known that nations gather information about each other. It is natural for us not only to collect information about potential foes, but also to attempt to prevent them from collecting information about us. The line between information collection and information protection is not always clear. I believe over-emphasis on the one may lead to a diminution of the other. Lieutenant Colonel Roy Peterson, wrote in his *American Attaché in the Moscow Maelstrom*, "Security was the number one priority in Moscow for the Defense Attaché Office. At least for me." My thought (then and now) was: If security was that important, it might have been safer not to send attachés to Moscow in the first place. As General Michael Hayden wrote in his memoir *Playing to the Edge*, "Caution isn't always a virtue. Not if you're serious about doing your duty."

In order to go after information, we might jeopardize our own personal security. If we took a risk and failed, that would reflect poorly on our own professional record and put our immediate supervisors in an awkward position. Consequently, it was always safer—read 'more career-enhancing'— to pull in one's horns and be careful not to get into trouble. (In general, individuals who had gotten into trouble early in their careers seldom rose to the higher ranks of the military, or probably of any large civilian organization.) Powers refers to a sign over the desk of a CIA officer in Rome: "Big ops, big problems. Small ops, small problems. No ops, no problems."

Since it was becoming clear I would be unable to collect much significant military information in the USSR, I decided that during the rest of my tour I would mix more with Soviet citizens and try to exploit any opportunities that might arise. In other words, I would take more chances. I concluded that if I were to be effective here in the

Soviet Union, I would have to engage in activities that might ultimately backfire on me.

So I began to spend more time in the city. I used public transportation, shopped or pretended to shop in Moscow stores. On weekends I went to the Moscow parks. There I would wander around and occasionally stop to listen to a concert or watch a variety show.

I had few illusions about gathering significant information during those outings, but one never knows. Besides, I wanted to get a taste of how the Russians spent their weekends. Like many Europeans, they seemed to love to walk in the parks. I usually went alone. Before I left the United States, I had shopped for clothing in the Fort Myer thrift shop. Wearing those older clothes when out in the city or traveling, as well as having changed my wedding ring from left to right hand (the Russian custom) before arriving in Moscow, made it possible to move among Russians without being conspicuous.

In my free time, or when the workload in the office was light, I went out into the city parks. The Economic Achievements Park was located in the northern sector of the city and was easily accessible by Metro/subway. Known by the initials V-D-N-Kh (pronounced Veh-Deh-En-Khah), standing for "Exhibition of the Achievements of the National Economy," it was very large—nearly 600 acres—and always had interesting pavilions to visit. The famous gigantic statue of the worker and the collective farm woman that one sees at the beginning of many Soviet movies made at Mosfilm decorated the entrance to VDNKh. I "people watched" hundreds or even thousands of Soviet tourists each time I visited. An estimated 11 million tourists visited the park annually.

Sokolniki was another park to spend hours walking, watching outdoor shows and sampling the food. It was not always the case that one could find food in the parks, but in Sokolniki, I discovered an excellent sausage: the *sardelka*. Sardelkas are similar to German Rindwurst (pure beef Wurst). They are short, plump, dense and brown. As I write this, thoughts of a sardelka, some strong *gorchitsa* (mustard) and a bottle of beer make my mouth water. Sokolniki was more of a nature, walking park. Not so many people, not so much activity, but a pleasant place to spend time. Occasionally I caught concerts or variety shows.

I preferred VDNKh and Sokolniki to the more famous Gorky Park near the center of the city. Gorky Park also had food and concerts, but it was always more crowded. Probably because it was in town and offered many rides (called *atraktsiony*), it always seemed to have too much hustle-bustle for me. In the winter, authorities watered the walkways, which became paths for ice-skating.

Another new activity for me was to attend various public lectures at the *Znanie* (Knowledge) Society. The Society was established in 1947 as a public forum for dissemination of political and scientific knowledge. Various experts in science and the arts gave free lectures. One in particular I remember took place in mid-summer 1980. The U.S. was embroiled in a presidential campaign. The *Znanie* lecture was to be about American presidential politics.

The speaker impressed me with his knowledge of both principal U.S. political parties, of the individual candidates at the time—Jimmy Carter, Ronald Reagan and Independent John Anderson—of the primary system, national conventions and the Electoral College. However, when someone from the audience asked a question about the relationship of the presidential election to the state and local elections, the speaker was at a loss and quickly brought the subject back to his own area of expertise. To me it was evidence of a weakness in the Soviet education system. Soviet scholars displayed high degrees of specialization. There were many top-notch experts in narrowly defined fields, but to go beyond those fields and deal with more general subjects was not one of the goals of the Soviet education system. I likened their system to one of training, not education. In the first category, students become highly skilled in one field. In the second category, students are taught to think, associate, address unknowns and be better rounded in their outlook on life.

An Evening with the Great Vishnevsky

I asked my passenger, Sergei Vishnevsky, a top correspondent at *Pravda*, for directions to his home.

"You can just drop me off at the Belorussky Train Station."

As we approached the station, Vishnevsky said, "I've changed my mind. Take me to my office at the *Pravda* building."

We went a couple of blocks and turned onto Yamskova Polya 1 Street. I followed his directions to Pravda Street and pulled up outside the newspaper building.

I waited for him to get out.

"Come on up and see where the Great Vishnevsky does his work for the most important newspaper in the Soviet Union."

I hesitated. What might I be getting myself into? In the first place, I was alone. Attachés were supposed to travel in pairs when out working. But then, the Army Attaché had left me alone in that village on our way back from Murmansk. Secondly, Vishnevsky was inviting me into a building that was full of Communists and who knew what kind of security personnel? But this was a rare opportunity to get into one of the most important centers of propaganda in the USSR. Pravda was the most influential newspaper in the Soviet Union since it was the mouthpiece of the Communist Party.

I decided that here was a chance to broaden my area of operations. This was an opportunity to see where some important Soviets worked. It was certainly a far cry from photographing antennas or driving by military installations in which we could see little of value. I recalled reviewing my reports for the IG just a few weeks earlier and telling myself I was going to strike out and look for something of real value in Moscow. Perhaps this would be a good start?

This first chance to test my decision to become more aggressive occurred shortly after the IG visit. On 21 May, the U.S. Embassy Press Attaché invited me to his apartment for a taped showing of a 14 April interview with Zbigniew Brzezinski. In attendance also—and the real reason for this get-together—were six Soviet correspondents: Vishnevsky from *Pravda*, Matveev and Kondrashev from *Izvestiya*, Gerasimov from *Novosti* Press Agency, Nikolaev from *Ogonek* and Prudkov from *Literaturnaya Gazeta*. They all spoke passable English. Rounding out the American contingent were a couple of embassy officers and some U.S. correspondents. Vishnevsky had been *Pravda* bureau chief in Washington, DC during the 1960s.

The videotaped Brzezinski interview should have been of keen interest to the Soviets, since it took place not long after the failed Iran hostage rescue attempt and the resignation in protest over this fiasco by Secretary of State, Cyrus Vance, a few days later. The Soviets, however, were more interested in personalities in the Carter administration and made some pointed remarks about the new Secretary of State, Edmund Muskie. This period was definitely one of the "lows" in the Cold War and U.S.-Soviet relations. The Soviet invasion of Afghanistan had taken place five months earlier and President Carter had established a grain embargo against the USSR. There was serious talk about the U.S. and many other countries boycotting the Moscow Olympics that were to begin in a couple of months.

When the Soviets learned I was a military attaché, a couple of them complained about my being there: "This is a journalists' gathering, not one for military spies!" My host countered by stating I was not a spy, but rather a specialist on all things Soviet, not just military subjects. (He and I had been drawn together by our shared interest in Soviet jazz.)

"I disagree with you," Vishnevsky said to his journalist colleagues. "Of course he's an all-around Russian specialist. Just look at how he speaks Russian. I think it's refreshing to know up front he's a military attaché. At least we know who he is and what he does. Not one of those civilian embassy officers whose real status we're never sure about."

I felt the need to say something. So I came up with a polite, but bland response. "I appreciate meeting representatives of the Soviet press. The press is an important element of society." I resisted saying anything about the Soviet press being little more than a mouthpiece for the Communist Party.

Vishnevsky shook my hand. "I'm glad you're a military officer. We can understand each other. I worked at the Soviet military newspaper *Red Star* for two years. I'm now a senior lieutenant in the reserves. You outrank me, sir."

There was some muttering among the other Soviets as they turned away and began talking to the American correspondents. Vishnevsky lost no time.

"What do you think about this latest stage of the arms race? I'm talking about the cruise missile."

"Frankly, I don't know much about it. I'm a military attaché, not a strategic planner or maker of policy."

"You have to have some opinions about all this."

"You should know that American military officers don't debate U.S. national policies. We do have our views, but we express them at the ballot box. The American military professional is apolitical."

He tried to get me in a *tête-à-tête* on other political-military issues. I kept trying to stay involved with the discussions the others were conducting, but then I became curious and decided it might be of some value if I allowed him to pursue his apparent line of questioning.

As the social event was about to break up, I asked Vishnevsky if I could give him a ride home. He immediately accepted. We left the apartment about 11:30 that evening.

Once I had decided to take Vishnevsky up on his invitation to come into the *Pravda* building, my imagination began to race ahead. I admit I had visions of something really significant possibly happening. I recalled how the Soviets used NBC's John Scali during the Cuban Missile Crisis in 1962 to pass informal word to the White House that Khrushchyov was prepared to negotiate.

As indicated above, relations between our two countries at this point in 1980 were at a very low stage and many channels of communications were closed or clogged. In fact, the U.S. reaction to the Soviet invasion of Afghanistan included an order from the U.S. Joint Chiefs of Staff (JCS) to avoid all official and unofficial contact with the Soviet military. I certainly was in no position to send any messages to the Soviet government, but what if Vishnevsky wanted to use me as a conduit on some issue of concern between our two countries? At the very least, his questioning might give me some idea of the primary concerns of the Soviet government. Vishnevsky was believed to have high connections within the Soviet Communist Party and the KGB.

"Comrade," Vishnevsky said to the policeman at the door—loud enough so all the *Pravda* employees in the entrance lobby could hear— "This is an American military attaché. We've just come from a party and I've invited him up to my office."

The policeman just nodded his head. Apparently Vishnevsky carried some weight here in the office if the policeman simply let us pass without checking, at least, my documents.

When we got to his office on the third floor, Vishnevsky turned to me.

"I don't want to keep calling you 'Mr.' Holbrook, or even 'Major' Holbrook. What's your first name?"

"I go by Yasha or Jim."

"Yasha's not a nice name. It's Jewish. I'll call you Jimochka."

"And I'll call you Seryozha."

"Good. I'm sorry the canteen is closed. I don't have anything in my office to drink but tea. We should have taken a bottle from the apartment before we left." He put a kettle of water on a hotplate in a corner of his office.

"Tea's fine with me. Remember, I'm driving."

Vishnevsky had a small, private office. It reminded me of the offices of some of my university professors. In the clutter were several English-language magazines and books. I had never met Vishnevsky before, but I knew his name from reading *Pravda*. He was ten years older than me, overweight and scruffy. When he saw me looking around his office, he smiled and told me that two weeks earlier he had received the "Vorovsky Prize," which, according to him, was the Soviet equivalent of a Pulitzer for his writing on international affairs.

"Well, Jimochka. What should we talk about?"

"What's on your mind? Afghanistan seems a logical place to start."

"Afghanistan! Afghanistan! You Americans overreacted to that event."

"Protesting one nation attacking another without a serious threat to its own security doesn't seem to me to be an overreaction."

"Obviously, you don't understand what was at stake. I'll tell you why the Soviet Armed Forces went into Afghanistan." He explained, "It should be obvious to any realist that the Soviet Union has a genuine and legitimate interest in the affairs of countries on its borders. Once Taraki established a socialist government there, how could the USSR allow it to be brought down by Amin and replaced by a government which, for religious or nationalistic reasons, might pose a threat to our border area?"

Vishnevsky added, "The United States can justify military actions allegedly for national security reasons anywhere in the world, but the USSR is not even permitted to protect its borders. This is particularly illogical and deceitful."

As he poured our tea, he continued. "We feel surrounded, and have for many hundreds of years. And for good reason. You Americans can't understand that because you still feel like frontiersmen, cowboys. You're always looking outward for new frontiers to conquer. We, unfortunately, must keep looking inwards, must continue to build fortresses around ourselves."

"I can see some logic in that," I said, "but invading another country, assassinating its president and taking over all the elements of power seems to me to be a little overboard."

"Perhaps we miscalculated on Afghanistan, but the United States is partly to blame."

"How is that?"

"If the U.S. was so concerned about Soviet influence in Afghanistan, why did it stand by and let Taraki take power in 1978?"

"I don't know what to say. I don't know Afghan history and I'm no student of U.S. foreign policy," I answered. I immediately recalled, however, that Dean Acheson, U.S. Secretary of State in 1950 received post-Korean War criticism for just this type of policy. Acheson apparently had made a statement that excluded Korea from the U.S. area of vital interests and that, supposedly, gave North Korea the confidence to attack the South.

"I'll tell you what, Jimochka. American foreign policy is unpredictable and destabilizing to the international environment. Other countries don't know what to expect, especially when there's a change of administration. Hell, you yourselves don't know what to expect."

"I wouldn't put it that way. American goals are pretty well formulated and admired around the world. I would say, however, that we do have to be flexible in the face of turmoil in the world."

"Nonsense, Jimochka. The problem lies in the fact that your foreign policy is based on your domestic politics. Whatever the party in power thinks will help them get votes. I see that Reagan, Carter and Anderson are relatively close in the most recent Gallup poll. How do we know what to expect from any of them?"

"Well, public opinion does play a certain role in our government's policies. That's what our country is all about. You know, of course, Lincoln's statement "of the people, by the people, for the people.""

"Well, that's all nice. But the people don't understand enough about strategic arms development. That's a matter for the experts. And we never know which experts have the ear of your president."

"It's a very complex matter," I agreed.

"Your cruise missile, for example. How can it be controlled? It's a tiny weapon that cannot be detected—and with so much destructive power. And the MX Missile—a stupid idea. Our generals and admirals would be traitors to their country if they didn't come up with a counter-weapon. I'm sure they're already working on it."

"Once again, you're talking about matters way above my head," I said.

He dropped the strategic arms topic. He asked me what was going on in Miami. There had been some race riots there. I told him I knew only what was printed in our newspapers. He said he was required to write an item for tomorrow's paper on the topic. He had hoped I would be able to help him out. (When he saw I would be of little help, he told me he had already written the news item and submitted it for the morning newspaper.)

We talked about Iran—the hostage crisis and the failed rescue mission, "Operation Eagle Claw." As a military officer, I was very uncomfortable about his remarks on our effort to rescue the hostages. I told him it was late and I had to get back home. As I was leaving, he asked what my "bosses" would say if they found out I had spent several hours with him.

"Oh, I don't think they'll mind so long as I report our conversation."

I did just that the next day. Not long after I sent that report in (it's one of the declassified IRs DIA later sent me), I received kudos from the White House for my visit to the *Pravda* building. I'm sure those kudos came from then Brigadier General Bill Odom, who was on Brzezinski's staff at the time. In any case, the kudos made me feel that my branching out to meet people was the way to go.

"It Don't Mean a Thing..."

Knock my socks off! Those cats could swing!

Soviet jazz pianist Igor Bril and guitarist Alexei Kuznetsov were doing *It Don't Mean a Thing If It Ain't Got That Swing*. Never had I heard such a marriage of melody and rhythm. It was magic. To this day, I've not heard the piece done better.

I had come to a jazz concert in the Musicians' Union House in Moscow with a Soviet acquaintance, Georgii Bakhchiev (pronounced BAKH-chee-eff). During my tour of duty in Moscow, Georgii provided many opportunities for me to hear jazz and to meet jazz musicians.

This Soviet came close to being a real friend. Under the circumstances, I felt I could never really trust a Soviet. The safest way to view events that touched my life in the USSR during those years was to assume the KGB orchestrated almost all the events. Soviet citizens were subject to various pressures from the KGB. This was particularly true of Soviets who were allowed to associate with foreigners.

Georgii was associating with an American military attaché, a diplomat who was in the USSR to collect military information. Embassy officers warned me about him. I had to assume he was either working for the KGB or at least reporting our contacts to them. But I didn't blame him. I reported my contact with him to my own people.

Whether Georgii was working for the KGB or not, his relationship with me was completely benign. Maybe he collected some biographic information the KGB didn't have, but unlike many other Soviet citizens with whom I established a relationship, Georgii never asked me about my work, where I traveled or with whom I met. He never asked me to get him western clothing or buy anything in our special stores. The one thing he did ask for, frequently, was a pinch of my pipe tobacco, which he would use to roll a homemade cigarette from a piece of Russian newspaper. Striking up this relationship was part of my effort to take some chances and to mix with Soviet citizens. Georgii never made me regret that we "befriended" each other.

I first met him in the summer of 1979 at the home of the American cultural attaché, who was also a jazz fan. We had a common friend in Washington, Dick Baker, who wrote articles on jazz and other cultural events in the U.S. Information Agency's magazine *Amerika*.

At the cultural attaché's apartment that night I met two Soviet jazzmen: Igor Bril and Georgii. Igor was not only an accomplished pianist, he was also a jazz theoretician who had written a book on jazz composition and later became a professor at one of the Moscow jazz academies. Georgii was a jazz impresario (called an *organizator* in Russian), who traveled about the Soviet Union giving lectures and playing jazz records for Soviet citizens who were far from the city life of Moscow or Leningrad. He also organized jazz concerts in various cities. Our talk that evening was all about jazz. At the end of the evening, Georgii invited me to attend an upcoming jazz concert. I accepted and thus began our long, friendly relationship.

Elaine and I spent time with Georgii's family—Anna, his wife; Vera, his 8-year-old daughter; and his mother, Alexandra Ivanovna Bakhchieva, whom we called *Babushka* (Grandma). Babushka was a devoted Communist, but for a 69-year-old Bolshevik, she had an unusually independent outlook on life. She relished the idea that her son had brought home an "American spy." We had several friendly arguments about politics. What fascinated me most about her was that she had witnessed many of the historic events in Soviet history. I often tried to get her to talk about her youth and her experiences during World War II.

All I was able to glean was that she was a young girl at the time of the Bolshevik coup and was in her thirties during the Battle of Moscow. During the war she was evacuated, along with her two children, to Tbilisi, Georgia. On a boat along the way, a woman kidnapped her youngest son, Sasha, in order to be counted as a mother with children and, thus, be excused from heavy work. Babushka pinned Georgii to her skirt (he was three years old at the time) and went searching for Sasha. She found him and was able to get him back. (Alexandra Ivanovna Bakhchieva passed away in 2009, at the age of 99.)

Alexandra Ivanovna's mother had been a Hero of the Civil War, for which the government awarded her a dacha on the outskirts of the city. Several times Elaine and I, or occasionally I alone, visited and stayed overnight at this dacha. On one occasion, we all went mushroom hunting, a favorite Russian pastime. Georgii pointed out which mushrooms were edible and which were poisonous. We then returned to the dacha, where we cooked and ate them.

One of the things that drew Georgii and me together was that neither he nor I played any instrument, but we were both devoted fans of jazz. My role in the jazz world was to listen and enjoy. Georgii, on the other hand, was quite involved in Soviet jazz. In addition to his travels around the Soviet Union spreading the jazz gospel, he wrote liner notes on some of the Soviet jazz records that were produced in Moscow. At his apartment, he prominently displayed a photo of himself with Duke Ellington, taken during the latter's tour of the Soviet Union in 1971.

On this evening, Georgii and I had just entered the Musicians' Union House. The 300 or so jazz fans in the auditorium were silent as we quietly moved up to our seats in the front row. The audience was focused on the duo on the stage. When they finished, the hall erupted with prolonged applause.

I shouldn't have been so amazed at the performance of these two jazzmen. When I first arrived in the Soviet Union, the high level of Soviet jazz shocked me at first, but by now I was getting used to it. This performance by Igor Bril and Alexei Kuznetsov was one of the two most memorable ones I've ever witnessed. The second occurred when the Soviet Army Orchestra opened a big band festival by playing Glenn Miller's *In the Mood*. That gave me goose bumps.

American jazz was one of our most influential gifts to world culture. Born in New Orleans, jazz "went on the road" after city officials closed the famous red-light district—Storyville—on 12 November 1917, coincidentally five days after the Bolshevik Coup in St. Petersburg. Until the last decades, when Americans started traveling abroad more, we tended to think that since jazz was American-born, only Americans could excel at it. But, no. Jazz not only went on the road in the USA, it also traveled abroad.

Frederick Starr's *Red and Hot: Jazz in the Soviet Union* provides the best English-language summary of jazz history in USSR from its beginnings through the 1970s. (My bibliography contains also two comprehensive Russian-language books on Soviet jazz history.) Most of the highlights and lowlights in early Soviet jazz discussed below are from Starr's book.

Although jazz, as such, didn't get to Russia until 1922, American popular music was already a favorite in certain circles in St. Petersburg. Before the First World War, for example, the military band of the Sumskoi Hussar's Regiment had issued a record of *Alexander's Ragtime Band*. The Volynia Life Guards Regiment played two-steps and the cakewalk at public gatherings. The night in 1916 when Prince Felix Yusupov poisoned Rasputin, the gramophone in his house played *Yankee Doodle Went to Town*.

When Russian Valentin Parnakh arrived in Moscow in 1922 with jazz instruments, Russia became one of the very few countries in the world where jazz was not introduced by Americans, but rather by a native son. During 1920s, 30s and 40s, jazz was dance music in both America and Russia. (In fact, Benny Goodman began his performances with *Let's Dance*.)

As with all the arts during the Soviet era, jazz traveled a very rocky road. The official government attitude toward jazz varied from viewing it as bourgeois decadence to, at times, accepting it as the folk music of the downtrodden American Negroes. For example, in 1926, the Soviet Commissar of Cultural Affairs, Anatolii Lunacharsky, was so taken by the music, he sent Leopold Teplitsky to Philadelphia to learn as much as he could about jazz and to buy up music arrangements and instruments. In 1929, however, Lunacharsky had Teplitsky arrested. In 1937, Valentin Parnakh likewise was arrested and never heard of again. In 1945, according to *National Geographic*, due to a lack of recording materials, two jazz enthusiasts in Leningrad used discarded x-rays on which to record music smuggled into the USSR.

At one high point in the history of Soviet jazz the Komsomol (Young Communist) organization set up special cafes where young people could come to hear jazz and dance to the popular music. At a low point in the history of jazz in the USSR, however, Komsomol meetings were taken up in debate over "Can a young Communist like jazz?" In one special Moscow high school, several girls in the senior class were expelled for admitting they loved jazz. In both 1929 and 1949, officials attempted to ban the saxophone. Komsomol members went around to the various music venues to ensure no saxophones or trumpet mutes were being used. The government wanted to replace the saxophone with the cello.

During the good years for jazz, however, several prominent Soviet musicians took a great interest in it. The composer Dmitri Shostakovich arranged *Tea for Two* as a foxtrot and called it *Tahiti Trot*. Sergei Prokofiev, composer of *Peter and the Wolf,* kept abreast of new developments in jazz by staying in contact with young members of the American Embassy. Jazz combos were popular in the military, especially during the Second World War. At a Kremlin reception to mark the anniversary of the "Great October Revolution," Commissar of Defense, Marshal Kliment Voroshilov, and his wife led the others present in dancing the foxtrot. As a cultural affairs officer at the American Embassy once put it, in the Soviet Union "The whole business of jazz was a political question, not cultural."

One of the more interesting aspects of Soviet jazz is that it made a major contribution to American jazz in the person of Joseph Schillinger. A musician, teacher and theorist, Schillinger ran into official opposition in Leningrad in the 1920s. By 1929 he had emigrated to New York. His theories and teaching had a significant influence on many American jazz greats, including Benny Goodman, Tommy Dorsey, Eubie Blake, Gerry Mulligan, Quincy Jones and John Lewis. He is indirectly responsible for Glenn Miller's *Moonlight Serenade* and George Gershwin's *Porgy and Bess*.

Voice of America's Willis Conover and his program, "Music USA," was an invaluable source and inspiration to Soviet jazzmen. Russians would listen, record and distribute tapes of the music he played. One Russian wrote to Conover: "You are a source of strength when I am overwhelmed by pessimism, my dear idol." As a result primarily of Conover's broadcasts, I found Soviet jazz musicians were more than just well informed about American jazz history and developments. Conover inspired them to create and perform their own jazz.

I was fortunate that jazz was now (1979-1981) more or less officially condoned in the Soviet Union. It seemed the biggest threat to jazz in the 1970s was the invasion from the West of rock music. As touchy as the authorities were about whether to approve or disapprove of jazz, the musicians themselves were apolitical. Like professional musicians around the world, their primary concern was their music.

This is what allowed me to socialize with them. I didn't want to associate with political dissidents or Jewish refuseniks (Russian Jews who had requested permission to emigrate, but were refused). If I spent time with those two groups, although it would have been interesting and potentially the source of much non-official information, I would be asking for even more attention from the KGB. I sought no information from Soviet jazzmen. They came to realize this and to accept me.

I concentrated on the Moscow jazz world. When I arrived in Moscow, I was by no means a jazz aficionado. My introduction to both jazz and classical music occurred during my teens in the mid-1950s, when my brother bought a wind-up phonograph. The phonograph came with a classical record: Carl Otto Nicolai's *Overture to The Merry Wives of Windsor* and a jazz record by the drummer Cozy Cole. Neither jazz nor classical music could be found on radio stations in rural Wisconsin. But my brother's records hooked me from that time forward on both music genres. My experiences with Soviet jazz music and musicians deepened my knowledge and appreciation for this American gift to the world.

Nikolai Ogarkov
Marshal Of The Soviet Union

Did Soviet military doctrine call for a first, preemptive nuclear strike if war loomed? Or would the MAD (Mutual Assured Destruction) doctrine prevent a nuclear holocaust? According to MAD, the threat of destroying civilization was so frightening that our governments supposedly would never start a thermonuclear war.

Not all strategic analysts, however, were that confident about this doctrine. From time to time, a political or military leader on one side or the other would say something in public that caused doubts about MAD's viability as a deterrent. Such was apparently the case in 1980, when Chief of the Soviet General Staff, Marshal of the Soviet Union Nikolai Ogarkov, made some public comments about "first strike." I don't remember what it was, but it might have been some version of the debate about whether any country could "win" a nuclear war. (Ogarkov reportedly had objected to a statement in the 1979 Vienna U.S.-Soviet Communiqué that no one could win a nuclear war.)

Prior to his becoming the next Chairman of the Senate Foreign Relations Committee, U.S. Senator Charles Percy had planned a late-November 1980 trip to the Soviet Union at the invitation of Ambassador Watson. He would use part of his time in Moscow to discuss arms control issues with Soviet leaders. During a 3-hour meeting with Leonid Brezhnev and Soviet Minister of Defense Dmitri Ustinov, Senator Percy expressed concern over Ogarkov's earlier remarks. Ogarkov was present at the meeting and denied ever saying or writing that the Soviets could win a nuclear war. He offered to bet his dacha and year's pay that no one could prove he had suggested that.

Ustinov apparently decided at the last minute to have Marshal Ogarkov attend a previously scheduled luncheon the next day at Ambassador Watson's residence. It was to be an opportunity for Senator Percy to meet with some of the top Soviet specialists on the United States—Soviet "Americanologists." Ustinov hoped Ogarkov could allay Percy's fears. Any discussions at the luncheon would be conducted in English since all the Americanologists spoke English. But with the addition of Marshal Ogarkov, who did not speak English, the ambassador needed an interpreter. The embassy asked me to fill this need.

Senator Percy was scheduled to meet with Soviet Foreign Minister Andrei Gromyko that morning at the Ministry of Foreign Affairs. The luncheon was to take place at noon at Spaso House. The chief of the embassy's political section, Ed Djerejian, and I arrived at Spaso House about 11:45. No one else was there yet. Earlier in the year, Ed and I had traveled to Armenia together, so we chatted about that trip, all the time glancing at our watches.

I was a little nervous about meeting and interpreting for Marshal Ogarkov. He wasn't just some high-ranking military officer. He was *the* senior military officer of the Soviet Armed Forces. As Chief of the Soviet General Staff, he was equivalent to the Chairman of the American Joint Chiefs of Staff. He had a reputation as a highly intelligent military intellectual and a leader in Soviet efforts to upgrade the technical basis of their military. I was sure Ogarkov would not remember meeting me during the 1980 May Day festivities on Red Square. (As a sign of our displeasure with the Soviet invasion of Afghanistan the preceding December, the embassy selected me—one of the junior assistant military attachés—to appear on Red Square that day. I was introduced to him as "the American.") On Red Square I had been in uniform; here I was in civilian clothes.

At precisely 12:00 noon, I opened the door and saw the imposing figure of Marshal Ogarkov. His Hero of the Soviet Union Red Star—similar to our Medal of Honor—was among the many medals and ribbons covering his uniform blouse. That he was alone, without an interpreter of his own, was probably due to the fact that he knew all the other Soviets at the luncheon spoke English and would step in if an American interpreter didn't do his job well enough. He appeared taken aback that no one else was present.

Ed and I greeted him in Russian.

"I'm Ed Djerijian, head of the Embassy Political Section."

"Marshal of the Soviet Union Ogarkov, I'm Major Holbrook of the Defense Attaché Office. I will be your interpreter today." (I had to use the full military title, as this was the highest rank among various other kinds of marshals in the Soviet Armed Forces.)

He nodded and we shook hands.

"Where is everyone?" the marshal asked.

"They are apparently delayed at the Ministry of Foreign Affairs," I replied.

A few seconds of awkward silence. I knew we couldn't just stand there, but I wasn't sure how to get a conversation going. "How are you?" would have been a ridiculous question. To ask any substantive questions, however, would have been inappropriate since even though Ogarkov didn't know me, I'm sure he considered me to be some kind of intelligence officer.

"Would you like a cigarette or a cup of tea or coffee?" I asked.

"Thank you, no."

"I'm sure they will be here shortly. Have you ever been to the American ambassador's residence before?"

"No."

"Well then, let me show you around the house while we wait for the others to arrive."

Built in 1914, Spaso House once belonged to a wealthy Russian merchant. Its main hall on the ground floor was 82 feet long and boasted a large chandelier of Russian crystal—reportedly the largest house chandelier in Moscow.

One thing I was sure would interest the marshal was the exhibition of paintings on Spaso House walls. Galleries loan paintings by American artists to embassies around the world. The ones currently on exhibit were very striking—large, bright paintings of houses and street scenes with sharp, almost cubist, lines—all against the background of the Spaso's white walls.

"Allow me to show you some very interesting paintings by American artists," I offered. "Here they are in the reception area of the ballroom. That door there leads to the room where the luncheon will take place."

"Fine," said Ogarkov. He followed me into the ballroom and seemed to take a genuine interest in the paintings, pausing for some time before each one. Soon, however, he was looking at his watch.

"Are you sure the luncheon was scheduled for noon? Is it possible I was given the wrong information?" he asked.

"No, sir. You are correct. The senator and ambassador are with Minister Gromyko now. He has apparently held them a little longer than expected."

"I'm a military man. When I'm supposed to be some place at a particular time, I'm on time. I expect others also to be prompt."

"Understood, sir. But I'm sure they would not leave Minister Gromyko's office until he felt their discussions had been concluded."

By the time he had finished looking at the last painting, about half an hour had gone by. He looked at his watch again.

"I'm not going to wait around. I'm going back to my office. When the party arrives, call me," he said, addressing both Ed and me. "It's a short ride on the Metro from the General Staff building and Spaso."

He said this with a straight face, although we knew he had come in a limo. As a matter of fact, there was no convenient metro station near Spaso.

"Fine, sir. Could I get your phone number?" I asked.

Marshal Ogarkov hesitated, then said, "Call Colonel Tikhomirov. He'll know how to get in touch with me. I'm sure you have his number." The marshal then departed.

Colonel Tikhomirov was the MOD Foreign Liaison officer who dealt with the attachés from English-speaking countries. I carried his number with me in the event I needed his help in a difficult situation.

"I don't think Ogarkov was too keen on coming to this luncheon in the first place," I said to Ed.

"No, and he didn't seem to appreciate being stood up by civilians," Ed replied.

Finally, Ambassador Watson, Senator Percy and the Soviet American experts arrived, after what had turned out to be a 4-hour visit at the Ministry of Foreign Affairs. I explained to the ambassador what had transpired with Marshal Ogarkov.

"Fine. Call him now and tell him we're here and we'll hold up starting lunch until he gets here."

I went to the phone and dialed Colonel Tikhomirov's number. Some lieutenant answered.

"This is Major Holbrook, American Assistant Army Attaché. I need to talk to Colonel Tikhomirov."

"Just one minute," the lieutenant said. In a few seconds, he returned to the phone.

"Colonel Tikhomirov isn't here right now."

"Listen," I said. "I'm calling on behalf of Marshal of the Soviet Union Ogarkov. He instructed me to contact Colonel Tikhomirov."

"Just one minute."

Almost immediately, Colonel Tikhomirov was on the phone.

"Sir, Marshal of the Soviet Union Ogarkov is scheduled to attend a luncheon here at the American Ambassador's residence. He was here, but the party was late in arriving so he returned to his office and told me to call you when the others got here. The ambassador promises not to start the luncheon until the marshal returns."

"OK, give me a minute," the colonel said.

I waited for a least a minute before Tikhomirov came back on the phone.

"Marshal of the Soviet Union Ogarkov sends his regrets," said the colonel. "He's gone to the Kremlin on business and will not be able to attend the luncheon."

I told Ambassador Watson that Marshal Ogarkov wouldn't be coming to the luncheon.

"Since everyone else speaks English, you won't need me and I'll leave."

"No, no. You stay and enjoy the lunch. You interpreters seldom get a chance to have a decent meal," said the Ambassador.

The Ambassador was very understanding. It was as if he had read an article by a CIA officer who wrote of "the occupational diseases, nervous indigestion and undernourishment, contracted in [an interpreter's] attempts to gulp food while translating banquet conversations."

Marshal Ogarkov was the Soviet face on TV after the KAL 007 shoot-down in 1983. Possibly because of conflicts he had with the Soviet political leadership, the Minister of Defense relieved him from the post of Chief of the Soviet General Staff in 1984. Marshal Georgii Zhukov had had similar difficulties with political leaders after WWII.

I was surprised to find out later that Ogarkov opposed the Soviet invasion of Afghanistan. General-Major Alexander Lyakovsky, formerly of the Soviet General Staff, described this in his 1985 *The Tragedy and Valor of Afghanistan*. According to Lyakovsky, on 10 December 1979, Defense Minister Ustinov summoned Ogarkov and told him of the Politburo's decision to introduce troops into Afghanistan. "Ogarkov was surprised and outraged by such a decision" and called it "reckless." Ustinov said to him, "Are you going to teach the Politburo? Your only duty is to carry out the orders." On the same day, the principal members of the Politburo called Ogarkov to a meeting. He told them the Afghan people "never tolerated foreigners on their soil." He lost his case, however, and the Soviets invaded Afghanistan on 27 December.

This attitude toward Soviet involvement in Afghanistan is indirectly corroborated by Marshal of the Soviet Union, and another former Chief of the Soviet General Staff, Sergei Akhromeev. He reportedly said during a television interview in 1990: "As I have said on more than one occasion, the military top brass was against the war...We feared that the whole Islamic world would rise up against the USSR."

AFGHANISTAN AND THE 1980 MOSCOW OLYMPICS

The 1980 Moscow Summer Olympic games were going to increase the prestige of the USSR. But the Soviet leadership shot itself in the foot.

As stated in the previous chapter, on 27 December 1979, the Soviets invaded Afghanistan. KGB and GRU Spetsnaz troops killed Afghan President Amin and occupied all key government buildings in Kabul. The international community reacted angrily. Nothing could be done in the U.N. Security Council because the Soviet Union wielded veto power there. The U.N. General Assembly, however, voted 104 to 18 for a "total withdrawal of foreign troops" from Afghanistan.

President Carter called the invasion "the most serious threat to peace since the Second World War." He urged all countries to condemn the USSR actions and imposed a grain embargo on the Soviets. One of Carter's subsequent moves was to assist the anti-Soviet forces in Afghanistan (the Mujahideen) by purchasing all of Israel's captured Soviet weapons and sending them to Afghanistan. Additionally, the idea immediately arose of boycotting the summer 1980 Moscow Olympics.

Perhaps even more effective than a grain embargo was Soviet nuclear physicist and humanist Andrei Sakharov's public support for strong U.S. action against the USSR. Sakharov, one of the fathers of the Soviet hydrogen bomb had become over the years a strong voice for reform and human rights. Among his brave acts was the use of foreign correspondents to get his opposition to the Soviet government known to the outside world. His world fame as a scientist protected him to some extent against KGB retribution for his dissident activities. Sakharov was awarded the Nobel Peace Prize in 1975 and received a personal letter of support from President Carter. He backed the Western boycott of the Olympics. In January 1980, however, less than one month after the Soviet invasion, the KGB arrested him and sent him with his wife, Elena Bonner, into internal exile to Gorky—a city that was closed to foreigners, including, most importantly, foreign correspondents.

I believed an Olympic boycott was one of the surest ways to punish the Soviets without resorting to military force. The Russians are extremely self-conscious when it comes to how their cultural, political and economic status is perceived by the civilized world. Even if they wouldn't admit it, they sensed that Sergei Witte spoke the truth when he said, "The world bowed not to our culture, nor to our bureaucratized church, nor to our wealth and prosperity. It bowed to our might." The Soviets viewed the 1980 Summer Olympics as an opportunity to show the world that not only were they a military superpower, but also a modern and sophisticated society. The Soviet approach to these Olympics paralleled that of Hitler in 1936.

For several months leading up to the summer of 1980, the Soviets spruced up Moscow and all Olympic venues (Minsk, Leningrad, Kiev and Tallinn). They renovated historic churches and other historic sites, carted off drunks and beggars to someplace beyond the city, and sent children off to summer camps. All Soviet individuals who would likely have contact with foreigners—store clerks, hotel personnel, cab drivers, etc.—found themselves outfitted with new denim clothing and taking lessons in basic English. Fewer noisy and stinky trucks roared through Moscow's streets. The city seemed almost empty. The stores, however, were well stocked for the first time.

When no decision had yet been made on a possible boycott, I sent a letter to Brigadier General Bill Odom, at the White House. I wrote the letter in Russian, believing that was the surest way to make sure it got to him. I knew from when we were neighbors at West Point that the general was a big enthusiast of the Russian language. In the letter I wrote:

24 January 1980

General Odom:

A couple of words from "the site of events" to corroborate a fact well known to you: The 1980 Olympics play an exceptionally important role in Soviet world propaganda. Consequently, the proposed boycott by the U.S. and other countries would deliver a serious blow to the status and prestige of the Soviet government.

History does not often give such opportunities to influence world events without the use of military force.

Warm regards to Anne and Mark.
Yasha Holbrook, Moscow

Holly sent a letter to President Carter with the same message. She received a response from the White House. I'm sure the final decision to boycott the Olympics was made without our input, but I was gratified to see the decision later announced in Washington and other world capitals.

The Soviets, however, continued their preparations for the Olympics. Foreigners began to show up all over town. Russians who had access to hard currency frequented the Beryozka shops with fistfuls of American dollars.

On opening day of the Olympics—19 July—I attended a party in the Soviet apartment of a female acquaintance, an impresario of non-official art. (I'll call her Natasha.) In attendance were about ten Soviets, including an official of the Soviet Artists' Union, the director of the Moscow River Transportation Office, a Soviet Georgian who was a hotel director, and some artists. I was the only foreigner.

In the Russian tradition, we all gathered around the dining room table. It was a pretty good-sized table, but no matter, since according to Russian custom, there is no limit to the number of people you can fit at a round table. It was no surprise that the conversation soon turned to the Olympics.

"So today's the big day. Who, in the end, is here and who isn't?"

"The most important countries are absent: America, Germany, Japan, Canada."

"All the better. Just that many more medals for us."

"Yes, but winning an event by forfeit carries no honor."

"A medal's a medal."

"Not true."

"Well, I for one think the American boycott ruined our Olympics."

"We ruined it ourselves by invading Afghanistan. I'm glad there's a boycott."

By this time, I realized not everyone knew I was an American. Although I usually allowed Russians to think I was one of them, tonight it didn't seem right. I didn't want them to be embarrassed by their anti-government remarks once they found out who I was. I pointed that out to Natasha and asked her to let everyone know that an American was present.

"Comrades. I want to introduce my special guest this evening. Yasha Holbrook is from the American Embassy."

"Why are you here?"

"Well, my government certainly wouldn't let me go to any Olympic festivities."

"Where does the name "Yasha" come from? Are you Jewish?"

"No. My American name is James, which is Yakov in Russian. A college professor gave me the nickname 'Yasha.'"

"What do you do at the embassy?"

"I'm a military attaché."

"Aha! You've come to collect information?"

"What kind of information could I get from a bunch of artists? No. I'm here to have a good time. Just like you."

"Well, I propose a toast to the Moscow Olympics."

"You know I can't drink to that."

"OK. Then we'll have a toast to the boycott."

"I'll drink to that."

The complaints about Soviet policy in Afghanistan became a little more muted but didn't end. I was gratified to detect a sense among the partygoers that the boycott was a blow to the Soviet/Russian self-image.

By the time the last Soviet soldier left Afghanistan in 1989, the Soviets had lost 15,051 soldiers killed. 53,753 were wounded and 417 were missing in action.

The Olympic boycott resulted in Moscow and the Soviet Communist Party leadership losing the opportunity to show the outside world how much they deserved to be considered an equal in the civilized community of nations.

"You May Call Me Natasha"

Here is the rest of the story about my relationship with Natasha, the hostess of the party I attended on opening day of the Moscow Olympics.

The occasion for my first meeting with her was a farewell party in the fall of 1979 given for our departing Defense Attaché in his embassy apartment. I saw Natasha and another woman across the room talking to other guests. I was attracted to her initially because of the way she was dressed. She wore a modern cocktail dress, but it also reminded me of a dress one might see at a 19th century ball. That was a period when women displayed their physical endowments in a way that was sure to attract men. (Bailey reports that the American Minister to Russia in 1837, George M. Dallas, was "impressed by the handsome dresses of the women but was somewhat shocked by 'a most profuse display of the bust.'")

Soviet employees at the embassy often attended social functions there. The four Soviet "girls" who worked in the embassy's Administrative Office were frequent guests at get-togethers in the Embassy. That they reported on these events to their KGB masters was made clear at least once. A flyer announcing an August farewell for the Army Attaché showed a Lenin caricature in shorts and an Army Runner t-shirt. The day after that party, the embassy received a complaint from the MOD. They claimed such a depiction of Lenin was in very poor taste (read: sacrilegious).

Natasha, on the other hand, was an outsider. I was surprised she had been allowed to be at this party. It turned out she was an art impresario. The fact that she was allowed to be at an embassy party suggested she was one of those special Soviets who had been given permission by the KGB to associate with foreigners. She was probably in her early 40s, as was I.

I walked up to her.

"Good evening, I'm Major Jim Holbrook, an assistant Army attaché. I've been in Moscow only a few months. I don't believe we've met."

"Pleased to meet you, Major Jim. I'm A. No, we haven't met yet."

She gave me the once-over, which was only fair, as I was doing the same to her. She wasn't what you'd call a "beauty," although, as I said, she was quite attractive.

"You may call me Yasha."

"That's interesting. Why do you go by that name?"

"A professor gave me the Russian version of James—Yakov—in college. And of course, Yasha is the diminutive name for Yakov. I've used it ever since with colleagues and Russian acquaintances."

"Very nice. You may call me Natasha."

"How is it you know General Larkin?"

"He and his wife purchased artwork from me. I have a gallery in my apartment. Are you interested in Russian art?"

"I'm interested in everything Russian," I said with a smile.

"Then you must come to my place someday to see the artwork I have. Much of it is from non-establishment artists."

"I would like that very much."

That was pretty much the extent of our exchange that night. I would have loved to go visit her, but had not yet reached the point in my attaché tour where I was prepared to take the chance of visiting a woman alone in her apartment. To me Natasha was an obvious KGB plant and I thought it best to stay clear of her.

I didn't see her again until the Fourth of July picnic at Spaso house in 1980. There were several Soviet guests at the picnic, including Sergei Vishnevsky, the *Pravda* columnist, and many of my Soviet jazz acquaintances. When I saw Natasha, I approached her, intending to reintroduce myself. Once again she was dressed provocatively. Before I had a chance to say anything, she spoke.

"Yasha! Long time no see. Why haven't you come by my place to look at the art?"

"Hi, Natasha. Just haven't gotten around to it. Nice to see you again."

"You really must come."

I was now past my May 1980 decision to start taking chances. The night with Vishnevsky had gone well. Perhaps this was another initiative opportunity.

"I will come by at the first opportunity," I said.

"Well, the first opportunity is a little party I'm giving on Opening Day of the Olympics. On the 19th. Will you come?"

"I have to check my schedule, but if I can make it I'll be there. Where do you live?"

"Just up the street from your embassy. Sadovaya Kudrinkskaya 5/12, apartment 27."

I did go to the party, which I described in the previous chapter on Afghanistan and the Olympics.

During the Olympic party I met two non-establishment artists, Boris and Sonya. I believe they were married. I visited them in their apartment sometime later. Boris and Sonya attached themselves to me that evening as soon as they knew I was an American. I wasn't sure whether they were looking to exploit their acquaintance with me to sell their art, to assist in getting them a visa to emigrate or what. But they were quite warm to me.

"Natasha has taken a real liking to you," Boris confided to me.

"She's quite attractive. And this apartment! How does she rate such a large apartment?" I replied.

"It belonged to her parents who are dead now. She uses it as an unofficial art gallery, which helps us artists a lot."

I later found in Andrew Nagorski's 1985 Reluctant Farewell a description of Natasha and her apartment:

> The exhibition was in the apartment of a woman
> who considered herself a patron of the arts; she allowed
> recognized and "unofficial" artists to show their work

there. The authorities must have known about these exhibits, but for some reason they made no movement to prevent them. As usual, theories abounded to explain the anomaly. To some, the woman was a true benefactor; to others, she was a possible KGB informer with the mission of flushing out independent artists.

Toward the end of the party, Natasha invited me into her bedroom to see some paintings on the walls. She sidled up close to me, smiled and out of nowhere said, "Later."

The party started winding down. It was nearing midnight. Several of the guests departed. I started helping my hostess clear the table by carrying dishes to her kitchen.

"Can you stay the night?" she asked quietly.

"I... I... don't know."

"I'd like to show you a sight from the roof of my apartment. There are too many people here to offer that to everyone."

"OK. I'll stick around a little after everyone's gone."

When all the guests had departed, Natasha took my hand and led me through her bedroom to a trap door near the ceiling. She opened it, lowered a ladder, and told me to follow her. We stepped out onto the roof. Since it was a clear summer night, we could see much of the city from there. It was an awe-inspiring sight.

"There's your embassy there. And you can see some of the Kremlin towers over there," she said. When we had finished marveling over all the sights, we went back down into her bedroom.

"Now will you agree to stay the night," she asked again.

I wanted to, but I was still nervous about it. There was no doubt in my mind the KGB would learn of this tryst. But maybe that was good. I wanted the KGB to know I couldn't be blackmailed. Perhaps if I did something so obviously wrong despite knowing the KGB would find out, that would convince them I was invulnerable to blackmail or their overtures. And I admit my mind was a bit clouded by other urges at the time. I had drunk some vodka during the party, but believed I was still in full control of my faculties.

"Yes, I'll stay," I said.

I didn't stay the whole night. I left her apartment around 4 a.m. But I returned to visit her a few more times that summer. Once she asked me what I would do if the KGB found out about our affair and tried to blackmail me. I told her they would fail because I would immediately report what I had done, both to my people at the embassy and to my wife.

The Mamas and the Papas

The Mamas and Papas in Moscow? Yes, but not the popular singing group of the late 1960s. Our MAMAs derived their name from the initials for the Moscow Association of Military Attachés. Attaché wives took the next logical step in this process by calling themselves the PAPAs. (The analogous association in Washington, DC, was the Washington Association of Military Attachés—WAMA. What could they do with that?) Our main activity as an organization was social and educational and consisted primarily of luncheons and dinners at one another's apartments. The PAPAs had their own get-togethers. Sometimes we would have a joint PAPA/MAMA event such as an evening boat ride on the Moscow River.

The MAMAs didn't, however, represent all the military attachés in Moscow. Although we invited every country's attachés to join, those from Communist, Soviet client states and many non-aligned countries didn't participate. Whether they had their own association I don't know. The exceptions were the military attachés from China, Poland, Czechoslovakia, Yugoslavia, Hungary and Rumania, as well as Switzerland and Sweden. Indian attachés attended occasionally. Our president was French Brigadier General J. Loran; the vice president was Indonesian Military Attaché Colonel Sudarmardi. I was the secretary. We had no treasurer since we didn't pay dues and the MAMA never financed any outings; it was always "pay as you go" if we did anything that involved costs.

As mentioned earlier, the Soviet MOD forbade us to have any social contact with Soviet officers, other than at official functions.

Furthermore, we had no normal social relations with attachés who weren't members of MAMA. Our dinners at each other's quarters always involved the same people. Official functions such as national days and armed forces days of the various countries provided the only real opportunity for us Western and friendly-country attachés to meet those from the other countries. But there was little real socializing at these events.

For Soviet military-sponsored activities, invitations went out to either the MAMA group or occasionally to all military attachés. During my tour in Moscow, the Soviets sponsored three activities to which they invited our military attachés. One was a military exercise in the Lithuanian Soviet Republic; one was a field trip to Borodino, site of a famous battle between the Russian Tsarist Army and Napoleon's Grande Armée during the War of 1812; and, finally, a trip to the Central Museum of the Soviet Armed Forces in Moscow.

The U.S. and Canadian attachés declined the invitation to the military exercise in Lithuania on the grounds that it might be interpreted as U.S. recognition of the Soviet Lithuanian Republic. None of the NATO countries recognized Soviet annexation of any of the three Baltic Republics.

The military exercise to which the Soviet military invited foreign attachés was named "Neman" after the Neman River that flows through Lithuania. Attachés from Great Britain, Belgium, Netherlands, East Germany, West Germany, Czechoslovakia, Sweden, Finland, France, Poland, Norway and Denmark attended. Since some Western attachés attended—several from countries that did not recognize the annexation—I was never sure what the U.S. accomplished by refusing to participate.

In any case, the Western attachés reported to our office all the details of the exercise. Despite the central Army newspaper *Red Star* reporting on a daily basis of a heated "realistic" exercise, our MAMA military attachés agreed it was a "set-piece demonstration," typical of all other Soviet exercises they had seen. By "set-piece" they meant that everything was well choreographed for the military attachés, with each Soviet military unit knowing ahead of time just where it was to go. For example, after an airborne drop, the attachés noticed the parachutists disappeared behind trees and bushes and could be seen lounging and having a smoke. Although attachés noted nothing of military significance, I sent in a summary of their reports.

As a signal to the Soviets about non-recognition of Soviet Lithuania, the NATO attachés did refuse an invitation to dinner with the mayor of Vilnius, saying that they "were there as guests of the Soviet Ministry of Defense and not of the Lithuanian government." They spent the evening in their hotel.

The other two Soviet-sponsored events were enjoyable and educational. Attachés and their families went on a field trip to Borodino, a famous battlefield in the War against Napoleon in 1812. The weather was nasty, so we were unable to walk the battlefield or view the original ruins of the battle. We could see, however, some trenches from the battles here in 1941 between the Red Army and the German Wehrmacht. Inside the visitors' center we saw an impressive diorama of the 1812 Battle.

Here I was to witness, and to participate tangentially, in another "Battle of Borodino." The battle on 7 September 1812 led to a crucial turning point for the Russian Army. Although they didn't defeat Napoleon's Grande Armée, it was his last offensive combat action fought in Russia. The Russian Army stopped Napoleon temporarily at Borodino, then withdrew, even abandoning Moscow to the French. But they preserved their combat strength, eventually allowing them to counterattack and force Napoleon out of the country. (Russians think of the battle as a draw and psychological victory, with the positive benefit of preserving the Russian Army.)

A week after the battle, Napoleon entered Moscow only to find it deserted with barely a few thousand Muscovites remaining. That night, fires erupted throughout the city. Shortly after Napoleon occupied the Kremlin, fires broke out there also and Napoleon had to flee. For three days the fires continued, destroying more than two-thirds of Moscow. As Napoleon led a freezing and starving army out of the city, Russian Field Marshal Mikhail Kutuzov began to attack his Grande Armée.

From a French-led Army that had attacked Russia with nearly half a million soldiers, only 23,000 Frenchmen returned home alive.

The Second "Battle" of Borodino resulted from the museum curator using the diorama to give the Russian version of the 1812 battle. The curator emphasized more the strategic significance of Kutuzov's withdrawal to preserve his army than the actual battle itself. The curator spoke, of course, in Russian. Several of the attachés in attendance, however, didn't speak Russian, so General Loran asked me to interpret into English for them. When the curator was done, he asked if there were any questions. General Loran spoke up.

"Thank you for your account of the battle. Would you be so kind as to permit me to present the French version?"

"Of course, General," the curator replied after a short hesitation.

General Loran told me he was going to give his account in English. Would I interpret it into Russian for the curator and the attachés who didn't understand English well?

The general then proceeded to give more details on the battle itself. He pointed out that by most interpretations, it was a clear-cut French victory. That's one reason, he pointed out, that Kutuzov withdrew his army. Military historians, including French, now conclude Napoleon made a fatal mistake by not committing his Guard to the battle. If he had done so, historians believe he would have destroyed the Russian army before they had a chance to withdraw.

The next ministry-sponsored event occurred in early May 1980, on the thirty-fifth anniversary of the defeat of Nazi Germany. MAMA attachés received an invitation from the MOD to visit the Central Museum of the Soviet Armed Forces. This was, indeed, an enjoyable outing. The museum holds many artifacts of Russian military history, but in the 90 minutes we were allotted, we were unable to visit all twenty-five halls.

I found two exhibits particularly interesting. One was the collection of Nazi banners the Soviet soldiers carried into Red Square and discarded at the Lenin Mausoleum during their victory parade.

The second fascinating exhibit was a medal, the "Order of Victory." It's made of platinum in the form of a star, studded with 174 diamonds.

The arms of the stars are made out of synthetic rubies. It was awarded twenty times: twelve to Soviet leaders—twice to Stalin, Marshals Georgii Zhukov and Alexander Vasilevsky—and five to foreign leaders. (In 1982, Brezhnev had one awarded to himself, but it was revoked after his death.) Among the foreigners who received the medal after the war were Field Marshal Bernard Montgomery and General Dwight Eisenhower. I saw General Eisenhower's Order of Victory at his museum in Abilene, Kansas, and later bought a facsimile of the medal at a shop in the Kremlin. I gave it to Dr. Les Grau, a friend and Russian military history expert at Fort Leavenworth.

Since I was a military history student myself (I later taught U.S. and Soviet military history at the Fort Leavenworth Command and General Staff College), I tried to take in as much of the museum as I could. Often I would pay no attention to the guide and would look around on my own, reading inscriptions on the exhibits. Little did I know that two weeks later my familiarity with the museum would come in handy.

INCIDENTS AT SEA

Our Naval Attaché asked me to come by his office.

"I have an unusual request of you, Major Holbrook," he said.

"What's that, sir?"

"A Navy delegation is coming to Moscow for the annual Incidents at Sea meetings. I would like you to be the interpreter for Vice Admiral Robert Foley, who's the head of the delegation."

"Would I be taking part in the meetings?"

"No. And neither will Admiral Foley until the end, when they have a final plenary session. But I'd like you to show the admiral around town."

"Be happy to, sir."

"The admiral will be in uniform all the time, although his activities outside the meetings will be unofficial."

"I can wear my greens, right?"

"No, that's the thing. I'd like you not to wear a uniform. I don't think it would look right for a high-ranking U.S. Navy officer to be accompanied by an Army officer in uniform."

"You want me to wear civilian clothes?"

"Right. Would that be a problem?"

"No sir. We wear civvies most of the time anyway."

Both the U.S. and Soviet Navies were formidable military forces during the Cold War. It was only natural for them to keep tabs on each other. Occasionally, they would test their opponent's defenses. This of course led to many collisions, aircraft buzzings and other incidents between the two navies that caused alarm and protests from the offended party. During the 1960s, more than 100 such incidents occurred each year. Fourteen were submarine-to-submarine collisions, the most serious of which was the June 1970 incident involving the USS *Tautog,* rammed by the Soviet submarine *Black Lila* near the Kamchatka city of Petropavlovsk. Sonar on the *Tautog* indicated the Soviet submarine had sunk, but years later it turned out that both heavily damaged boats survived the collision.

In 1968, the U.S. and the USSR agreed to discuss these issues and attempt to find a way to avert them in the future. The negotiations resulted in the May 1972 Incidents at Sea Agreement. Its main purpose was to find ways to avoid collisions, require surveillance ships to keep a safe distance and not to simulate attacks on each other. Each party was to notify the other of operations that might cause the threat of danger, to communicate through naval attachés and to hold annual meetings to review the past year's record. The agreement sharply reduced the number of incidents even though it did not completely eliminate them. It was inevitable that some incidents would occur so long as each navy continued to conduct operations and surveillance in waters near the other nation.

The annual Incidents at Sea meeting in 1980 was held in Moscow. First, there would be committee meetings to deal with specific issues. At the end of these meetings, there would be a plenary session to sum up progress and adopt new recommendations. Admiral Foley would attend that final session. While members of each navy worked in the committees, Admiral Foley would take in the sights of Moscow. That's where I came in.

He and I walked around inside the Kremlin, visited VDNKh and, of course, spent some time on Red Square. The highlight of our sightseeing excursion around Moscow, however, was a visit to the Central Museum of the Soviet Armed Forces.

A Soviet Navy officer met us at the museum entrance and stated he would be our guide. After a short meeting with the museum curator, we began our tour. The Soviet guide pointed out various exhibits and said a few words about them, which I then interpreted for the admiral. Occasionally, I pointed out an additional item and explained it to

Admiral Foley. I thought there were some exhibits that would interest the admiral that the guide was bypassing.

After about fifteen minutes, the Soviet naval officer turned to me and said, "You seem to be familiar with the museum. Why don't I just take you around and you can explain the things you think the admiral would like to know about? If you have any questions, I'll help you out." My visit two weeks earlier with the MAMA attachés made me seem more knowledgeable than in fact I was. I remembered much of what was shown us then, and knew enough about the Soviet side of WWII that I could recognize the significance of certain exhibits.

Official and Social Functions

During the years in Moscow, our social life consisted of three types of events: official, semi-official and unofficial. Official events occurred on some Soviet holidays, foreign national days, or when a foreign military celebrated its armed forces' day. On those occasions we wore dress uniforms. Otherwise, we traveled and went about our daily comings and goings in civilian clothes. These official functions were also the only events where we could expect to see Soviet military officers in attendance. High-ranking Soviet military and civilians often showed up at a function as a courtesy to the host country but, with rare exceptions, lower ranking "gate guards" cordoned them off so we couldn't engage them in conversation.

On major U.S. holidays, or to celebrate a visit to Moscow of some American VIP, the Embassy occasionally sponsored receptions at Spaso House. Spaso receptions gave us the opportunity to meet and talk with some prominent Soviets. That's how I met Soviet Cosmonaut General Leonov.

Leonov was, indeed, a Soviet hero, but there was another person who was a hero to me: Viktor Sukhodrev. He was the Soviet interpreter for Andrei Gromyko and Soviet leaders Khrushchyov and Brezhnev. He later interpreted for Andropov, Chernenko and Gorbachyov. He was a legend among English-Russian interpreters. Former NBC correspondent in Moscow, Marvin Kalb, once said, "Viktor was the best."

Sukhodrev had a reputation of being able to speak not only proper English, but also regional dialects. I decided to test him when I met him at a Spaso House reception. I introduced myself to him in Russian. I then began to comment on his interpreting skills.

"Mr. Sukhodrev, I too am an interpreter."

"Well, you certainly speak good Russian."

I switched to English.

"And legend has it you speak several varieties of English," I said.

"To some extent."

"Could I hear you say something in English Cockney?"

"I learned Cockney as a young boy in England," he said in a clipped cockney accent.

"And southern American speech?" I asked.

"Ah ain't never bin ta Jo-ja or Al-bamy," he said slowly with a southern drawl.

Viktor attended the Soviet Embassy school during his six childhood years in London, but his playmates were English and he soon became fluent in our language. He later studied at Moscow's Military Institute of Foreign Languages.

It was also at a Spaso reception that I met Soviet poet Andrei Voznesensky. In the mid-1960s, I had attended one of his poetry readings at the Library of Congress. Voznesensky frequently attended Spaso receptions. He was one of three very popular Soviet poets who often toured outside the USSR. The others were Yevgenii Yevtushenko and Bella Akhmadulina. In the Soviet Union each of these poets could draw whole stadiums full of poetry lovers. I attended a Yevtushenko reading at the Library of Congress in the 1960s, but never had the opportunity to meet him. My favorite poem of all time is Yevtushenko's "The City of Yes and the City of No." I had hoped to meet him someday and show him my videotaped performance of his "City of Yes…" Unfortunately, he passed away in 2017. I never saw or heard Akhmadulina.

When we attended receptions at other embassies, it was always interesting to note who among the Soviet military and other foreign attachés attended or didn't attend. For example, at the Chinese Armed Forces Day reception in July 1979, we noted the highest-ranking Soviet military officer was 3-star Admiral Novoytsev. He had also attended our Armed Forces Day reception that June. Perhaps more interesting was the fact that there were no officers at the Chinese Embassy from Mongolia or North Vietnam. (Earlier in 1979, the Chinese Army had made a brief incursion into Vietnam over a dispute about Vietnamese activities in Cambodia.)

At the 1980 Finnish Defense Forces Day reception, the Soviets went all out by sending Chief of the General Staff Marshal Ogarkov and Head of the Military Political Directorate, Army General Aleksei Yepishev. There were 40-50 other Soviet officers, including many generals and admirals. When I arrived at the Finnish embassy, I at first wondered if I had come to the wrong place since there were so many Soviet officers milling around. Later, when I asked a Soviet colonel why the Minister of Defense, Marshal Ustinov, was not there, he replied, "Don't worry. Nothing unusual is going on." The 5 June issue of *Red Star* reported this reception and listed most of the high-ranking Soviet officers who attended.

It was interesting that the Soviets devoted so much attention to this Finnish reception, as the Soviet Union had a troubled history with Finland. They shared a long border in the Soviet northwest. For over 100 years, until the end of WWI, it had been part of the Russian Empire. In 1939, the Soviet Union attacked Finland, hoping to reclaim the territory it had lost after WWI and to use it as a buffer defense for Leningrad. The Red Army, decimated by Stalin's purges in the late 1930s, got its nose bloodied by Finnish Armed Forces in what is known as the "Winter War." By the end of the three-month conflict, the Red Army's casualties—dead, missing and wounded—totaled 323,000. Finnish casualties numbered 70,000. In the end, however, the Soviets prevailed.

Since the end of WWII, Finland maintained foreign policies that were designed not to provoke the USSR. Finland's behavior toward the USSR during the Cold War gave birth to the term "finlandization," which refers to any country that avoids foreign policy conflicts with a neighboring country that is much more powerful. I noticed that some of the Finnish attachés and Finnish officers whom I met during my travels appeared to be pro-Soviet.

This particular reception at the Finnish Embassy would have been an excellent opportunity for U.S. attachés to approach high-ranking Soviet officers—there were too many of them to all be cordoned off— and engage them in conversations about Afghanistan, Poland, etc. But no, this was *verboten* by the January 1980 instructions from our JCS, forbidding any official contact with Soviet officials as "punishment" for the Soviet invasion of Afghanistan in December 1979. At the end of my report on this reception I requested updated guidance about this restriction, but never received a response. Although we did avoid approaching Soviet brass, we still occasionally talked with more junior officers.

The official functions often provided interesting observations and, on occasion, a chance to discuss political and military issues with foreign attachés. The rumor mill was always quite active at those times. Foreign attachés often approached us with questions.

One country's attachés openly carried a list of questions. Most often our answers were taken from open press statements from Washington or similar pieces in the Soviet press. If the information was classified, we pleaded ignorance or, in some cases, stated we would check with our headquarters to see if such information was available. Some foreign attachés would volunteer information to us, either allegedly from their country's intelligence services or a rumor they had heard.

In late June 1979, at a reception in honor of our departing Defense Attaché, I talked with a Chinese Assistant Attaché. According to him, the Chinese viewed the recently signed SALT II Treaty as more advantageous to the USSR than to the U.S. Recent Soviet overtures toward the People's Republic of China, he pointed out, were overshadowed by many items critical of China in the Soviet press. He didn't believe anything positive would come of the Soviets' efforts and said "one should always be wary when Soviets ask to negotiate." He added that even after the death of Brezhnev, China was not looking forward to significant improvements: "Russia today is like Russia 100 years ago." He said he based his views on a recent report by the Chinese Communist Party leader, Hua Guo Feng. In October, at the Egyptian Embassy, during a reception in honor of Egyptian Armed Forces Day, the same Chinese Assistant Attaché reiterated his opinion about Sino-Soviet negotiations. According to him, they were "at a standstill."

At a reception in the Chinese embassy, I also learned the interesting history of an excellent Chinese beer—"Tsingtao." I had discovered it earlier in Berlin. I told a Chinese Attaché it tasted like German beer.

"Well, you could say it *is* German beer," he replied.

"I don't understand."

"Oh yes. Many years ago some German brewmasters immigrated to China and settled in the city of Tsingtao. There they set up the brewery that makes this excellent beer." Since then, I've read where German beer specialists have traveled to Tsingtao.

It was impossible to determine whether the Chinese Assistant Attaché, with whom I most often spoke was army, navy or air force. The Chinese all wore the same uniform, didn't wear military insignia and each was listed in the official Attaché Protocol booklet as an assistant for all the services. We assumed the senior Chinese Attaché was a general-equivalent, although the MOD included him in the list of colonels. The assistant with whom I usually talked spoke very good Russian.

All the Chinese attachés seemed to favor me at official functions, perhaps because I would always exchange greetings with them in their language. The Chinese general even visited me in my embassy office where we discussed high-level changes in the Warsaw Pact and the situation in Poland. I pointed out to him that the information I was providing him was taken from the Soviet open press. The Chinese usually said they were basing their judgment on cables from their embassy in Warsaw. As late as December 1980, at a time when the Polish Solidarity movement seemed to becoming more active in its anti-government protests, the Chinese insisted the Polish Communist Party and government had things under control. Although the Chinese agreed with the U.S. estimate that the Soviets had completed all preparations for an invasion, they did not believe the Soviet Army would initiate military actions there.

In July 1980, attendance at the Polish National Day reception allowed us once again to fix the location of Army General Ivan Pavlovsky, CINC, Soviet Ground Forces. Washington was very interested in keeping track of him. He had disappeared from the public before the Soviet invasion of Afghanistan. Lately, once again, Pavlovsky hadn't been seen or reported to be in Moscow.

At this reception a Soviet major approached me and greeted me in Arabic.

"I'm Major Skorobogatov from the Ministry Liaison Office," he said.

His name intrigued me because it meant "soon rich." Even more interesting was the fact that he spoke to me in Arabic. We exchanged some pleasantries in Arabic.

"You do speak Arabic, don't you?" he asked in Russian.

"Not really. I know a few phrases, but that's all."

"I'm an Arab specialist at the Liaison Office. I deal with the Arab-speaking countries."

"Why did you think I speak Arabic?" I asked.

"It's well known you speak several languages so I thought I'd try out some Arabic on you."

"I did study a little Tunisian Arabic, but I can't really carry on a conversation in the language."

Skorobogatov's approach was a surprise for me. The more I thought about it, the more suspicious I became. The only Arabic I had spoken in Moscow was with the Egyptian Army Attaché. Had he told Skorobogatov that I spoke some Arabic? Surely, the Soviets didn't know that earlier I had taken some private lessons from a Tunisian student I had met in Alexandria, Virginia.

The two of us chatted in Russian for a few minutes about languages until I spotted Pavlovsky.

"Is that Army General Pavlovsky over there?" I asked Skorobogatov.

He turned and looked in Pavlovsky's direction.

"Yes it is. Would you like me to introduce you to him?"

"No, but thank you for offering," I replied.

Ordinarily I would have jumped at the opportunity. But on this occasion, I had in mind the JCS message. How could I report the results of a conversation with Pavlovsky when we had been instructed to have nothing to do with the Soviet military? Besides, I thought it would be interesting to be unpredictable. Skorobogatov probably assumed any attaché would welcome a chance to talk to a high-ranking Soviet. How would he report back to his boss or the KGB that I had actually said no to his invitation to talk to the Soviet general who was the focus of attention by many observers of Soviet military policy?

I found out later that either I just hadn't gotten the word on new instructions from the JCS or some of our attachés were ignoring it. It turned out that at that same reception our Naval Attaché reported a long conversation with the Soviet admiral who was editor in chief of the main Soviet Navy journal *Morskoi sbornik.*

There was one topic that made me quite uncomfortable whenever I did get to talk to Soviet officers—the U.S. April 1980 attempt to free the Iranian-held hostages. The Soviets sarcastically remarked that, although they understood how a couple of helicopters could have had problems, they would have built in operational redundancy by using not five, but fifty, or even 500 aircraft, if they thought that was necessary. When American involvement in the Vietnam War was brought up, I quickly changed the topic to their own involvement in Afghanistan. There were already signs that the Soviet military was being drawn into a quagmire.

Semi-official social functions involved liaison visits to and from other attachés. Sometimes attachés would come to our embassy office with information or questions. At other times, we entertained each other at dinners in our quarters. During the course of those dinners, we might pick up some interesting information, but by and large they were simply social events among those of us in the tight-knit Western attaché community.

I remember being pushed to and beyond my foreign language proficiency limits. The Italian Attaché always placed me at the table beside his wife who didn't understand English or Russian. My Italian was quite limited at the time. It had been over 15 years since I studied it. I could still carry on a simple conversation, but I certainly couldn't translate all that was going on. I explained that to the attaché's wife. She was very understanding and enjoyed the simple conversations we had.

The Chinese Defense Attaché enjoyed exchanging a few phrases with me in his language. But alas! My Chinese was worse than my Italian.

We considered dinners among friendly attachés semi-official because we had small government-financed expense accounts to help cover costs. We did, however, report anything of interest stemming from the dinners and movie get-togethers. For example, during a dinner at the Canadian Attaché's apartment, I reported that the Finnish Military Attaché expressed concern about a U.S.-Norway agreement involving the pre-positioning of military equipment there. Since the Soviet press had complained about this development, it appeared at the time the Finnish officer was taking the Soviet side. In retrospect, however, given Finland's tenuous relationship with the USSR, the attaché may have viewed the pre-positioning as a legitimate threat.

Due to the evolving Polish crisis, during the summer and fall of 1980, we sent in many reports that were based on rumors or from sources for whom we couldn't vouch. Rumors included reports in October that some border crossings with Poland were being closed, in November that mail to and from Poland was being cut off, and that Polish forces were withdrawing from the Soviet border.

By now I was also seeking sources outside of official channels. Unofficial socializing usually involved contact with non-military Soviets. In the summer of 1980, Elaine and I attended a Soviet wedding ceremony. An American "Manny," the name we gave to male nannies, married a Russian girl. It was nothing like an American wedding. First of all, it didn't take place in a church (if so, that was very rare, even outlawed) but rather occurred in a Wedding Palace. Every weekend couples lined up outside the door of the official (almost always a woman) who was going to handle the exchange of wedding vows. Before the vows came a reading of the duties of the new bride and groom to the Party, the State and to each other. More important than saying "I do" to loving each other in all circumstances was the "I will" carry out the obligations of good citizenship.

Even though our bride was the daughter of a Communist Party member, the couple didn't follow the tradition of visiting Lenin's

Mausoleum, the Eternal Flame of the Unknown Soldier behind the Kremlin, or the ride to the top of Lenin Hills overlooking the city. After the wedding ceremony, we went directly to a restaurant for a "wedding feast." It was here that I had my first opportunity to talk with the bride's father.

In September 1980, I visited the father at his apartment. (I'll call him Andrei.) I was curious whether Party members discussed high-level political issues, and if so, how were they dealing with the Polish situation? The legend in the Party was that it practiced "democratic centralism." This meant that any and all discussions were allowed at local party meetings, but once the leadership made a decision, all members had to follow the Party line. But my sense of what Andrei related to me suggested there were no local Party discussions on Afghanistan, the Olympics or the Polish situation.

Andrei was a member of the Moscow Philharmonic Orchestra. Although he, like many Soviet professionals, appeared to be a Communist for career purposes only, he was still required to go through the drill of attending periodic Party organization meetings. Since his daughter had married an American, I could sense the family was considering emigration to the U.S. Consequently, Andrei was most hospitable and willing to discuss a variety of topics with me. I think he actually enjoyed talking about politics with someone outside his normal circle of acquaintances.

I was careful not to push him too hard, as our relationship was based on my friendship with his daughter and I didn't want to come off as an aggressive collector of information. Over a few drinks, however, I was able to broach the subject of Solidarity and Poland. The following was taken from my reports of meetings with Andrei.

I expressed concern that the Polish situation was beginning to appear to the Soviet government as similar to Hungary in 1956 and Czechoslovakia in 1968.

"No," he said, "Poland is a horse of a different color. I agree the situation is looking worse and worse, but with Poland we have a serious dilemma."

"How is that?" I asked.

"Poland won't knuckle under so easily if we intervene. The last thing we want is to get bogged down in a protracted conflict in Poland, especially given the situation in Afghanistan."

"What do you think about the Polish intellectuals joining with the workers at Gdansk? Together they're demanding concessions from their government that here would be unthinkable."

"That's the crux of the dilemma. The Polish intellectuals know that the workers have the power. When our intellectuals attempted revolutionary action in the 19th century, they got nowhere. Marx taught us the power of the workers and Lenin showed us. How can the Polish or Soviet Communist parties justify an armed struggle against the Polish workers?"

Andrei assured me the Soviets would not attack Poland.

On another occasion, Andrei insisted Premier Alexei Kosygin's recent resignation was voluntary because he was upset at the drift in Soviet domestic policies. He no longer wanted to be associated with the failure of the Soviet economy. In both instances, I was unable to ascertain whether Andrei's views were his own or were shared by other low-level Communist Party members.

Later, at an early December 1980 dinner with Andrei, he was more pessimistic about the final outcome in Poland.

"So how's the situation in Poland," he asked.

"Bad," I said.

He then gave me his new views on the situation.

"I doubt the workers will be able to gain anything more than chaos, given the fact that all weapons and communications are in the hands of the Communist Party. A real workers' revolution in the Socialist Commonwealth is virtually impossible. The Polish workers and intellectuals should recognize this and be satisfied with what they've achieved, which is already remarkable from a Soviet's point of view."

Another unofficial contact took place with an underground artist who, paradoxically, was a member of the Komsomol and who provided the following comments on Poland:

"Polish workers have it much better than Soviet workers. I don't understand why they are striking."

"There are troublemakers in the new union who are endangering the future for all workers."

"There are forces and money coming into Poland from the West."

"The Poles are creating trouble for themselves.

"Will the Soviet Union intervene? Of course. The Poles will give up just like the Czechs did."

I considered each of my informants to be less than doctrinaire. In fact, they were often cynical about the Soviet Communist Party. It was all the more interesting then that they all seemed to accept, in one way or another, the Party's propaganda.

Other instances gave me opportunities to deal with civilians. One day I was out walking along Leninsky Prospekt, smoking my pipe. I noticed two black men standing on the edge of the street attempting to hail a taxi. Sometimes a taxi would slow down, but then speed by. I walked over to them and asked where they were from. They told me they were Nigerians attending Patrice Lumumba University—a school that was almost exclusively for foreign students.

"We can't get a taxi to stop for us," one of the men said.

"It's because we're black," the other one added.

There was a policeman out in the center of the 8-lane street. I excused myself and walked out to where he was standing.

"Do you see what's happening over there?" I asked.

"What do you mean?"

"Your taxis are refusing to pick up those two men because they're black. I'm surprised, since your country invited them to come to the Soviet Union to study. I should think you would want them to take home a positive impression of your country, not one that shows discrimination against blacks."

The policeman hesitated for a moment and then said, "I'll take care of it."

I walked back to where the two Nigerian students were standing.

"I think you'll get your taxi now," I told them.

Sure enough. The policeman pulled over a taxi driver and stuck his head in the window of the driver. Soon the taxi pulled over to the curb where the Nigerian students and I were standing. I gave them my card and said if they ever wanted a home-cooked meal to give me a call.

A few days later, they called and I invited them to our apartment for dinner. During the course of the meal, they were eager to talk about their troubles in Moscow that they blamed on their being black. I had heard stories of racism in the Soviet Union. My guests were simply corroborating those stories.

Mapping Moscow

Yes, I did some work for the CIA in Moscow. I drove two of their cartographers around the city as they gathered information to be used for an unclassified map.

The result, published in 1980, was the *Moscow Guide*. Andrew Nagorski, who served there as the *Newsweek* correspondent in the early 1980s, called the map "The most highly prized possession of even the officially assigned Russian drivers of diplomats, journalists, and businessmen." Earlier, Soviet-produced maps of Moscow contained very little detail or reliable information. The CIA came to the rescue.

Maps were hardly known in the USSR. We tried to pick up local maps in every city where we traveled. If we found one, however, it would be frightfully inadequate. The local map might show some of the tourist sites in the center of a city, but too often streets on the map would just end with no explanation. Or the information would be incorrect. We viewed this as an obvious attempt by the Soviet government to keep aspects of their cities unknown to tourists and, especially, foreign visitors.

This was just another example of Soviets regarding the most common features of their society as "state secrets." It's important, however, to note that this was not just a Communist phenomenon, but rather the continuation of a long Russian tradition. The Marquis de Custine, traveling in Russia in the 1830s noted, "No bookshop sells a complete index of sights of Petersburg [later Leningrad]… on the map of the city of Petersburg you find only the names of the principal streets."

In fact, according to Joseph Baclawski, in a 1997 article published in the CIA's *Studies in Intelligence*, for a time after WWII, if the Soviet police caught one displaying a map in a Soviet city, he or she might be arrested for espionage. This lack of a "map culture" in the Soviet Union is illustrated by an instance in East Germany when a USMLM team came upon a Soviet Army unit commander who was trying to find the way back to his home installation. He was attempting to read a map but with little apparent success. The American team stopped, showed him how the map worked and then offered to guide him and his unit back to their garrison. The Soviet major accepted.

The CIA published the first Moscow map in 1953 and revised it over the years. These maps were "flat sheets and folded to facilitate insertion in a pocket. The maps carried no attribution to the CIA." Once U.S. intelligence was able to obtain satellite photography of Moscow, the maps began to take on a more realistic representation of the city.

In 1979 and 1980, the CIA sent a couple of mapping specialists to Moscow. These men needed automobile transportation around town to check out and fill in various informational gaps for the latest map. Several of us attachés took turns chauffeuring them. Of course, the KGB kept close surveillance on us. I'm sure they knew who these individuals were and what we were doing, but we stayed in our vehicles and didn't violate any traffic laws, so they didn't bother us. Baclawski notes, however, that a side benefit of these mapping trips was that "the systematic field checks of hundreds of streets in all parts of the city temporarily diverted much of the time and attention of Moscow KGB personnel from their normal surveillance targets."

The 1980 version of the *Moscow Guide* to which we contributed included: streets, subway stations, public buildings, hotels, theaters, universities, institutes, academies, churches, cemeteries, the location of gas stations and auto-repair stations. The map was in booklet form and contained 203 pages.

Some swore they saw a copy of the CIA Moscow map for sale in a Soviet store. I knew many diplomats and attachés from friendly embassies actively tried to get copies. I'm sure the Soviets, including the KGB, got their hands on it. In fact, Soviet KGB General Krasilnikov recounts a mix-up that went bad for a CIA officer and his agent because the street name had changed and was different from the one in the CIA *Guide*.

Even the CIA map didn't, however, show everything. Although the KGB Headquarters was identified, the GRU Headquarters was not shown. On one occasion, I got lost in the city and found myself driving down a street that led, unbeknownst to me, to the main GRU building. When I saw how many Soviet military were mingling around, I left the area as fast as I could. I'm surprised now, looking back, that the KGB surveillants didn't detain me. Perhaps I was free of surveillance at the time.

In the last few years, especially since the demise of the Communist Party and the Soviet Union, the Russian government has produced some good maps of its own. It's no wonder these maps resemble that of the CIA. An item about the CIA map appeared in *Pravda* in 2002. The author of the article wrote, "Not many people know that the first detailed version of the [Russian] maps was made by the CIA."

That 1980 *Moscow Guide* was invaluable to me during the writing of this memoir, since it showed the Moscow I knew in 1979-1980. Without the *Guide*, I would have been hard pressed to orient myself for some events during my attaché years. Today, in 2018, many streets have different names and the landscape of the city has changed significantly.

INFORMATION COLLECTION IN MOSCOW

GENERAL

Except for troop rotation and the parades on Red Square, the Moscow collection environment differed very little from that in other Soviet cities. Just as we often did in the capitals of the Soviet republics, we were tasked a few times to cover ministry buildings in Moscow—what were called "government control" buildings. I never quite understood why we were doing this, as each ministry had a plaque attached to its building identifying what it was. It was hard to believe Washington didn't already know about them. Why would we photograph such ministries as the Russian Federation Ministries of Education and Procurement? Why was it that the nine Soviet ministries on Prospekt Kalinina, just around the corner from the American Embassy, were the targets of attaché collection? In preparing to write this memoir, I revisited those questions and believe I found a plausible answer. Some of the ministries we covered in Moscow were not listed in the CIA *Moscow Guide*. It's likely the CIA was updating its map of Moscow and needed that information.

One target we worked was the alleged "large self-propelled (SP) gun" at Kubinka Army Barracks and Tank Training Facility, not far from Moscow. My first trip to Kubinka was in August 1979. An Allied attaché thought he saw a large gun there. Before our first trip, another American attaché and I parked the car around the corner of the apartment building.

We walked out early in the morning, dressed for jogging. Consequently, I believe we had no surveillance on our way to the target.

When we arrived, we saw all vehicles in the barracks area under tarps, so we couldn't confirm the presence of the SP gun. In January 1980, another attaché and I made a trip back to Kubinka. This time we got photos of a larger-than-usual vehicle, also tarped, but with a gun muzzle. It was a good candidate for the "large SP gun." A third trip, in June 1980 was likewise not too productive. At that time, summer foliage interfered with our attempts to photograph. We did see, however, that the suspected SP gun was still tarped and in the same location it had been the previous January. The only real take-away from those trips was photography of apparent modifications to an anti-ballistic missile radar.

As I mentioned in earlier chapters, whenever we left Moscow on a road trip, KGB surveillants would be with us. They followed our car, traveled on the same train or plane and stayed in the same hotels with us. Surveillance in Moscow, however, was spotty. The KGB's First Department of the Second Directorate, together with surveillants from the Seventh Directorate, was responsible for targeting American Embassy personnel. General-Major Rem Krasilnikov was its head from 1979-1982. In his book, *Ghosts from Chaikovsky Street*, Krasilnikov makes several references to the American DAO. Krasilnikov believed his officers "had to deal with… DIA and military service intelligence officers of the Defense Attaché Office." According to this KGB general, the DAO was a "favorite place" for CIA officers. He claimed the first Chief of the CIA Station in Moscow used the position of Naval Attaché for his cover. Krasilnikov was of the opinion that the attaché system was the "second most important agency in the intelligence community."

In Moscow, the KGB had a lot of help keeping tabs on us most of the time. For example, our vehicle license plates were of the reverse colors of regular Moscow plates; ours were black numbers on white backgrounds. Further, each embassy had its own number. For example, the U.S. was 04, the U.K. 01. The cars of all our diplomats had plates that showed D-04, plus a serial number. All American correspondents had K-04. Since there were policemen at almost all the important intersections in the city, it was a simple matter for them to note and report the passing of a foreign-licensed car. Furthermore, we assumed any Soviet citizen who was allowed to socialize with foreigners reported to the KGB. Waiters and hotel personnel reported on foreigners. More insidious, however, were the employees in the embassy or in the homes of diplomats.

The Soviets used standard surveillance as well. But the time and expense to cover all foreigners in Moscow would have been prohibitive, even for the KGB. We believed that when a new diplomat arrived at the embassy, he or she would be the target of close surveillance for a certain amount of time. Then, depending on what the KGB believed that diplomat was doing in Moscow, they might lift the heavy surveillance or use it only on occasion. Another KGB practice was to concentrate on one embassy for a certain period and then switch the focus to another.

I don't remember much vehicular or foot surveillance during my trips around the city. In my reports DIA sent, there was only one occasion when I referred to surveillance. And that was a little strange. During the coverage of one of the "government control buildings"—the Russian Federation's Ministry of Education on Chistoprudnii Boulevard—we observed three males and two females whose attention to us suggested they were KGB. Of course, it was likely that we had surveillance on several other trips about town, but none of it was obvious.

In view of the meager results of attaché collection efforts, I'm convinced the KGB's biggest concern and the reason for surveillance of attachés was to determine whether or not we met with Soviet citizens who were our agents during travels in and outside of Moscow. Soviet military attachés the world over did just that; they attempted to recruit and run agents who would work for Soviet intelligence. Here we were dealing, once again, with mirror imaging. Their second priority was likely to determine what kind of targets we went after during our travels in order to identify what our interests and priorities were.

TROOP ROTATION

Thirty combat-ready Soviet divisions and four air armies lined up in Eastern Europe, facing NATO forces. More than half a million men.

In order to replenish these forces, every spring and fall, thousands of soldiers arrived in Eastern Europe by air and rail from the USSR. We hoped that, correspondingly, thousands returned to the Soviet Union. This was what we called Troop Rotation. Who and how many were arriving and who and how many were departing was of utmost interest to NATO. Although Troop Rotation had been going on for several years, during each rotation we still had to ask ourselves the question: Were the Soviets reinforcing their units in Eastern Europe or was it a routine replacement of demobilized draftees by new ones just called up at home?

During the Cold War, the Soviet forces in Eastern Europe were organized into "groups." In the 1970s, there were the Northern Group of Forces in Poland; Central Group of Forces in Czechoslovakia; Southern Group of Forces in Hungary; and most important and formidable, the Group of Soviet Forces in East Germany (GSFG). GSFG alone had deployed approximately 400,000 troops, almost twice as many soldiers as in the entire East German Army. It was the Headquarters of GSFG to which USMLM in Potsdam was attached. I served at USMLM in 1976-1977.

Soviet troop rotation was one of my areas of expertise. In fact, my Moscow assignment brought me full circle on the Troop Rotation event. My introduction to it came on the intelligence staff of Headquarters, U.S. Army Europe (USAREUR) in Heidelberg. There, as part of my putting together a daily intelligence summary, I received reports from USMLM and our Moscow attachés of Troop Rotation activity. I also had the advantage of receiving reports from other agencies watching the rotation, what we called "all-source" intelligence. At USAREUR I submitted a special study of the probable system and the effects of troop rotation on GSFG combat effectiveness.

From Heidelberg I moved on to USMLM and became the author of many of those reports back to HQ on observations we made of Soviet Troop Rotation in East Germany. All around East Germany, we and the other allied missions (British and French) would stake out rail lines and airfields day and night, counting planes and troop trains arriving from and leaving for the USSR. By reporting the numbers painted on the aircraft tails, our national collection assets had ways of following the planes back and forth between the Soviet Union and Eastern Europe.

Now, two years after leaving USMLM, I found myself watching Troop Rotation from Moscow. Other Soviet cities beside Moscow were also being used to stage flights and rail transportation to and from Eastern Europe. Occasionally, other NATO attachés or we would spot Troop Rotation in those other cities as part of our routine travels about the USSR. But our main collection activities centered on Moscow.

The Soviet Armed Forces filled their ranks primarily with conscripts/ draftees. According to the 1967 Law on Universal Military Service, all males 18- to 27-years-old were eligible to be called for military service. For the Army and Air Force the term of service was two years; for the Navy it was three years. Some exemptions occurred, especially for those attending higher education institutions. They, in turn, might be given ROTC-type training and leave school as reserve officers.

Young men were required to register as soon as they turned 17. Over 400 registration/recruitment points (*voennye komissariaty* or *voenkomats*) handled the processing of these conscripts/draftees. This process included physical examinations and reviews of their pre-military DOSAAF records. Based on this information, young men were assigned to the various services. The Airborne, for example, accepted new conscripts only if they had had parachute training with DOSAAF.

When I arrived in late April 1979, troop rotation was already underway. When I sent in my first report about observing 66 fresh conscripts (draftees) at Domodedovo Airport, I signed off with the statement: "Pleased to be back in the Troop Rotation business."

Due to my experience with Troop Rotation, I became the coordinator of Moscow-based NATO collection and reporting for the fall 1979, Spring and Fall 1980 Troop Rotation. We began our collection around the end of August and February by checking on train schedules to and from Eastern Europe and forwarding them to DIA and other intelligence agencies and headquarters. We held our final planning meetings in late September and late March, just after the official troop draft notice was published in the Soviet papers.

We were able to identify the new draftees because they had all their hair sheared off (we called them "skinheads"). Groups of them would often be seen with newspapers, folded in the shape of hats, covering their shiny untanned heads. They were apparently ashamed to be seen with shaved heads in public, although one group was observed removing their paper hats once they boarded a train. Shaving a head has long been a sign in many cultures of humiliation and was an ominous start to the treatment the soldiers would endure before their two-year hitch was over. (U.S. forces also shaved the hair off our new draftees and recruits.)

Being able to get up close to the Soviet soldiers was also a unique aspect of attaché collection in Moscow. From time to time we would note unusual badges or rank insignia, which could help our analysts in Washington put together some idea of the internal organization of the Soviet military. For example, in June we saw ten soldiers with "MVO" patches under their service stripes. I never found out what the "MVO" stood for, although it could have been the initials for "Moscow Military District." One group of ground force soldiers wore anchors on their sleeves. Another group had Soviet Air Force initials on their red, ground-force-colored shoulder boards. A few soldiers were wearing the rank of master sergeant (*starshina*), but also the "SA" (Soviet Army) letters of draftees. Could it be, we wondered, that draftees could rise to the rank of master sergeant in less than two years? If so, what did that say about the Soviet Army non-commissioned (NCO) corps? That was important in light of the seasoned and professional NCOs in the U.S., British and French military. I saw a warrant officer and three soldiers at the Belorussky train station wearing crossed sabers on their collars, the insignia of horse cavalry. Although the early Red Army had horse cavalry units (Marshal Semyon Budyonny is said to have sent horse cavalry against German tanks at the start of WWII), there were no such units in the modern Soviet Army. We speculated these soldiers were from a special horse cavalry unit made up of active-duty soldiers who were assigned to MosFilm Studios, the Soviet equivalent of Hollywood movie production studios.

Many new draftees on their way to Eastern Europe were Asiatics, from Tadzhikistan, Uzbekistan, Turkestan, Kirghizia or Kazakhstan. Almost always they were speaking their native languages, not Russian.

In fact, one of the training problems the Soviet military faced was dealing with soldiers who didn't speak Russian very well. This in spite of the Soviet education system that required Russian be taught in all schools. On occasion, we would observe European-looking soldiers who also were not speaking Russian. They were probably from the Baltic republics: Latvia, Estonia and Lithuania.

In May 1980, a Soviet open source magazine—*Rear Services*—provided unique insights into the organization of Troop Rotation, as well as information about transportation problems. That article showed the unique kind of information that can be gleaned from the open press. Such information would never be available to ground observers. The authors, a general-major and a colonel, wrote that before each rotation period a meeting is held at the Military District with representatives of *voenkomats*, military transportation services, rail lines, train commanders and their political deputies.

Among the shortcomings in the rotation transport area were: poor scheduling, overloading of trains, poor sanitation and food services, vandalism to seats on trains and planes, and to tables and compartments on trains. Mix-ups included, for example, in the fall of 1979, a planeload of troops arrived at Domodedovo airport and was to travel on with another aircraft. But the troop commander took them to the train ticket counter, as a result of which the troops were forced to wait two more days before continuing their trip. According to the authors, the airport assistant military commandant should have met the troops and assisted them in transferring to another aircraft. The authors recommended that the percentage of troops transported by air be increased. They predicted use of the new wide-body IL-86 in the near future. But that plane had developmental problems and never saw much use.

In the fall of 1980, a 30-something private first class was noted at an airport being seen off by his father and wife. His father's advice to him was: "Don't go to bed with a woman when you're drunk. Don't shoot women. And above all, respect the people." One group of new draftees was seen standing at attention in an airport for a shakedown inspection conducted by an officer. The officer found and confiscated some food packages from the soldiers.

Perhaps the most important contribution we attachés made on the Moscow end of the rotation was to verify that experienced soldiers were, indeed, returning home from the groups of forces in Eastern Europe. We could read the badges on their uniforms and the decals on their suitcases that identified one of the Eastern European countries. For example, when the soldiers' decals read Arnstadt, Templin, Neubrandenburg or Leipzig, we were confident we were seeing soldiers who had just returned from East Germany.

At one point early in the fall of 1980, we saw plenty of new draftees around the city at airports and train stations. But there were few signs of returnees. I went to Domodedovo airport by myself. When I saw a group of young men, apparently civilians, sitting on a bench, I joined them. After awhile I struck up a conversation with one, telling him I was waiting for my nephew, a soldier, to return from East Germany. I definitely gave him the impression I was a Soviet. He told me his brother was also coming in from Germany.

I was a little nervous because I knew there must be surveillance nearby and I had misrepresented myself to the soldiers. I simply got them involved in a casual conversation. I was careful, however, not to tell them I was a Russian. I just acted like a Russian. But I knew someone was watching me and would learn that I had "passed" as a Russian. I had violated two rules—one Soviet and one American. The Soviet rule didn't allow us to talk to their military personnel without permission from the MOD. The Americans forbade us to pass ourselves as Russians, something tantamount to clandestine spying. After I returned to the embassy and wrote my report, I told the Army Attaché how I had acquired the information. One reason I did that was there was a chance the KGB would report my misbehavior and I didn't want my boss to get blindsided. The Army Attaché chastised me and told me not to do it again. We never heard a word from the Soviets about the incident. It was just inconceivable that they didn't know. Why didn't they protest my activities at the airport?

On another occasion the previous spring, I approached a group of young soldiers who were on their way west. Upon questioning them I discovered that shortly after they were drafted they found themselves in electronics school and were now junior sergeants. Unlike the above instance, however, I said nothing to suggest I was a Soviet citizen. At the same time, I didn't advertise the fact that I was a military attaché. This was within the boundaries of American guidelines.

Each of the posts from which I worked troop rotation had its advantages and disadvantages. In Heidelberg, for example, I had access to all-source intelligence and could more easily see the big picture. I was limited, however, by having to rely on these reports, without actually seeing any of the activity. At USMLM, we were able to see the groups of soldiers on trains and, sometimes, in busses and trucks. We saw them actually boarding or disembarking from planes. We could not, however, get close to most of them and could not determine from where or to where they were traveling. In Moscow, we often got up close enough even to talk to the draftees arriving from Eastern Europe or departing for Soviet units there. But we couldn't determine exactly where they were headed.

Domodedovo airport, to the south of the city, served as the primary airport for planes flying between the USSR and Eastern Europe. Soviet authorities apparently felt the soldiers would be inspired to serve the Motherland when they saw the "*ikonostas*" of Lenin and the Politburo displayed near the entrance to the airport. The Russian Orthodox iconostasis in churches and cathedrals presents a variety of saints, as well as Christ and the Holy Mother. Such a portrayal of the Politburo, seen often around the Soviet Union, was just another reminder of the Communist Party's efforts to supplant religion with Communist ideology.

At best, we could only approximate the numbers of troops going back and forth. Still, there was room for exaggeration. On one occasion, the Army Attaché and I observed a group of skinheads at Belorussky Station. When later he passed his report to me for review, I noticed he had stated the number was 60. "No, I told him, it was more like 20." "Then we'll compromise and call it 40," he said. Overall, though, the importance of our reports was that we actually saw newbies going to Eastern Europe and veterans returning to the USSR.

For an event that was repeated twice a year, there might have been a temptation for us not to give it the attention it deserved. But the movement of tens of thousands of Soviet soldiers between the USSR and countries that bordered NATO forces was something we could not take lightly.

RED SQUARE

I felt a little foolish being hoisted up by another attaché in order to look over the fence into Central Airfield, the military assembly area for Red Square parades. If the KGB was watching, there just wasn't any way we could deny what we were doing. Peeking over the wall at Central Airfield was one effort to identify whether the Soviets would parade any new equipment across Red Square on 7 November. We tried various approaches to Central Airfield. It was during one of those approaches that I found myself going down a dead-end street that led to GRU Headquarters, which bordered the airfield.

Late October and early November were active times for attachés in Moscow. Both Troop Rotation and, in the fall, Red Square military parade preparation for the anniversary of the "Great October Revolution" (held in November) took place during these months. Tanks, armored personnel carriers, rockets, artillery pieces, and other military equipment came rolling into town. They all headed for Central Airfield. For the three of us in the Army Attaché Office who had served at USMLM, it almost reminded us of old times. In East Germany we chased convoys of military vehicles, counting equipment, trying to determine the nomenclature of any weapons seen, and recording the vehicle bumper numbers. In Moscow, however, the equipment usually came in during the night and ended up at Central Airfield.

Our DAO coordinated the parade coverage in Moscow with some of the attachés from other NATO countries. Although I'm sure our satellites covered the parade, perhaps even photographed Central Airfield, we could perhaps alert those national collection assets to something that bore special attention. When parade day arrived, some of our attachés would be on Red Square to watch and take pictures.

Others would spread out in the city looking for choke points where the military equipment would slow down or even stop.

During my tour, I spent one May Day and one 7 November celebration on Red Square. Even with an official invitation card, it wasn't easy getting to our designated area. One American correspondent with a Red Square pass writes that he had to pass through 13 checkpoints, eight in his car and five on foot.

In May 1979 and November 1980, I stood next to Lenin's Mausoleum with other military attachés to observe parades. During my tour as an attaché, we saw no new equipment, with the possible exception of a new version of an armored personnel carrier. But I did get some pictures of the Soviet hierarchy reviewing the parade.

Before the parade began, columns of combat equipment lined up on streets that fed into Red Square. This was an excellent chance to get close to the equipment. Once, when I wasn't going to be on Red Square, I went to Gorky Street with two cameras. One was the Minox in my coat pocket. The other was a Canon with a 50mm lens. I hung the Canon around my neck under my overcoat. I then unbuttoned my coat so the lens of the camera could peek out onto the street. After taking a few surreptitious photos with both cameras, I noticed several Soviet citizens were walking out into the street and taking pictures at close range. My caution seemed to be unfounded. Consequently, I took out my Canon and walked out into the street and took pictures like the others.

I then moved to a choke point near an underpass. I had no trouble getting up close and even taking pictures of the undercarriage of a Soviet tank.

Red Square had seen many Soviet military parades. Troops and military equipment preceded "workers" who marched past the tribunal above Lenin's Mausoleum, where the Politburo and military leadership stood waving. Two earlier parades in particular were historic. On 7 November 1941, while Moscow was under siege by the Germans, troops and military hardware went directly from Red Square to the front lines to face the Wehrmacht in the Battle of Moscow. On 24 June 1945, a month after the Allied victory over Hitler's forces, the Soviets conducted a victory parade. On that occasion, Soviet soldiers threw 200 captured German military banners and standards at the foot of the Lenin Mausoleum (the ones I saw in the Armed Forces Museum). This was reminiscent of Russian troops throwing Napoleon's banners at the feet of Tsar Alexander I after victory in the War of 1812.

In Moscow everything was centered, both figuratively and actually, around Red Square and the Kremlin. One travel guide for Moscow points out that on the four sides of Red Square "stand the Kremlin, GUM Department Store, State Historical Museum and St. Basil's Cathedral—centers of government, commerce, history and religion." Whenever I came up from the Eternal Flame of the Unknown Soldier behind the Kremlin, rounded the corner, and walked up the slight incline past the Historical Museum, I could not help but be thrilled at the sight of Red Square ahead of me. Once again, I thought of Disneyland. Even though I had made this walk before, when St. Basil's Cathedral came into view, it was always a "wow" moment.

St. Basil's is perhaps the most recognizable symbol of Russia. Ivan IV (the Terrible) had the cathedral built to commemorate his victory in Kazan against the Tatar Mongols in 1552. According to legend, when St. Basil's was completed, Ivan had the architect, Postnik Yakovlev, blinded in order to prevent him from building a more magnificent building for anyone else. (This is a favorite folk legend in several countries with spectacular architectural structures. For example, a similar story is told of the Taj Mahal's architect.) In any case, an apparently "blind" Yakovlev did later built a similar cathedral in Vladimir.

Another legend has it that Napoleon ordered St. Basil's blown up, but according to legend, God made it rain on the gunpowder kegs' fuses. More current and more credible is the story that the famous architect, Peter Baranovsky, saved St. Basil's from destruction by Stalin. He reportedly stood on the cathedral's steps and threatened to cut his own throat if the masterpiece was destroyed. Stalin apparently gave in but sent Baranovsky to prison for five years. Although St. Basil's Cathedral escaped Stalin's campaign against Russian Orthodox churches (as did the spectacular Church of the Savior on Spilled Blood in Leningrad), Kazan Cathedral and Iversky Chapel in the northwest corner of Red Square did not. He had them destroyed to "make room for heavy military vehicles driving through Red Square." (Both were rebuilt after the demise of the Soviet Union.)

In addition to the architectural wonders of Red Square, including the Kremlin, there is no other place in Russia that holds as much drama and history. I first walked onto the Square in 1971 from the Rossiya Hotel, where I stayed during my first trip to the USSR as a tourist with my friend Dex Dickinson. With St. Basil's on the left and the Kremlin straight ahead, it was a breathtaking sight.

The name *Red* has nothing to do with the association of that color with socialism or communism. The word 'red' in Russian is *krasnaya*, which in Old Russian meant "beautiful." The square was called *"Krasnaya"* in the 17th century. The square's name might just as well have come from the color of blood, much of which was spilled there over the centuries. Between Ivan the Terrible in the 16th century and Peter the Great in the late 17th century, many noblemen, their servants and mutinous soldiers were slaughtered on Red Square.

If the Kremlin was the nerve center of the Soviet Empire, the little granite structure outside the Kremlin wall on Red Square—Lenin's Mausoleum or Tomb—was, according to the Communist Party, the heart. This was the final resting place of the revolutionary and founder of the modern Communist Party, Vladimir Ilyich Lenin (his real last name was Ulyanov). In Tsarist times, many revolutionaries used pseudonyms that later became the names history remembers them by. Lenin supposedly took his name to honor the victims of a massacre at the Lena River gold mines. Stalin's ("steel") real name was Dzhugashvili, Trotsky's ("opposition" or "defiance" in German and Yiddish) name was Bronstein, and Molotov's ("hammer") was Skriabin.

Lenin died in 1924. Political and medical experts decided his body would be embalmed in such a way that it could be preserved "forever." An ancient Russian religious belief was likely the motive for Lenin's preservation. The Russian Orthodox Church interpreted the lack of decomposition of a corpse as a sign of special holy status. An illustrative example is found in Dostoevsky's *Brothers Karamazov*, when young Alyosha is shocked and disturbed by the fact that his hero, Father Zosim, begins to decompose a few days after his death. (Naturally preserved mummies of "Saintly" monks can be seen in the cave-catacombs of Kiev.)

Lenin's body has been available for viewing by the public almost every day since his death (with the exception of during the Second World War and various interludes for "refreshing" the secret embalming treatment). The line of people waiting to see Lenin's body usually extended up Red Square past the Historical Museum and, occasionally, wrapped around the Kremlin walls.

I went down into the crypt a total of three times. Once as a tourist in 1971 and twice while assigned to Moscow. When I came out of the Mausoleum, I followed a path that took me past the graves of major Soviet notables such as the former presidents of the USSR, represented by busts on individual grave markers. Stalin, who died in 1953, had himself placed beside Lenin in the Mausoleum. In 1961, however, as a result of the anti-Stalin campaign, Khrushchyov removed his body and buried it in the line with other former leaders. Khrushchyov himself is buried in Novodevichy Cemetery.

I sometimes walked on Red Square at night. There was a special aura of history in the area. Originally in the center of Red Square, but now on the end near St. Basil's was the *Lobnoye mesto* (in my *Oxford Russian Dictionary* defined as "place of execution"). It was, in fact, actually a platform for announcement of official decrees from the tsar. Given the number of executions that took place near it, however, the name seems appropriate. *Lob* means 'forehead' in Russian.

The only statuary on Red Square is dedicated to Kuzmin Minin and Dmitri Pozharsky, who led a people's uprising to defeat the Poles in the early 17th century. This was during the Russian "Time of Troubles," just before the start of the 300-year reign of the Romanov dynasty. Although the statue was also originally placed in the middle of Red Square, Stalin moved it to the front of St. Basil's Cathedral in 1931 to make room for official demonstrations and parades.

The Kremlin wall and the land between it and the cobblestones of Red Square form a Communist necropolis. The Kremlin wall contains the ashes of 107 men and eight women who were in one way or another

Communist heroes. Three Americans' ashes are there: John Reed, the American journalist who wrote *Ten Days that Shook the World*; Bill Hayward, a U.S. Socialist Party leader and one of the founders of the Industrial Workers of the World trade union; and Bill Hayward, founder of the Communist Party USA. Also entombed in the wall are Nadezhda Krupskaya, Lenin's wife, and Yurii Gagarin, the first man in space. The land around the wall contains mass graves of early Bolsheviks during their battles to gain control of Moscow. Those at the very foot of the northeast Kremlin wall are burial grounds for Bolsheviks who fought at that spot to take over the Kremlin.

THE MOSCOW KREMLIN

One Moscow target I found particularly special: the Kremlin.

Napoleon occupied the Kremlin for five weeks in 1812, then began his retreat. Hitler never reached the Kremlin. I refer to *the* Kremlin, but in Russia there are several such structures, originally meaning "fortress." Three other kremlins, for example—in Novgorod, Kazan and Suzdal—are World Heritage sights. Astrakhan, Kolomna, Nizhny Novogorod, Pskov, Smolensk, Tobolsk and Tula have their own kremlins. To foreigners and many Russians, however, the word "Kremlin" denotes the one in Moscow. Like 10 Downing Street or the White House, it is often used to refer to the Soviet/Russian government.

I entered the Kremlin through the Trinity Gate, the only pedestrian entryway. Each time I went there, I could not help but think to myself, *Here I am in the Kremlin*! Certain sights have a way of never being taken for granted. Whether it be the Alps in Bavaria, the Rocky Mountains, or the view of the National Mall and the Washington and Lincoln monuments from Capitol hill, certain locations give one a special sensation.

So it was for me when I was on Red Square or in the Kremlin. The Russian poet Mikhail Lermontov wrote, "It's impossible to describe the Kremlin and its serrated walls, dark passages and lush palaces. One must see, see … one must feel all that it bespeaks to the heart and imagination!" Napoleon first viewed the Kremlin and Moscow from the top of Sparrow Hills (the Soviets renamed it Lenin Hills, but today it is once again Sparrow Hills.)

The Soviet invasion of Afghanistan in December 1979 caught many Americans, including our DAO, by surprise. How much of a surprise it was in Washington, however, is doubtful. Zbigniew Brzezinski told the French magazine *Le Nouvel Observateur* "We didn't push the Russians to intervene, but we knowingly increased the probability that they would. The day the Soviets officially crossed the border, I wrote to President Carter: 'We now have the opportunity of giving to the USSR its Vietnam War...'"

Further evidence of the fact that Washington knew what was going to happen in Afghanistan is provided by Milt Bearden, a high-ranking CIA officer, who wrote in his *The Main Enemy*, that the Soviet military action in Afghanistan "began incrementally" in June 1979. The Soviet Politburo became obsessed that an "American-fomented disaster" was to take place. The massive invasion took place in December.

Partly due to our apparent surprise, Washington decided we should develop a program to monitor Soviet governmental activity in Moscow in order to determine whether something big was about to happen. Of course, the chickens had already flown the coop, but we decided to try to do something positive about our alleged lack of preparedness. By the summer of 1980, the Polish crisis raised the specter of another possible Soviet military operation. One of our tactics was to drive around Moscow defense locations at night to see if there were more or fewer lights on in the offices. More lights might tell us people were working overtime and something might be up. (The Soviets also traveled about Washington, checking on our government building activity.)

Another approach was to send someone to the Kremlin from time to time to establish norms of activity and to watch how that activity might vary. In 1980, I spent time at the Kremlin as more than a tourist.

The Kremlin was closed on Thursdays for Politburo meetings. The Communist Party Politburo, a committee of some 12-14 members headed by a General (or First) Secretary (Lenin, Stalin, Khrushchyov, Brezhnev), was the *de facto* Soviet government and dictated all Soviet policies from the time of the Bolshevik Coup in 1917. There did exist a government on paper, but all government leaders were members of the Communist Party and took their orders from the Politburo. The Party had organizations in every government office, the legislature, educational institutions, the military, as well as every factory and research facility. These Party organizations saw to it that their particular institution carried out the orders of the Politburo. It was as if, during a Democratic Administration in the United States, the Democratic National Committee had representatives everywhere in our society to make sure the President's orders were carried out. To further that analogy, if that were the case in the U.S., there would be no Republican Party to challenge the White House.

There was one location in the Kremlin that might yield signs something unusual was up. The Borovitsky Gate was the main entry point for vehicles (the main exit was through Spassky Gate). Soviet limousines—Chaikas and Zils—entered here. If I saw groups of these cars coming in, that could mean Politburo and Central Committee members were gathering.

In fact, I really couldn't tell a heck of a lot of what was going on in the Kremlin. Everything appeared normal each time I visited. The Party and government office buildings there were off limits. I don't remember ever writing reports on my Kremlin observations. But it was a kick to think that the Kremlin was "my beat."

Borovitsky Gate was near the Armory Museum, which I never tired of visiting. The museum contains, according to one brochure, "a staggering collection" of Tsarist artifacts. Here one can find the ivory throne of Ivan the Terrible, the double throne of Peter the Great and his brother Ivan, the world's largest collection of Fabergé eggs, and the awesome collection of Russia's gold and diamonds. No student of Russian history should miss visiting the Armory when in Moscow.

I walked around the Kremlin grounds that were open to the public, trying to identify who the KGB officers were. At first, when there were a lot of tourists milling around, it was a little hard to identify the KGB. One day, however, the weather was terrible and there were very few tourists. The KGB men then stood out like sore thumbs. They seemed to have permanent posts. I made a note of these posts so I could observe them on days when the Kremlin was busy.

I sometimes engaged the KGB in small talk, always playing the role of a dumb tourist. Once several Chaikas (second-tier limousines) entered the Kremlin through Borovitsky Gate when I was waiting to get into the Armory Museum. I walked up to a KGB guard and asked, "Are those Mercedes?" He growled back at me, "No, they're Soviet cars. Chaikas." Had I been able to be near that gate on a Thursday, I would have seen several Zils (first-echelon limousines) coming through the gate with Politburo members. But since no tourist could get into the Kremlin on Thursdays, I never observed more than 2-3 Chaikas or Zils at a time.

A Dark and Stormy Night

Writers usually deride the phrase "a dark and stormy night"—voted the worst opening line of a novel, but used by Snoopy in the novel he's writing atop his doghouse. For me it *was* a dark and stormy night in Moscow that started the events I recount here.

A hand shot toward my car door window as I backed out of a parking space at the American housing complex on Vernadsky Prospekt. It struck with a muffled thud in the din of heavy rain that was beating down on the car. The hand belonged to a woman. As we made eye contact, she drew back and shouted something. I looked around quickly to see if she was alone. I couldn't be sure. It was already dark and the windows had steamed up. The woman's shouts were completely inaudible. I cracked my window and spoke to her in English.

"What is it?"

She answered in Russian. "Are you going into town? I need a ride."

I switched to Russian. "Are you by yourself?"

"*Da, da*. Please give me a ride."

"Go around and get in." Muscovites often hitched rides but I had never picked anyone up before. If it hadn't been raining so hard, I wouldn't have considered it then.

As she passed in front of the headlights, I could see she was young— maybe in her twenties. She had no umbrella and her long dark hair was soaked and clung to her neck. As soon as she got into the car, I made another 360-degree inspection of the parking lot. No one else in sight.

"*Spasibo* (Thank you)," she said as she pulled the door shut.

"Lock your door."

"How do I do that?"

"Push down on the knob at the bottom of the window. There, by your shoulder."

"Thank you so much. I didn't expect this rain. It just came up a few minutes ago."

"What were you doing here in an American housing area?"

"I was visiting in the neighboring apartment complex and was just passing through here on my way to the Yugo-zapadnaya Metro Station. Then I saw you get into your car. My name's Dunya."

"*Ochen priyatno* (Pleased to meet you), Dunya. My name's Yasha."

"This is a nice car. Is it American?"

The license plate, D 04-25, marked it as an American diplomat's car. "No, it's German. A BMW."

"Well, it's still nice. But I like American things. I love American jazz. I have a daughter Rita whom I named after Aretha Franklin." Then, in English she said, "I know small English."

"You're welcome to speak English with me."

"*Nyet, nyet.* You speak Russian too well. Why do you speak Russian like that?"

"My grandfather spoke Russian. I'm going to the embassy. Where do you want me to drop you off?"

"Will you be going near Kalinin Prospekt?"

"Yes, of course. It's on my way to the embassy."

"I'm sorry, I... Yes. Near Kalinin Prospekt, if you don't mind."

Then as quickly as she had begun chattering, she stopped talking altogether. As we rode north on Vernadsky Prospekt toward the center of Moscow, I wondered what was going on. Since arriving in Moscow nearly a year ago, I had come to believe it's rarely a coincidence when a Soviet citizen unexpectedly meets an American diplomat. Although I had several Soviet acquaintances, I considered each of them to be either full-fledged KGB operatives or, at the very least, subject to making regular reports to the KGB. At first this had bothered me, but I soon grew accustomed to it. For Soviet citizens it was a way of life. For me it was either accept that all my Soviet acquaintances were reporting to the KGB or have no contacts. After all, wasn't I also making reports on many of the Soviets I met?

I began to run down the checklist I had devised for each time I met a new Soviet citizen. Was Dunya the young woman in distress she appeared to be or was she an *agent provocateur*? Did she know about my love of jazz and my connections with the Soviet jazz community in Moscow? Was she an *invalyutka*—a prostitute who specialized in Western clientele? Not likely, out here in the outskirts of the city. How clever the Soviets were in devising new words. *Invalyutka* derived from two Russian words—'foreign' and 'hard currency'—and rhymed with *prostitutka*. Did Dunya know she had hitched a ride with a military attaché assigned to the American Embassy in Moscow?

I turned left onto Lomonosov Prospekt, which would take me to Kutuzov Prospekt. Then a straight shot to Kalinin Prospekt, a short distance from our embassy on Chaikovsky. Although traffic was light at this hour, I had to keep my eyes on the road because the rain made for poor visibility. The last thing I wanted was to hit some Soviet pedestrian who had decided to run across the street rather than use a pedestrian underpass. We called them "dark darters." They were a real hazard for drivers at night. Moscow streetlights were always dim or not on at all.

All I could discern about Dunya's appearance was that she was well dressed for a Soviet girl—chic leather boots, a short skirt and what looked like a foreign-made jacket. She had unzipped the jacket and I found the combination of her boots, legs and short skirt quite tantalizing. From my brief glances at her face, I could see she had large sparkling eyes. Her mouth seemed to be formed in a smile, even when she wasn't talking. I found her quite attractive.

I tried to get the young woman talking again.

"Dunya, aren't you a little worried about being in a car with an American diplomat?

"Why should I be? Soviet citizens are allowed to associate with whomever they wish. Besides, no one knows I'm hitching a ride with you."

"I just wanted to make sure you knew what you were doing."

"Thanks. Don't worry about me. My mother works as a secretary at the General Staff, so I have some privileges. Marshal Malinovsky once visited our apartment."

The General Staff, I thought. *How interesting.* Marshal Rodion Malinovsky was the Soviet Minister of Defense when I served in Berlin in the early 1960s. If I could meet some Soviets who worked for the government, I might learn something about the war in Afghanistan or the situation in Poland. Or maybe meet some Soviet officers, despite the Soviet MOD's rule on that. I had had some casual encounters with officers when traveling—in restaurants or on trains. Otherwise, I pretty much observed the restrictions the Defense Ministry had placed on us about not making military contacts in Moscow without special permission. With the war in Afghanistan and the crisis in Poland, however, surely there had to be somebody who would inadvertently drop tidbits. And who knows, maybe even something more substantial? I certainly wouldn't mind insinuating myself into the company of someone who worked for the General Staff.

Just before I reached Kalininsky Bridge, Dunya interrupted my thoughts.

"I'll get out here. Can you pull over?"

"Sure, but I thought you wanted to go to Kalinin Prospekt."

"I'll walk from here."

I pulled over to the curb. Dunya fumbled with the door handle. I reached across with my right arm and opened the door. In doing so I caught a light, pleasant aroma. It didn't seem to be perfume. Perhaps it was soap. Perhaps it was nothing but her natural smell. She smiled as I straightened up quickly in my seat. She didn't move for a few seconds, then looked at me.

"Thank you very much, Yasha. May I see you again?" she asked. Without waiting for a reply, she reached into her purse and pulled out a piece of paper. "Here's my telephone number."

"Ah... Sure, I guess. I'll... I'll give you a call."

Dunya jumped out without saying another word. Instead of walking up to the corner of Kalinin, she ran across the street in the direction of the Ukraina Hotel. I would have liked to see if she went into the hotel, but when she reached the sidewalk on the other side, she turned and stood waving, apparently waiting for me to drive off. As I proceeded to the embassy, I realized she already had had her phone number written on a piece of paper. Not believing in coincidences in the first place, everything about this "casual" meeting was too pat. I decided I was probably dealing with a *provokatsiya*, a set-up.

When I pulled up and parked at the curb outside the embassy, I was still a little dazed by this strange encounter with this attractive Soviet girl. Who was Dunya? She seemed naïve in many ways, but when she dropped the tidbit about Malinovsky visiting her apartment and the fact that her mother worked at the General Staff, she got my attention. She offered that information knowing I was an American diplomat, but before I told her I worked in the military attaché office. The jazz connection was particularly suspicious. She was slightly off on that score. Aretha Franklin was known as the "Queen of Soul," not jazz.

It was a general rule that we report our contacts with Soviet nationals. Of course, living in the middle of Moscow, it would have been ridiculous to report all contacts. "I had a long discussion about the weather with a man at the bus stop?" or "I met an outstanding soprano saxophone player last night?" On-going contacts, like the one I had with Georgii and his family, were another thing. But even with him I didn't account for every contact. Instead, I reported that I had a Soviet acquaintance with whom I shared an interest in jazz, visited his family, and often went with him to jazz concerts.

The encounter with Dunya was an entirely different story. I hoped she had the potential to lead to some meetings with people who might be of intelligence value. If I intended to pursue this, however, I needed approval from someone higher up in the embassy. I needed an official green light. In this case, it was the CIA Station Chief.

I recalled my orientation at the "Farm," as it was known to CIA officers—the CIA training center in Virginia. Its location and very existence used to be a secret, but in my research for this book I found at least eleven open sources that referred to it. This included Soviet KGB General Krasilnikov, as well as retired CIA Deputy of Operations, Jack Devine in his memoir, *Good Hunting*.

Before leaving for Moscow, Lieutenant Colonel Tom Spencer and

I, together with some attachés going to other countries, spent three weeks at the Farm. Although it is still listed as a military base, in 1961 it became the CIA main field tradecraft center. Tom and I didn't go there to learn how to become spies. I've already pointed out that attachés didn't engage in clandestine work. The purpose for our training was to become familiar with some of the aspects of information collection and the role we were to play in that endeavor. We learned that if a Soviet approached us with any hint of clandestine potential, we were to report it immediately.

Our most practical lesson at the Farm dealt with foot counter-surveillance. Officers took us into town with the most basic low-level collection assignments. Our primary task, however, was to identify our surveillants. When we returned, we would have a debriefing and meet the CIA officers who had been tailing us. The exercise presented some surprises, as we recognized several individuals during the debriefing whom we had not pegged for surveillants.

Foot surveillance in East Germany was rare, probably because we did so much of our work from cars. Even vehicular surveillance in East Germany was not a big issue, since we could easily outrun the East German Stasi. In Moscow, it was a different story altogether. Besides, in Moscow it wasn't smart to attempt to outmaneuver KGB surveillance. Any effort to do that could easily lead to a protest from the Soviet MOD and our possibly being declared *persona non grata*. Our training helped us learn to identify any type of surveillant.

The CIA Station Chief usually had breakfast in the embassy snack bar. I thought that would be a good place to get in touch with him. The next morning I went to the snack bar, but he wasn't around. So I went to the CIA spaces in the embassy and told the receptionist I needed to talk to the Chief.

"He's out of town, but I can call the Deputy."

The Deputy came out and met me. "Let's go into the Bubble," he said.

As I pointed out earlier, the "Bubble" was a room in the embassy specially designed to thwart any Soviet listening devices, including the microwaves the KGB had been beaming at us from across the street for several years now. There were two or three Bubbles in the embassy.

I explained to him the encounter the night before.

"She started out very talkative. I've never seen that in a Soviet stranger before. And then she quickly made the point that she was really a big American music fan."

"In what way?"

"She said she likes jazz. She claimed she even named her daughter after Aretha Franklin."

"Hmm. And she wants to get in the car with one of the embassy's biggest jazz nuts. A little obvious, don't you think? Sounds like a *provokatsiya*, a set-up, to me."

"Yeah, of course. That's what I thought too. It's just that I remember from your agency's instructions at the Farm that we were to be alert to possible HUMINT inroads and to let you folks know about them immediately. A chance to meet some people in the General Staff is worth some risk."

"You're right. And I appreciate your coming to us on this."

"What do you think? You think I should make contact with this Dunya?"

"Did she ask for anything? Western goods? Help getting a visa?"

"No. Not yet."

I didn't want to let Dunya get away. I was wrestling with feelings about whether I was attracted to her because of the way she looked. Or did I really think she might turn out to be a conduit into a lucrative collection situation? I decided that I wouldn't let this become another relationship like the one I had had with Natasha, which we had ended. Dunya, on the other hand, would be a work-related contact.

"If we go into this with our eyes open," I told the Deputy, "we might be able to get something of value before they try anything. If it's a set-up, how far will they let me go? Or let one of *your* people go. I'd prefer to introduce one of your officers to Dunya down the road."

"No, I don't think that would work. If it's a set-up, it looks like you're the target."

The Deputy paused, as if he were trying to decide what to say.

"I'm tempted to tell you to go ahead and make contact with her again. It could be useful to see where this might lead. What would your wife think about your meeting a Russian woman?"

"I never tell my wife what I do here in Moscow. Oh, yeah, she travels with me sometimes when we go to other cities, but that's about it. No, she wouldn't know anything about this. How about my boss? Should I say anything to him?"

"Absolutely not. Especially him. He would get all flustered. I'll take responsibility for this. So go ahead and give her a call. If it turns into something, the fewer people in the know, the better."

I tried to keep my mind on work during the rest of the day. It was no easy task, as I kept thinking about what I might be getting myself into. Just before I left the embassy at the end of the day, I dialed the number Dunya had given me.

"Dunya?"

"*Da.*"

"This is Yasha. Remember me? I gave you a lift last night."

"Of course I remember you. How nice of you to call."

"Well, you asked me to. So I thought maybe we could meet somewhere and visit under more normal circumstances."

"Yes, yes. That would be nice."

"How about tomorrow?"

"That would be great."

We arranged to meet at the Moscow Zoo, which is close to the American Embassy. With the CIA Deputy giving me the green light, I could rationalize this rendezvous as part of my work. Maybe it was all starting to come together. My second year as an attaché could yet turn out to be useful.

I took the Metro to Krasnopresnenskaya Station, just across the street from the zoo. I often used the Metro to go into town. First of all, surveillants outside our apartment usually waited for us in cars. If I left the apartment on foot, I'd be able more easily to see anyone getting out of a car to follow. Secondly, there was the matter of parking. Although I could park just about anywhere I wanted to in Moscow, I didn't like to flaunt my diplomatic status with the police. Finally, I enjoyed riding what was undoubtedly the best underground transportation system in the world.

Dunya was waiting for me as I came out of the metro station. Again, she was wearing a mini-skirt, high boots and a leather jacket. My pulse quickened. *Remember your resolve*, I thought.

She saw me approach, smiled and made an abbreviated wave.

"Hello, Yasha."

"Greetings, Dunya. Nice to see you. Let's get across the street."

I bought two tickets and we entered the zoo. I casually looked around for obvious surveillance, but no one stood out. I assumed, however, there was someone there.

When we were cleared of the turnstiles, Dunya took my arm.

"Let's walk around the lake," she suggested.

"Fine."

We began to walk along the path around what was called the "Big Pond." Ducks swam nonchalantly, while flamingos were more skittish and walked away when we approached. Dunya's arm around mine quickened my pulse. I reached into my pocket and brought out a pack of Marlboros. I didn't really smoke cigarettes, but smoking a pipe here would make me a little too conspicuous. A man smoking a cigarette here at the zoo would blend right in.

"Mind if I smoke?"

"No, of course not. I'll smoke too if you will make me a present of a cigarette."

We stopped. I disengaged from Dunya and took out two cigarettes. I lit hers with my lighter and then lit my own.

She then placed her arm around my elbow again and we continued to walk.

After a few minutes of walking and puffing on our cigarettes, Dunya began the conversation.

"What should we talk about?"

"What would you like to talk about?"

"Let's talk about American jazz."

"How about Soviet jazz? You know anything about it? I've never seen you at a jazz concert."

"No, I'm not familiar with Soviet jazz. I like American jazz. I listen to Willis Conover and Marie Ciliberti on your Voice of America."

"You should get to know Soviet jazz also. It's very good."

"Do you have any jazz records?"

"I do. I buy them at a department store in Helsinki."

"At Stockmann's?"

"How do you know about that store in Finland?"

"You're not the first foreigner I've met, Yasha. I work at the Intourist Hotel."

Dunya stopped and turned toward me.

"Would you let me listen to one of your records? Do you have Ella or Count Basie?"

"Yes, of course. Of course."

"It would be great if you could visit me at my apartment and bring some records."

As much as I wanted to visit her apartment (perhaps she lived with her mother), internal red flags flared up again.

"Dunya, do you know who I am? I'm a military attaché."

"Does that mean you're a spy?"

"Of course not. Although that's what your government thinks. I'm simply a representative of our Army for any contacts we might have with your Army. I don't know anything about spying."

"To tell you the truth, Yasha, I wouldn't be here if I thought you were a spy. I love my country and would never give away secrets to a foreigner."

"My God, Dunya. I'd never ask you to do that."

"Good," she said as she squeezed my arm.

"But still, you need to be careful because of the way your security agencies view us attachés."

"Yasha, I like you. You just continue to be a nice guy. I don't think we have anything to worry about. Can we *tykat*?"

Tykat is the Russian verb that means to address one another with the familiar 'you' (ty) form, a sign of a familiar or close friendship.

"Yes, that's fine with me."

"Are you married, Yasha?"

Her question startled me. I swallowed audibly. This was a whole different matter. Now we weren't talking about spies.

"Yes, I am. And I have three children."

"How old are they?"

"The oldest is 16. My daughter is 14 and my youngest son is 10."

"What's your wife's name?"

"Elena."

"That's a pretty name. Now about the jazz records. When can you come over to play them for me?"

Dunya tugged on my arm and drew closer.

"I'm not sure, but I'll find a time."

By now we had gone almost all around the lake and were approaching the point where we had started, near the zoo entrance.

"I need to go now, Dunya. I hope we can get together again."

"Absolutely. What's your telephone number?"

"My office phone is 555 24 24." I resisted the urge to give her my card, which identified me as a military attaché.

She took out a scrap of paper and wrote it down. "I'd like your home phone too, if that's possible," she said, still holding the scrap of paper.

"Let me write it down for you. Please don't call me at home unless it's really important."

We left the zoo. When we reached the sidewalk, Dunya said she was going in the other direction. She gave me a soft peck on the cheek, turned and walked away.

I decided to cool it for a while. I decided to let several weeks go by without phoning her. If she was working for the KGB, I knew that sooner or later she would contact me. When she did, it came as a shock.

One night the phone rang in my Moscow apartment. My wife answered it.

"Yasha, it's some woman. A Dunya."

I immediately took the phone.

"Dunya. What's wrong?"

"I've had an abortion."

I didn't know what to say. "I'm sorry?" "Congratulations?" Abortions were the standard form of birth control in the Soviet Union. Some women had had several of them.

"I don't know what to say."

"I would like you to come to my apartment. I need to see you."

"Do you need help? I don't know what to say or do."

"No, I'm fine. I'd just like to see you."

Elaine asked me who this Dunya was. I told her she was a lead on a possible good contact.

The next day, full of trepidation, I showed up at Dunya's apartment. A man opened the door.

"I'm Yasha Holbrook. Dunya called last night."

"Come on in. She's in the bedroom."

I found her in bed. She seemed happy to see me. I looked around to see if there was anyone else in the apartment but saw no one else. She introduced me to Sergei.

"He's my brother," she said.

Sergei wasn't very talkative, which was all right with me. I asked Dunya how she was doing. She said everything was fine. I didn't ask her about the abortion. I wasn't sure she really had one.

"Sergei is going to Germany in a few days. He promises to bring back medicine for me."

"That sounds good."

"Yes, but he doesn't have any hard currency. Only rubles. Is there any chance you could buy some rubles from him for dollars?"

"Oh, no. That's a serious violation of Soviet law. We could both get in trouble for something like that."

Dunya looked at me for a few seconds, then at her "brother."

"Well, I don't want you to get into trouble. But I thought I'd ask, just in case. I thought maybe if no one knew about it, you'd be OK."

"Dunya, the KGB has ears everywhere. They would surely find out. The last thing I want is to get in trouble with the KGB by breaking Soviet law."

I heard Sergei leave the apartment. Dunya and I talked for a few minutes about the jazz records I had promised someday to bring for her to listen to. I told her that when she got back on her feet, I'd get in touch with her and we would do something together again. I then excused myself and left.

As I drove back into the city toward the embassy, I began to doubt Dunya was going to be as valuable as I had hoped. When she was talking about spies and making a point to tell me she would never give her country's secrets to a foreigner, I believed it might be useful to meet her mother. This request for dollars, however, didn't set too well with me. It may have been that she was just a Soviet willing to take chances contacting foreigners in order to exploit them in any way she could. If so, there was a good chance she was working with black marketeers, not the KGB. Or maybe both.

I reported to the CIA Deputy that things weren't going very well. He told me to be patient. I did plan to contact Dunya again in a few weeks, but other dramatic events intervened. As it turned out, I left the Soviet Union before I ever saw her again.

Open Sources

"Papa, there's Brezhnev over there."

I looked across the hockey rink and, sure enough, there sat Leonid Brezhnev, the Soviet Communist Party and government leader with his entourage, enjoying a game of hockey between two Soviet teams, Spartak and Dynamo. Spartak won, 7 to 1.

It was fall 1980 and Brezhnev had been out of sight for several weeks. We didn't know if it was because of his health or some secret Soviet planning session to invade and occupy another country. If either were the case, it would be important. My 11-year-old son, Misha, had helped us find the answer to a question that had concerned us for a long time: Where was Brezhnev? Now we had just answered that question without recourse to any collection operation. If one kept his or her eyes open and used common sense, there were some things one could glean in the open.

These were turbulent times in the Cold War. The Iranian hostage crisis in November 1979, the Soviet invasion of Afghanistan in December 1979, and the American-led boycott of the Moscow Summer Olympics had diminished any U.S.-Soviet good relations that had arisen from the SALT II signing in June 1979.

More immediate, however, was that the Polish situation was heating up. As I mentioned earlier, the Polish workers at the Gdansk Shipyard had formed an independent trade union, called "Solidarity." The union, with its outspoken leader, Lech Walesa, had the earmarks of becoming a major political force in Communist Poland.

Western political-military analysts and policy makers eagerly sought information on current developments in Moscow regarding the budding Polish rebellion. This obviously had an effect on DAO activities. Of course, we still couldn't talk to Soviet military officers because of the taboo the U.S. JCS had placed on us after the Afghanistan invasion. Not that it would have made much difference, given the meager information we might get from them. We needed to know, however, where Soviet leaders were and what they were up to.

When Minister of Defense Marshal Dmitri Ustinov appeared in Moscow on 29 October, 1980, but disappeared again for some time, we reported it. (Ustinov was reportedly in poor health, which might have explained some non-appearances.) On 27 November, he met with U.S. Senator Charles Percy who was in Moscow as a guest of Ambassador Watson. It was after this meeting that the luncheon at Spaso House took place. Ustinov didn't attend the luncheon, but sent the Chief of the Soviet General Staff, Marshal Ogarkov. (See my chapter on Ogarkov.)

When the Warsaw Pact was planning a military operation, East European governments usually recalled their attachés home from Moscow for consultations. So, of course, since we were concerned about Poland, we wondered where the Polish Military Attaché was. No one had seen him for a few days. I reached him at his office and invited him to dinner at my quarters the following week. "I'm sorry," he said. "My wife and I will be out of town. We'll be in Warsaw for a few days."

We were not always able—in fact, it was very, very rare—to have face-to-face contact with high Soviet officials. So we were forced to turn to the open press for whatever we could find. Although woefully inadequate in substance, the press provided the best available source on who was where. Editorials and special articles by influential Soviets sometimes gave us an idea of what they were thinking and doing.

Of course, the Soviet leaders weren't going to broadcast or print their war plans, but years of observing them in crisis situations suggested some clues. Articles on the Polish situation and the location of Soviet leaders were two of those clues. Carefully reading the Soviet press was one element of "Kremlinology" that provided trained analysts with various kinds of information.

Milovan Djilas wrote a book, *The New Class*, in which he attacked

Communist regimes for being hypocritical about their "classless" societies. Among high Communist officials, it was often a matter of where you stood or in what order your name appeared on Party announcements. Analysis of the names and the order in which they appeared in obituaries and ceremonies, or where they stood on the Lenin Mausoleum during Red Square festivities, often revealed the status of Soviet officials. This phenomenon permeated all levels of Soviet society. Vasilii Aksyonov, the Russian novelist, told us during a seminar I took with him at George Washington University that everyone at the Soviet Writers' Union was keen to see "who sits with whom" (*kto s kem sidit*) at the writers' club in order to determine who was in favor and who was not.

Analysts in Washington and Europe worried about a Soviet military incursion into Poland to eradicate Solidarity. The Soviet track record with opposition to communist rule on its borders was ominous. Soviet troops were behind the East German forces that had put down a major anti-government strike in Berlin in 1953, they had invaded Hungary in 1956 and Czechoslovakia in 1968. Not to mention their December 1979 invasion of Afghanistan.

I began reading Soviet newspapers while still at the Army Language School in Monterey. When I was a student at American University in the 1960s, I subscribed to *Red Star* and *Pravda*. (That was toward the end of the Joe McCarthy era and often I would take a newspaper out of my university mailbox only to find a note from the postmaster that said: "This is propaganda and you do not have to accept it.") While an analyst of Soviet political and military affairs in the Army Chief of Staff's Intelligence Support Detachment at the Pentagon and at U.S. Army Headquarters in Heidelberg, I found Soviet newspapers and journals a valuable source of information. I reiterate, however, in both the above cases, I was an analyst.

In Moscow, I continued to monitor *Pravda, Izvestiya, Red Star* and the occasional military journal or book. Of course, I didn't have time to do this on a permanent or regular basis, but at times I would identify information that I felt needed to be reported quickly to Washington. For the most part, my reports were meant more as a heads-up to analysts in Washington than as an intelligence item. Occasionally, we received requests to monitor open press coverage on certain areas of interest in Washington.

There was, of course, a downside to reading the open press; one could not or should not rely on it exclusively. Especially the Soviet press, which was infamous for its dishonesty. In the United States, however, Soviet spies were more fortunate. Under great pressure to produce intelligence from their sources, they often reported open press items as though the information had come from their agents. According to a book authored by two American scholars and a former KGB officer, *Spies: The Rise and Fall of the KGB in America*, Soviet spy handlers "sometimes listen to commercial radio news reports or read newspapers, summarize them, and send the results back to Moscow as if they'd gathered top-secret information through their spy networks."

Jeffrey Richelson, in his *Sword and Shield*, gives a frightening picture of the open U.S. sources that are available to the KGB, GRU and other foreign spies for political, military, economic and technical information. He lists at least twenty-two open publications that are sources of military intelligence. Zacharias writes in his *Secret Missions* that a prominent German agent believed "on the surface, the United States has no secrets which an efficient and alert foreign operative could not procure." He pointed out that a trip to the United States Government Printing Office in Washington "usually yielded data at a nominal price which agents elsewhere would have had immense difficulties in obtaining. Most of the Army and Navy manuals were offered for sale. The document rooms of the Senate and House were other sources of information." A friendly foreign military attaché in Moscow, who had once been an attaché in Washington, told me I should be grateful information was so hard to come by in the USSR. When he was in Washington, he was inundated with open source information and could hardly sort out what deserved to be reported back to his capital.

But overreliance on open sources could be a weakness among news reporters and some foreign attachés in Moscow. Especially those who didn't know Russian. Consequently, not only could they not move around in Soviet society and converse with Russians, they were forced to rely on the Soviet-produced English-language summaries. Andrew Nagorski, in his book, *Reluctant Farewell*, points out that the problem of relying on the Soviet press was a serious shortcoming for the foreign press. He wrote:

> Only one of the Associated Press correspondents had even a passable knowledge of Russian. Only about half of American press corps spoke Russian well. Most Western reporters… were merely dependent on three less-than-reliable sources of information: The English-language TASS news service and whatever was gleaned from the Soviet press by their Russian translators; English-speaking Russians, most of whom were likely to be Soviet journalists and officials who were the mainstays of the foreigners' social circuit; and Western diplomats, many of whom were as isolated from Soviet life as most correspondents themselves. The vast majority of copy produced by Western correspondents amounted to a rewriting of dispatches and articles issued by TASS and the Soviet Press.

Nagorski singled out Anne Garrels, the ABC TV reporter, as "the only network correspondent with a background in Soviet studies and who spoke Russian." I too was impressed by Anne. Not only did she have a Soviet studies background, but she was fearless in her efforts to acquire newsworthy information. Once she stood outside the military store *Voentorg*, attempting to interview soldiers going in and out. I had earlier lent her, at her request, the declassified DIA *Handbook on Soviet Forces*. The KGB later set Anne up and ABC had to bring her home for her own safety.

Hedrick Smith, author of the best selling *The Russians,* pointed out in a 2016 interview: "[To] me it was, if not insane, at least enormously shortsighted of a major news organization to send somebody to a place as important as Russia without at least giving them some Russian… but most of them did."

Our DAO was much better prepared linguistically than the foreign correspondent corps and some other foreign attachés. We had several speakers of adequate Russian. We did not rely exclusively on the Soviet press for our reporting. Those of us who did read the Soviet press found that it took a lot of time. I felt that analysts in Washington had more time for this and could have done the work better. Almost all Soviet publications were available in a few days to our agencies in Washington, DC.

As I look back over my reports based on open sources, I see there was no immediacy for a report about the Soviet reaction to the U.S. proposal to set up a Quick Reaction Corps. The same goes for my report on a newly revised edition of Soviet military regulations. When *Red Star* published a picture of an armored assault vehicle without its usual turret and Sergei Vishnevsky refused to get me a copy of the original picture in return for the cruise missile picture I had sent him earlier, I should have dropped it at that. The fact that the Black Sea Fleet was building a new fishing trawler (trawlers were often used for voice intercept and other electronic warfare collection off the coast of the U.S.) likewise was not urgent. I have already commented on an article in a Soviet military journal that discussed transportation problems associated with troop rotation. In retrospect, I have no idea why I reported on the lack of progress in the Baku, Azerbaijan, underground sewer construction. Possibly, it was in response to a specific request from Washington.

After spending considerable time culling through seven months of newspapers to provide biographical updates on Soviet military officers, I ended my report with the following:

```
Reporting officer notes that all
the above information was taken
from open sources. Since Red Star is
readily available at DIA, I suspect
this report represents an unnecessary
duplication of effort, or at least is
a report that could be better done in
```

Washington than in Moscow. Welcome
your comments.

I never received any feedback.

I admit I did indulge in some comments and analysis when the news involved General of the Army Evgenii Ivanovsky. I had a unique perspective on this officer since I had met him several times when I served at USMLM in East Germany and was directly involved in his visit to CINC USAREUR, General George Blanchard in 1977. Ivanovsky was perhaps the only Soviet commander who had first-hand knowledge of the U.S. Army in Europe. As I pointed out earlier, I was General Blanchard's interpreter and at the end of the visit became General Ivanovsky's interpreter as well, when he sent his own interpreter away. I quote from my earlier memoir, *Potsdam Mission*:

> "Go get something to eat," Ivanovsky said to Yegorov [his interpreter]. He then addressed my general.
> "General Blanchard," he began, "I want you to know how much I appreciate what you have done for me and my staff." He continued, "I've looked carefully for signs that events were being staged, but all I saw were realistic demonstrations. I had open access to your officers and soldiers. You obviously have a well-trained army in which you have a lot of confidence. This visit has been one of the highlights of my career."

I think I knew Ivanovsky better than any American officer, with the possible exception of Nick Troyan. Before I arrived at USMLM, Nick had interpreted during Ivanovsky visits to social events in Potsdam and at Headquarters, GSFG. I believed Ivanovsky would never forget his visit to West Germany in 1977. He understood the U.S. Army better than any Soviet general. It's unlikely he shared his true views with the Soviet command back in Moscow. There was a long Soviet tradition of telling the boss what he wanted to hear. David E. Murphy, Sergei Kondrashev and George Baily, in their *Battleground Berlin,* described the situation thus: "Rarely was the social or political reality of the West portrayed to Soviet leaders for what it was. Most often Soviet leaders would be told what they wished to hear and would see what their ideology told them they must." Still, General Ivanovsky would never be able to erase his impressions of that 1977 visit.

Ivanovsky's assignment to the Belorussian Military District came as a surprise, since we assumed he would go to a high position at the Ministry of Defense or the Soviet General Staff. I believed that his assignment to this Military District, which shared hundreds of miles of border with Poland, was related to the Solidarity crisis. This assignment did enhance the status of that military district. No former CINC GSFG had been subsequently assigned to a military district, except for Marshal Ivan Yakubovsky, who later became CINC of Warsaw Pact Forces. Ivanovsky later did become CINC of all Soviet Ground Forces.

I began to think my sending in reports garnered from the open press was a waste of my attaché time. I continued, however, to report on items that I thought might escape the attention of analysts in Washington, but could be valuable to those who needed to understand the Soviet military. But my efforts with the Soviet open press gradually diminished. Based on the declassified reports DIA provided me, it appears I sent in very few reports taken from the open press after 1979.

In January 1980, however, I did report on a *Red Star* article containing unusual criticism of a small unit exercise where the battalion commander lost track of one of his companies and his chief of staff was completely in the dark once the battle had begun. My question at the end of the report was: "Don't Soviet commanders and their staffs prepare for the 'fog of war'?"

In December 1980, I sent a report about an interview with Deputy Chief of the Soviet General Staff, Army General Sergei Akhromeyev, published in *Red Star*. Such interviews often provided insights to high-level Soviet military policy. This one, however, only reiterated the Soviet position that any attempt to renegotiate SALT II would be met with Soviet opposition and counterdemands. Akhromeyev charged the U.S. had a new nuclear strategy that included "plans for preemptive strikes against the Socialist countries." He also managed to bring to readers of

Red Star a quote from President Carter: "If the U.S.A., having signed SALT II, refuses to ratify it, then we would assume the role of 'war monger,' having refused to take part in the joint attempt to limit the spreading of the most destructive arms mankind has ever known."

I justified that report by the fact that U.S. Senator Percy had just been in Moscow and met with Soviet political and military leaders. One of the topics of discussion during his visit was SALT II and the nuclear strategies of both countries.

I'm not saying open sources should be ignored. In fact, much information can be extracted from publications and broadcasts in a closed society. It's difficult to convey to non-Soviet specialists the utter lack of reliable information about the USSR and, in particular, its military forces. During the over 70 years of the Soviet Union, the most available source of information on virtually any subject probably was the open press. In a closed society like the USSR, where almost everything was considered a state secret, any tidbit of information was treated as valuable. I am suggesting, however, that exploitation of open sources could have been better done in Washington.

According to one CIA analyst, surveys put "the contribution of open sources anywhere from 35 to 95 percent of the intelligence used in the government." The FBI estimates that figure to be 90 percent. Ellis Zacharias in his book *Secret Missions*, writes that "Approximately 95 percent of our peacetime intelligence comes to us from open sources: from books published abroad; from reports of observing travelers; from newspaper articles or surveys in professional magazines; from foreign broadcasts and similar sources."

One of the advantages of open sources is that they are usually very timely. When I worked in the Pentagon, we prepared updated intelligence briefings (the "black book") for the Army Chief of Staff and his principle officers. Each morning before we left on our black-book rounds, we checked the *Washington Post* and were glued to TV network news to find out if anything dramatic had happened overnight that would have an impact on what we were going to tell the Army leadership.

The reader can easily sense my ambivalence about open sources.

The value of open sources for information about the Soviet Union suggested that, as 16th-century priest and scholar Erasmus wrote, "In the land of the blind, a one-eyed man is king." For the most part, as I've said repeatedly, in-depth reading and reporting of the Soviet press often yielded valuable intelligence information. But I believe it was a job that should be done primarily in Washington and not in the attaché office. At the very least, someone with good language ability could have been assigned to the DAO with the sole responsibility of scanning the Soviet press and TV. We had such a person in our office. Air Force Staff Sergeant David Baker would have performed that duty easily. Instead, the DAO chose to use him in the administrative section of the office.

PART V: ROVNO

ON TOWARD POLAND

No one in the embassy knew what to make of the fact that the MOD had approved this trip.

We had been trying to get an attaché team close to the Polish border area for weeks. Now, all of a sudden in January 1981, Tom Spencer and I received permission to do just that. It reminded me of an earlier trip to Baku that the Soviet MOD had denied several times. Washington had reported to us that military activity was taking place there, but when we finally received permission to travel, we found upon arrival that whatever had been going on was all over.

A military unit exercise was one thing, preparations for an invasion of another country was something else. Surely, if the Soviet Union was planning to send military forces into Poland, there would be some indicators along our way. We were to travel to Kiev by train and then take a DAO car to Rovno, Lvov and Uzhgorod. All three of these cities were relatively close to the Polish border. A restricted area along the border just west of Lvov prevented us from getting any closer. Little did we know we wouldn't even make it to Lvov.

The people of Poland had little love for Russia and its governments since at least the early 18th century and the first partition of their country. Historians note three partitions—1722, 1793 and 1795. The year 1939 should also qualify as a year of partition. In that year Nazi Germany invaded Poland on 1 September, occupying the western half of the country. On 17 September, the USSR invaded from the east and occupied the rest of Poland.

As I've mentioned earlier, in 1980, trouble had flared up again in

Poland. In July, the government of Edward Gierek raised the prices on consumer goods. A wave of strikes and factory occupations began at once. By late 1980, Solidarity was transforming itself from simply a trade union into a social and political movement. Using strikes and other protest actions, Solidarity sought to force a change in Polish governmental policies. The Polish government was losing control of the strikes. Brezhnev and the Soviet Politburo began to put pressure on Polish leaders to bring the situation under control.

It is likely the selection in 1978 of Krakow Bishop Karol Wojtyla, who became Pope John Paul II, increased Polish pride and hence their willingness to assert themselves against the Communist government. John Paul II visited his native country in 1979 and was cheered by millions. On 15 January 1981 (while Tom and I were on this latest trip), a delegation from Solidarity, including Lech Walesa, was meeting with Pope John Paul II in Rome.

Solidarity leaders and other anti-government protesters knew full well what might be in store for them. Soviet military intervention in Eastern Europe had become almost a tradition. Although the anti-communist riots in East Berlin in 1953 and Poland in 1956 had been put down pretty much by native units, the Soviets had taken direct military action in Hungary in 1956 and Czechoslovakia in 1968. Would it be Poland in 1981? On 5 December 1980, the *Washington Post* ran an article under the title, "Will Moscow Invade Again?" Given the Soviet track record in such crises, it was well within the realm of possibility that an invasion would take place. (I learned much later that the Soviets *had* made plans for an invasion of Poland in 1980, but abandoned the idea due to concern for Polish opposition and more grief in East-West relations.)

Fortunately, no military incursion into Poland ever took place, but, according to a 1992 UPI report, in December 1981, plans for such an invasion were once again well underway. Russian General Viktor Dubinin stated, "We were to enter Poland December 14, if General Wojceich Jaruzelski, the Polish prime minister, didn't declare martial law." Dubinin told the Polish newspaper *Gazeta Wyborcza*, "You were encircled by our troops who were stationed in Czechoslovakia [and] in Germany, and in one or two days Soviet troops would be in every Polish city."

The train ride to Kiev was uneventful. We shared our compartment with two probable KGB agents, but after months of traveling in the USSR, we were used to that. From Kiev's Moskovsky Rail Station we hired a taxi to take us to the Dnipr Hotel pay-parking lot, where we were to pick up a DAO car that had been left there earlier by other attachés. Although almost 500 miles south of Moscow, Kiev had more snow then the capital city. We had hoped our overnight train ride from Moscow would transport us to better weather. But no. Mounds of dirty snow along the curbs, sidewalks covered with three inches of ice, the grey, sunless sky and a bitter wind made us feel as if we were still back in Moscow.

When we reached our DAO car, we found it had one flat tire and was missing its windshield wipers. I walked over to the booth where the woman in charge was sitting and reading a book.

"What's going on here?" I asked. "We pay good money to have our car guarded and we expect it to be well taken care of."

The woman continued to read for a few moments as I waited for a response. She looked up slowly. "What's your problem?"

"See for yourself. A flat tire and no windshield wipers."

"So? The tire can go flat anytime. Nothing I can do about that. As far as windshield wipers are concerned, no problem."

She came out of her booth, walked over to another car, removed the wipers, and placed them on the American car.

"There," she said, "No problem."

We carried an extra set of wipers with us, but kept them hidden from the woman. Now we had to change the tire and find somewhere to have it fixed. When we got the spare on, we headed for the outskirts of town. According to our map, there was an automobile service station just outside the Kiev Ring Road on Academician Glushkov Prospekt. We could stop there to have the flat repaired.

As we drove out onto Khreshchatik, the main thoroughfare in downtown Kiev, we checked the rearview mirror and saw a light blue

Zhiguli following us with four male passengers. It followed us as we turned onto Taras Shevchenko Boulevard.

When we arrived at the repair station, there was a long line of cars. How long some of the Soviet drivers had been waiting was anyone's guess. Car owners came to repair stations and resigned themselves to waiting in line for a long time. Towards evening some would abandon their cars in the line and join with others for a ride into town. The next morning, they would all reappear, hoping this would be the day they would get their car serviced.

"This isn't going to work," Tom said.

"Right," I replied. "We may have to be a little assertive. I'll go in and see what I can do. Stay with the car."

When I entered the packed waiting room I saw a heavyset, middle-aged woman with bleach-blond hair and excessive makeup sitting behind the counter. The woman summarily dismissed each of the two men in front of me because they didn't have the right paperwork.

I said as pleasantly as possible, "Good morning."

The woman said nothing. She just scowled at me.

"Good morning," I repeated.

"I heard you the first time. What do you want?"

"I'm American Assistant Army Attaché Holbrook, and I'm…"

"I asked you what you wanted."

"We need to get a tire repaired."

"You'll just have to wait your turn. Cars are backed up in the garage."

"Yes, I understand. But we're American diplomats and…"

The woman interrupted me. "All the more reason."

This was a rare response. Usually being an American gave us preferential treatment in the USSR, as in the example of the butter and cheese store with Yasha. Another time, at an airport, a group of veterans was forced to stand out in the heat on the tarmac until another attaché and I boarded. I felt guilty so I complained to the Intourist agent and loudly apologized to the veterans as we went up the ramp to the plane. Elaine once got preferential treatment when her driver took her to the head of the long line at Lenin's Mausoleum by simply telling the hundreds of Soviets in line that she was an American. The attitude of this woman at the service station in Kiev, however, apparently was the flip side of the Russians' love-hate attitude toward us. David Shipler described it in his book *Russia: Broken Idols, Solemn Dreams*, as "being vilified and coddled at the same time."

"You see, we're on a tight schedule," I pointed out to the woman. "Your government expects us to get to Rovno by evening. We can't wait very long."

"Just because you're a foreigner, you think you can jump the line?"

"Well, I don't... we do need to get the tire fixed as soon as possible."

"Tough luck. You can wait with all the rest."

"Let me see your Complaint Book."

"My what?"

"The Complaint Book. You know what I'm talking about."

Every public service establishment in the USSR maintained a Complaint Book that was intended ostensibly to discourage rude behavior on the part of service personnel.

"I don't know where it is."

"How about the station manager? You know where he is?"

"Of course. Why?"

"I'd like to talk to him."

"His office is down the hall."

I walked down the hall until I found a door, partly open, with the sign *"Administrator"* attached. I could see a man sitting at a desk, talking on the phone. I knocked and pushed the door a little further open. The man looked up and motioned for me to enter. He then hung up the phone.

"Yes, what is it?"

"I'm sorry to interrupt you. My name is Major Jim Holbrook. I'm an American diplomat and I need your help."

The man glanced immediately at my shoes (*yes, they were Western*), then looked me up and down.

"Well, this is an honor Mr. Holbrook. I'm Oleg Krapchenko."

He offered his hand. "We've never had an American at our station before. What can we do for you?"

"I have an emergency. We need a tire repaired so my colleague and I can get to Rovno by evening. I know you're very busy, but is there any chance...?"

"No problem. Just go out to the receptionist and tell her what you need."

"I've tried that. The woman said we would have to wait like all the others. And, I might add... she was quite rude. Made disparaging remarks about our being foreigners. And wouldn't produce the Complaint Book."

"Is that so. Well, we'll take care of that in a hurry."

Krapchenko picked up his phone again. "Vanya, have Olga Andreyevna come in here."

A red-faced receptionist entered the manager's office. "Yes, Oleg Olegovich. You called for me?"

"I have two instructions for you, Olga Andreyevna. First you will apologize to Mr. Holbrook here. You will explain to him our policy on treatment of foreigners. Then you will put his request to have a tire repaired at the top of your list. Is that clear?"

"Yes, Oleg Olegovich." She turned to me with her head bowed.

"Look him in the eye."

"Mr. Holbrook, I'm sorry for my remarks. It is the policy of Repair Station RS 113 to treat foreigners with the utmost delicacy. We wish you to leave here with a positive impression of our enterprise."

She paused, looked at Krapchenko for his approval and then glared at me. I returned the glare.

"Thanks. I'll have my colleague bring the car up front. We're very grateful for your attention," I said.

Krapchenko waved his hand. "Now go on, Olga Andreyevna. Get their tire repaired."

Turning to me, he asked, "So, Mr. Holbrook, would you like to have a drink and some refreshments while you wait. I have some "Borzhomi" mineral water here, but I could open a bottle of cognac or vodka if you desire. Why don't you have your comrade come on in too?"

"Thank you very much, Mr. Krapchenko. But I think the tire repair won't take very long and perhaps it's better if I'm there when the work is done. In case there are some questions. I do appreciate the offer, though. And thank you very much for arranging to have this done quickly. I will take a positive impression of you and your station with me."

"I hope you will be happy with our service and won't need the Complaint Book."

"Oh, no. That won't be necessary now." As I left the office, I saw Krapchenko pick up a red phone.

The remainder of the trip went smoothly. Even the road to Rovno was in satisfactory repair. On the outskirts of the city we nearly hit a drunk who was walking down the middle of the road. In broad daylight no less! When we arrived in Rovno, we went straight to the hotel "Mir." Our Soviet map showed the "Mir" prominently on Kobilyanska Street. When we pulled up and stopped in front of the hotel, the light blue Zhiguli that had been with us since Kiev pulled in along the curb and parked. The four occupants remained in their car. We entered the hotel and were assigned to room 232.

HAPPY NEW YEAR!

The loud music and the crowd told us there was something unusual going on. When we entered the dining room, we saw it was decorated with flowers and red paper streamers. The *maitre d'* approached.

"Something special going on here tonight?" I asked.

"Yes, of course. We're celebrating the "old" New Year, the New Year according to the old calendar. Tonight's New Year's Eve."

"Of course. Let me be the first to wish you Happy New Year."

"Oh, no. Don't do that. It's not midnight yet. To say 'Happy New Year' before midnight is bad luck. You must be the Americans."

"Yes we are. So Happy Forthcoming New Year! We'd like a table for two in the smoking section."

"No smoking is allowed in the restaurant," the *maitre d'* said. "And we don't have any free tables. See for yourself." She pointed to an empty table in the corner. "That one's reserved."

Tom piped in. "Then just find us any two seats together. We're hungry."

The *maitre d'* looked over the dining area.

"Follow me." She led us to a table for eight. Two couples already occupied the table and were well into their partying.

When the rest of Europe changed over from the Julian calendar to the Gregorian in 1582, Russia did not. By 1918, the year Russia adopted the Gregorian, it was thirteen days behind Europe. The Russian Orthodox Church continues to use the Julian calendar so that Christmas (Old Style) falls on 7 January (New Style). The New Year (Old Style) is on 13 January (New Style). The 13-day gap has resulted in what are some interesting, sometimes confusing and apparent contradictions. For example, the February Revolution (when the Tsar abdicated) occurred in March (New Style). The "October Revolution" was now celebrated on 7 November (New Style).

Soviet hotel restaurants were just about the only place where locals could dine out and dance to live music. In fact, a dining establishment was required to provide live music in order to be classified a restaurant. The only unusual thing about the music tonight was that it was Tuesday. Normally, live music occurred only on Friday and Saturday. We had not paid attention to the date and thought at first maybe there was a wedding reception going on.

The "Mir" hotel was the largest in Rovno, Ukraine—a city of 250,000 people—and the only hotel the Soviets permitted foreigners to stay in. The restaurant was on the first floor and had high ceilings. Windows all around the restaurant were covered with dark green drapes that, among other things, prevented people on the sidewalk from seeing in. Not just anyone could get into the "Mir." Doormen guarded the entrance to hotels. One of their tasks was to keep to a minimum the number of locals who might make contact with foreigners inside. One had to have connections and prior reservations, or else be prepared to "tip" the doorman handsomely both when you entered and when you left for the evening. Doormen were good at remembering who tipped how much. This appeared to be the case for all hotels in the USSR that accepted foreigners.

Some of the tables had been pushed together to accommodate large groups. The restaurant was full. Most patrons were middle-aged, although a couple of groups of young men and women huddled at two separate tables. Most of the men wore white shirts and neckties, while the women were in brightly colored blouses or party dresses and heavy makeup. Several couples occupied the small dance floor. Three pairs of women danced with each other. This reminded me of the dances I had attended as a teenager in Wisconsin.

We ordered a bottle of cognac and sat back to watch the festivities. The two couples at our table were engaged in their own conversations.

The women talked to each other and the men did the same. They made no effort to include us in their party.

Two men came into the dining room and, without the assistance of the *maitre d'*, went straight to the "reserved" table in the corner. Tom tapped me on the shoulder and motioned with his head. "There're our 'buddies' for the evening."

We decided to bypass the menu and rely on the recommendation of the waiter. Experience had shown that despite the wide array of dishes printed on a menu, only a few items would be available. They were the ones with prices penciled in, although often even these were not available. Tonight the waiter recommended *bifshteks*, a tolerable piece of beef, together with noodles and cabbage.

I was starting to get a buzz from the cognac. I had to be careful. A couple of drinks with dinner were fine. We couldn't take a chance drinking the water. We ordered the bottle of cognac so we could break the seal ourselves. Besides, if other Soviets wished to join us later, there would be something to offer them. We had no intention of drinking the whole bottle by ourselves.

One of the advantages of traveling around the USSR was that it sometimes gave attachés a chance to meet genuine Soviet citizens, not the cosmopolitan Muscovites. People we ran into in Moscow were always suspect. Since contact with foreigners was virtually taboo, those Muscovites had to be considered KGB plants. Even if one were to meet a regular citizen casually, he or she would be subject to a debriefing by the KGB afterwards. Surveillance in Moscow was uneven, but it was rare to talk with someone who was not being watched by the KGB.

I poured myself another glass of cognac. I couldn't help but notice how many good-looking women there were in the restaurant. Outsiders too often gave Russian women short shrift. Some Russians were the most beautiful women I'd ever seen anywhere. One had to allow for primitive clothes and makeup, but the faces and the bodies! (A few years later, the editor of the Russian edition of *Vogue* estimated that "50 percent of the top models in the world issued from the former Soviet Union...")

We hadn't come to party. Our initial intention was simply to have dinner in our hotel as we almost always did when traveling. Still, we were enjoying the merriment going on around us. The band played some songs made famous by ABBA, the Beatles and various American groups. Right now they were playing and a girl vocalist was singing ABBA's *Money, Money, Money*. I wondered if the celebrants understood the lyrics. When that song ended, the bandleader announced the next dance would be a "white" dance. Women would choose their own partners from among the men. This was a Soviet version of Sadie Hawkin's Day in the U.S.

"I wonder how long it'll take for the word to get around that there are two Americans here," I mused aloud. I turned to Tom and said, "If anyone comes over and invites us to the white dance, we'll have to accommodate them or it'll be impolite."

"Yeah," said Tom. "Wouldn't want them to think we considered ourselves too good for their women?"

At that moment two girls approached our table. A redhead addressed me. She smiled and spoke English. "Please would you care to dance?"

"Well, I… I guess…Sure, of course," I answered in Russian. I got up and followed her onto the dance floor. Right behind me I saw Tom take the hand of the other girl as they too joined the dancers.

"My name's Katya," my dance partner said as she put her left hand on my shoulder.

"I'm Yasha," I said nervously as we began to dance.

Katya quickly moved close to me. I found this a bit awkward. The band was playing a Soviet rock and roll tune. Two loud saxophones, an even louder drum, two trumpets, a keyboard and a rhythm guitar blared out a "boom-boom-boom" beat. Older couples appeared to be jumping up and down, just like some of the swing music dancing I'd seen in early American movies.

When I put my right arm around her and placed it on her back in the standard dance position, I felt a rush. Katya moved even closer to me. I had known for some time that many Russian women were starved for genuine affection. To most Russian men a woman's role in life was to bundle the children off to school in the morning, work all day, shop during their lunch hour, pick up their children and then cook and wash clothes and dishes until they were ready to drop. And still be there on demand for their men. (See Anne Garrels's chapter "The Russian Family" in her *Putin Country*.)

Women had never been accepted as equals in Russia or, despite their propaganda to the contrary, in the USSR. The workplace for single (even married) women was often fraught with sexual harassment. In fact, in July 2016, according to Brian Whitmore in his daily "The Morning Vertical," the Kremlin introduced a bill to decriminalize domestic violence. The Russian Civic Chamber has warned that women who use excessive force in resisting rape attempts could face criminal charges.

I separated myself from Katya and began to dance a kind of twist, the way I would have danced to American music at this tempo. Katya followed suit and began to concentrate on her own dancing. I was still quite aware of who and where I was. I was a little self-conscious because I knew everyone was watching the two American diplomats. The main thing was to not let my guard down. When the music stopped, I started to escort my new partner back to her table.

"Wait. Please dance once more with me," Katya whispered.

Before I could react, the music began again. This time it was *Lara's Theme*, from the movie "Dr. Zhivago." I wondered how many people associated the music with Boris Pasternak. The Soviet government still banned the book in his homeland. Had anyone seen the movie? Katya placed her head on my shoulder. I felt her long red hair against my face. I was nervous, but was enjoying the dance-floor intimacy.

"How long will you be in Rovno?"

"A couple of days."

"Would you like me to show you the city tomorrow?"

"Thank you, but... my comrade and I are planning to drive around ourselves." I didn't tell her we would be looking for military targets to photograph. I looked over to the corner table where the two goons had taken a seat earlier, but they were gone. *Where are they? I know they're watching*, I thought.

I had always tried to stay ahead of the KGB. I varied my behavior when I was with Russians—drinking sometimes, tee-totaling it other times. Being lively in conversation sometimes, remaining very quiet other times. I wanted to keep the KGB off balance. I pretended I was unaware I was under surveillance and I always tried to appear as though I had nothing to hide.

The dance music finished. When I got back to our table, Tom was already there. He greeted me with a grin.

"You were getting pretty lovey-dovey out there."

"Yeah, she was all over me." I smiled. "I had to be polite, you know."

"I'll bet the goons put the band up to announcing a white dance," Tom said.

"Very possible, but I don't know what they think they can gain from it. Even if I were to take her to my room--"

Tom quickly interrupted. "I hope you're not considering that. Remember, we're on their territory and playing by their rules."

"On their territory, yes. But not necessarily by their rules."

"Yasha, you take a lot of chances."

"I have to, Tom. I've never gone in for truck counting, conscript sightings or taking pictures of antennas. That's what we did at USMLM. The real intelligence here will come from the people. And in order to get close to them, you have to pretend you have nothing to fear. And besides, who knows when another Penkovsky might come along and drop a letter in our pocket or a folder in our car window?" Colonel Oleg Penkovsky, whom I mentioned earlier, was a GRU officer who had worked for both the British SIS and the American CIA and was an invaluable source of information on Soviet moves during the 1962 Cuban Missile Crisis.

I poured myself another glass of cognac. As I thought about my new aggressive collection style, Dunya back in Moscow came to mind. Would I ever meet her mother? Would she invite me to a party where there would be officers or civilian workers from the General Staff? That's where I might get some real tidbits of important information. I wondered what Dunya was doing now. Had she tried to get in touch with me? As usual, I had said nothing to her about my trip to the Ukraine.

"I think you're hoping for too much," Tom interrupted my reverie.

"Perhaps, but unless we take some chances, we're not likely to get any valuable information."

The band took a break. I glanced over at the table where Katya was sitting. She was eating a piece of chicken. She saw me looking at her just as she was about to take a bite from a drumstick. She smiled and, instead of sinking her teeth into it, she put the meaty part into her mouth and just held it there. I drained my glass quickly and poured another drink.

"Hey, go easy on that, " Tom said.

"I've got you to keep an eye on me," I said. "How about it, Tom, how about tonight you're the designated driver?"

"Thanks a lot."

"Hey, Tom, did you notice something funny?" I said as I pointed at our table.

"What?"

"The other Russian couples never came back to our table."

Tom looked around the room and saw our former tablemates seated with another group of people. He motioned to me with his head.

"There they are. Over by the window. Maybe they hooked up with old friends."

"Or were told to get lost," I quipped. "To make room for someone else."

We were now sitting by ourselves at a table for eight.

"Uh-oh. Here comes your girlfriend," Tom said as he tapped my foot under the table. A smiling Katya came toward us, carrying a drink. Her figure, clearly visible beneath her tight, short cotton dress drew my attention and that of the other men seated nearby. Tom and I stood as she approached our table.

"My, what gentlemen you Americans are," Katya said as she placed her drink on our table.

"We noticed you were all alone. Would you mind if some of my friends and I join you? We have our own drinks."

I turned to Tom, who just rolled his eyes and shrugged.

"That would be very nice. Come on over," I said.

Katya waved to two men and three women. They got up, crossed the floor and joined us, bringing with them a half-full bottle of vodka, an almost empty bottle of "Sovetskoye" champagne, and an unopened bottle of Moldavian wine. One of the girls was the one with whom Tom had danced. She sat next to him, while my new "friend" pulled her chair up close to me. The Ukrainians told us they all lived in one apartment building in Kiev. The two couples were married.

Our conversation soon showed that the Ukrainians were very curious and very uninformed about America. Their views on American life showed they had never listened to Voice of America or Radio Liberty. Tom and I tried to set them straight on our political process, the selection and promotion of military officers and the so-called plight of our working class—what Communism called the "proletariat." The more we asked about their life in the Ukraine the more we were led to believe we were talking with Ukrainian nationalists. They had no love for Russians and occasionally spoke among themselves in Ukrainian.

A very large number of Russians lived in eastern Ukraine and it was they who tended to dominate political and economic matters there. But we were in western Ukraine. Inhabitants here particularly disliked how the "Great Russians" often called them "Little Russians." Our guests pointed out with great pride that 700 years ago, the now-Ukrainian capital Kiev was the actual capital of ancient Russia. Not only that, but Kiev ranked with Paris, Rome and London as a financial, artistic and political center during the height of the Middle Ages. The Mongol invasion at the beginning of the 13th century, according to our friends (and, incidentally, many historians), was the cause for Kiev and the rest of Russia falling behind the progress of Western Europe and thus not enjoying the advantages of a renaissance.

The drinks flowed freely. I ordered another bottle of champagne for our guests, but it soon became impossible to determine who was drinking from which bottle. I believed I was drinking only cognac and thought I was doing a good job of not mixing it with other alcoholic beverages. In the past, I often had reactions to drinking more than one type of alcohol at a time. In retrospect, however, I have no illusions that my senses were being blunted by alcohol.

Katya never asked to dance again. Instead, as we talked, she put her hand on my knee and walked her fingers up and down my thigh.

At the stroke of twelve, the restaurant exploded with cheers of "Happy New Year!"

After that it all got fuzzy. Tom appeared to be disoriented. I remember telling him that Katya was coming up to the room. The next thing I remember is helping Tom up to the second floor and asking the *dezhurnaya* (floor duty lady) for our key.

"Someone else has it already," said the old lady, giving us a knowing smile.

When we reached the room, the door was unlocked. We entered and I saw that Katya was in Tom's bed under the covers. I motioned to her.

"No, no. You come on over to my bed, Katya. Let's not pester Tom."

She pulled the blanket off and I saw she was wearing nothing but a pair of white cotton panties. She nonchalantly moved over into my bed and pulled the covers up over herself again. I could hardly get my clothes off fast enough. Just before I crawled into the narrow bed with her, I glanced over and saw that Tom had crashed and was sound asleep on his now unmade bed. He had taken some medicine earlier in the evening and I wondered if it had reacted with his drinks. I pulled the covers over us.

About half an hour later, someone slammed open the door to our suite and several people rushed in.

SURPRISE!

Forty years of having everything go my way ended the moment I awoke to the bang of the hotel room door being slammed against the wall.

The police and KGB rushed in. Repeated flashes from a camera temporarily blinded me as I scrambled out of bed and reached for my trousers. Katya sat upright and pulled the covers up to her chin.

In the next bed, Tom was just coming to. He sat up and rubbed his eyes.

"What the hell's going on?"

"It's the goons," I called back to Tom as I walked out in the living area of the hotel suite, snapping my trousers shut. "And they've brought an entire delegation with them."

"Who the hell you think you are?" I said to the police captain. "We're American diplomats, Comrade Captain. You have no right to bust in here like this."

Tom remained in bed. I wasn't sure whether he was really awake.

"Mister Holbrook, it is our duty to inform you that you have violated hotel rules by having an unauthorized person in your room for the night."

"You need the police and KGB to inform us of that? Is one of you the hotel manager?"

A tall man in civilian clothes at the rear of the delegation spoke up.

"I'm the administrator. I called the police because you are foreigners and I wasn't sure how to handle this."

"What about all these other guys?"

"They're hotel employees. Security."

"Security my ass. They're KGB."

"Mr. Holbrook. We advise you to conduct yourself in a gentlemanly way."

The floor *dezhurnaya*—the watchdog and holder of keys on each floor in almost every Soviet hotel—joined in. "And no swearing. Ivan Petrovich, did you hear him swear?"

"*Da*, I got it."

A police sergeant with a clipboard wrote something down.

"Captain, I advise you to take these people and leave immediately. I will report this to the American Embassy in Moscow. This is a violation of diplomatic protocol."

Tom said nothing. When I looked over at him, his eyes were closed again. He appeared to be sleeping in the sitting position.

The police captain smiled. "Mr. Holbrook, I think you realize you are not in any position to give orders. You yourself have violated diplomatic protocol by bringing this woman here."

"I didn't bring her here. She was already in the room when we arrived."

"Then you should have told her to leave," he answered.

The photographer continued to take pictures of the room, Tom, and the woman who still cowered in the bed. The others just stood and listened to the interchange between the police captain and me.

"Ha! This was a setup. Even your puritanical *dezhurnaya* played the game. Or she wouldn't have given the key to this woman, or smiled so at us when we later came up to the room last night."

"I think we can take care of this quickly, Mr. Holbrook, if you will just sign this *akt*, this statement of charges."

"F… you, Captain! And the horse you rode in on. Get out of here."

"You are just compounding your troubles, Mr. Holbrook. Will you or will you not sign this *akt*?"

"I will not. Now get the hell out of here."

"I too will report this incident to Moscow. To the appropriate authorities," the captain said.

He then nodded his head at the others and they slowly filed out of the room. I sat down at the table in the living area.

"Shit, Tom. This is all we need."

Tom heard nothing; he was conked out. I turned to Katya.

"You better get dressed and leave."

"What've I done? What'll happen to me? I'll lose my job."

"You just go on home. I'm sure you'll get a reward of some kind for this. You have a way home? How far away do you live?"

"About three kilometers out of town. At this hour, there won't be any public transportation. How can I go?"

"Look, just get dressed. We'll go down to the lobby together and get you a taxi. Hurry up."

Tom was snoring.

"Tom, wake up! Come down to the lobby with me. I don't want to be caught alone now." I shook him.

"What? What's going on...oh, it's you. What happened? I dozed off again."

"Come down to the lobby with us. C'mon."

We had no trouble finding a taxi, even at that hour. There was one right at the main entrance to the hotel. I gave the driver ten rubles and told him Katya would give him directions. We decided to walk the two flights back to our room. As we climbed the stairs, neither of us said a word. I tried to recall how all this had happened. What awaited me now?

We sat down at the table in the living area in our suite. After a few minutes of silence, Tom spoke.

"What're we going to do now, Yasha?

"I don't know. Maybe we'll call the embassy in the morning and tell them you're sick and we have to abort the rest of the trip."

"Are you going to report this when we get back?"

I pointed to the chandelier above the table and then to his ears.

"I don't know what I'm going to do," I nodded my head in the affirmative. "I think we should just get to bed and sleep on this. In the morning, we'll have clearer heads." As I said this, I wrote a note and pushed it over to Tom. The note said "We can talk out on the street tomorrow."

"Yeah, I think you're right," said Tom. "Let's sleep on it."

We both got ready for bed and turned the lights out. Before I got into bed, I walked over to the window. Parting the curtains, I looked out into the street and saw the same taxi I had just put Katya in. I could tell by the dent in the front door. Two men were standing by the back window talking to someone inside the vehicle. It was too dark to identify the faces, but I was sure the passenger was a woman.

THE PITCH

I awoke to rays of warm sunshine coming through the hotel window. This told me I had slept well into the morning, as the January sun didn't rise in Rovno until about 9 o'clock. Tom was still asleep. Or still passed out. I got up, went to the bathroom, splashed cold water on my face and let out a muffled "wheeew!" As my mind cleared, memories of the previous night's incident rushed forward. *What would today bring?*

I had considered calling the embassy last night, just after everyone had departed, but thought better of it. A call would have forced someone at the embassy to get up in the middle of the night and, besides, I didn't want the Soviets to think I was in a panic. I decided to call in the morning and tell the office Tom wasn't feeling well, which was true. For that reason we had decided to abort our trip.

I brushed my teeth with water from the faucet. I wondered how many bacteria got into my system in the process. In any case, I was confident whatever bacteria entered via my toothbrush would be killed by the stuff I took into my body the night before. I had no headache, which was a mixed blessing. Knowing I rarely suffered from hangovers, I had a tendency sometimes to go just a little too far when I drank. Generally, I was proud of my ability to drink with the Russians and, until last night's incident, thought I controlled my intake of cognac at the New Year's festivities. Of course, there was the possibility that someone had put something into the cognac bottle. I was sure someone had slipped Tom something. I went over to Tom's bed.

"Hey, old man. Get up. It's almost noon."

Tom made some unintelligible sounds and rolled over. I wetted a cloth with cold water and laid it over Tom's face. That did the trick. His eyes came open and he sat up abruptly.

"What the hell?"

"Tom, get up. We have to call the embassy and then pack up to go home. Let's go get something in our bellies."

"No way, man. I feel like I've been hit with a T-72 tank."

"Well, that might be the case, figuratively speaking. You were really out of it last night. Do you remember anything?"

Tom stared into space for a few seconds.

"Yeah, I remember we had some kind of Chinese fire drill here in the room last night. What happened? Who were those people?"

"I'll tell you about it at breakfast. Let's go down to the restaurant and at least get some kasha and coffee."

"The coffee sounds good. Give me a few minutes." He got up and tried to straighten out the clothes he had slept in.

The *dezhurnaya* was a different woman. Still, she smirked at us when we turned in our key and started down the steps. When we entered the restaurant, which had been cleaned up from last night's party, everything looked normal. Although there were other people in the restaurant, I recognized no one from the night before. The KGB had apparently changed surveillance teams and there were no obvious goon candidates. The *maitre d'* took us to an empty table.

"You think everyone knows about what happened last night?" I asked.

"If they do, they know more than I do," Tom said laughing.

"After breakfast we'll go for a walk and I'll fill you in."

I called to a waiter standing near the kitchen.

"Two kashas and a pot of coffee."

"No kasha today. Besides, it's noon. I'll bring the coffee while you look at the menu."

After what turned out to be a lunch of noodles and an unidentifiable cut of beef, neither of which Tom could eat, we stepped outside the hotel. I lit my pipe and we started walking down the street. When I explained what had happened the night before, Tom became agitated.

"Did they get pictures?"

"I'll say. And they tried to get me to sign an *akt*. I told them to piss off."

"What's next?"

"First let's check out the car. If it starts, we'll drive back to Kiev and fly or take a train out of there back to Moscow. We'll use the excuse that you're sick. That's what we're going to tell the embassy."

When I tried to start the car, nothing happened. No ignition.

"I was afraid of this. The bastards have been messing around with the car. They don't want us to leave today."

"Christ, Yasha. What're we going to do?"

"First we'll call the embassy and then I'll go to Intourist. I want to get out of here as soon as possible. The main thing is we don't want the Soviets to know how we're going to react when we get back to Moscow."

"How are we going to react? What do you plan to do?"

"Well, I'll definitely report the incident. If I don't, they've got me."

"And me."

"Don't worry. I think I can get you off the hook. Someone slipped you a Mickey. You had nothing to do with my fiasco."

The telephone circuits in Moscow were busy when I tried to call the embassy from our room. On my second attempt, an operator came on and said the lines to Moscow were temporarily down. I was to try again later. Tom and I went down to the lobby where I inquired whether we could get a plane or train out to Moscow. The Intourist agent was a petite blond.

"I'm sorry. We have no flights to Moscow today and there are no seats available on the train."

"Surely, you can find something. Even third class. We'd be willing to sit up all night. We're American diplomats and must return to our embassy in Moscow."

"Yes, of course. I know who you are."

The girl smiled. I wondered how much she really knew.

"But I'm afraid I can't do anything for you today. Maybe tomorrow. Just enjoy your stay in Rovno and we'll see what we can do for you."

"Sure. Thanks a lot."

I tried to be as nonchalant as possible. I didn't want the Soviets to think I was desperate. Tom was completely passive, still attempting to straighten out his head.

As we were returning to our room, I noticed two men standing at the elevator on the second floor. The "down" light was on. They caught my attention because it was unusual for people to use an elevator to go down. The rule of thumb was "ride up, walk down." It was supposed to save on wear and tear of elevators. A good rule also because using an elevator was always a chancy thing anyway. I thought one of the men at the elevator looked familiar. I walked by them and then stopped.

"Just a second, Tom."

I turned around and looked back. Neither man paid any attention to me. I stared at the one man, who turned away from my gaze. I was right. I knew who he was.

"What was that about?" Tom asked.

"You go on to the room. I'll be right there and explain."

I walked up to the two men who were still standing by the elevator.

"Colonel Kanavin?" He looked at me, as if he didn't know who I was.

"Yes?"

"I'm Major Holbrook."

"Yes. And you... you're an American?"

"Right. We know each other from the Military Liaison Mission in Potsdam."

"Of course, of course. You're Mr. Holbrook."

We shook hands. Kanavin introduced the other man as his brother-in-law Ivan Ivanov. (That name is as common as John Smith in the U.S.)

"What are you doing here?"

"I'm traveling with my colleague, Lieutenant Colonel Spencer, whom I believe you know also. We're military attachés in Moscow."

"Well, this really is a coincidence," Kanavin said. "Why don't the two of you join me for dinner this evening."

"That would be very nice. What time?"

"Let's say 8 p.m."

"Fine. We'll see you then.

When I got back to the room, I said to Tom, "Guess who I just ran into in the hallway."

"Who?"

"Our friend Colonel Igor Kanavin. Remember him from Potsdam?"

"Of course. What a coincidence."

"That's what he said, but I have a feeling this is no coincidence."

"What do you suppose he's doing here?"

"I think we're going to find out soon what the next step is in their plan."

Both Tom and I had served at USMLM in Potsdam, East Germany, before being assigned to the American Embassy in Moscow. Tom departed just before I arrived at Potsdam. Consequently, we had never traveled together in East Germany. But we both knew Colonel Kanavin, who at the time was the Soviet Army's chief contact with the military liaison missions from the US and British armies. Kanavin had attended many official U.S.-Soviet social events and was well thought of by the Americans as an intelligent and sophisticated officer. It had been three years since I last saw him.

Curious about Kanavin and a bit nervous about the immediate future, we decided to go back down to the street and try to start our car again. No luck. We agreed to stay away from the hotel for the rest of the day and spent the afternoon looking for tourist attractions. During our excursion about town, Tom and I picked up a couple of surveillance teams. Completely normal. Nothing suggested that something special might be brewing.

When we returned to the hotel in the late afternoon, I tried again to reach the embassy in Moscow. I was told the embassy switchboard wasn't answering. By now it was clear the Soviets were holding the two of us incommunicado. No way to contact the embassy. No way to get out of town. Surely something had to happen soon.

During the afternoon walk, Tom and I discussed what we would do when we finally got back to Moscow. I assured him I intended to report the incident fully. Things might not work out too well for me, but this was one of those eventualities for which I had planned for years. It was something I had always promised myself I would do as a way of keeping myself immune to KGB pressure. There was no question in my mind about it.

All my adult life, I had developed certain scenarios and programmed reactions to them. For example, if I were asked to try drugs, I would refuse outright. If someone ever jumped into my car at a stoplight, I would gun the car in order to cause an accident. And if I ever got in trouble with the KGB or any other foreign intelligence service, I would report it immediately. I had never expected the KGB to go this far; I thought they knew me better than that. But now that it had happened, I was going to see it through. It was time for me to prove my resolve. All day long I tried to reassure Tom that I would take all the responsibility on myself.

When we got to the restaurant, Colonel Kanavin was already seated at a table by himself. We walked up and greeted him.

"So, Colonel Kanavin. You remember Lieutenant Colonel Spencer?"

"Sure. Nice to see you again Mr. Spencer."

He shook hands with Tom.

"Would you like a glass of cognac?" I asked.

"No, thank you. I'm drinking wine. Beside, cognac does funny things to me. It's a dangerous drink, Mr. Holbrook."

"Yes, perhaps. Incidentally, Colonel, I've been meaning to ask this question of a Soviet officer for some time. Why don't you ever address us by our ranks? You always call us 'mister.'"

"It's that... We don't... We use ranks as a form of address only among our socialist brothers and comrades-at-arms. For foreigners we use "Mister," or "Herr" or "Signor," depending on the foreigner's native language. We consider "Mr." a polite form. But if you would like me to call you by your ranks, that's OK too."

"It doesn't matter, I guess. I was just curious."

Tom spoke up. "What are you doing in Rovno, Colonel?"

"It's like I told Mr. ...er, Major Holbrook here, my brother-in-law and I are shopping. I'm looking for a hair dryer for my wife. The one I bought in the GDR has burned up. But it was five years old anyway. Having a devil of a time finding one here. And you? What are you doing here, Colonel?"

"Well, as you know, military attachés like to travel all around their host countries and observe how things are going. All diplomats do that as part of their duties. Your Soviet attachés do the same in the U.S.," Tom replied.

"I see your Russian has improved."

"Yes, he works on it all the time," I said. "What a small world, Colonel. Imagine running into each other like this. In a country as big as the USSR."

Kanavin nodded and smiled. "I was just thinking the same thing."

We discussed our families. Kanavin said he had a dog now. We asked what kind. He said a "dog." After a little confusion about just what kind of a dog it was, Kanavin drew a picture on a piece of scrap paper. It turned out "dog" was the Russian name for a Great Dane.

So do you enjoy Rovno? How has your trip gone so far?" Kanavin asked.

Tom looked at me. I quickly answered, "Fine. But we haven't found many tourist sites in town."

"Where are you going from here?"

"We were on our way to Lvov..."

"But I've caught a bug or something," Tom said. "I think we should return to Moscow."

"I live in Lvov. I'm assigned to the Military District HQ there."

Colonel Kanavin pulled out a pack of cigarettes and offered one to each of us. We politely declined. Just as he lit up a cigarette, a waiter came over to the table.

"No smoking in the restaurant."

Kanavin looked surprised. He said nothing to the waiter, but looked around the restaurant. No one was smoking. He snuffed out the cigarette on a saucer and put it back in the package. I assumed either the waiter didn't know Kanavin was GRU or this was all staged. Soviet security people seldom bothered to observe such signs as "no smoking" or "no parking." Kanavin appeared to quickly recover.

"Would you like to step out for a smoke? It's getting so one can't smoke anywhere these days. And I remember you smoke a pipe, Major. Isn't that right?"

Did Kanavin remember Tom was not a smoker? Did he want to separate the two of us? Should I decline? Or should I continue to press to find out what was going on? I realized I was going to have to start making a lot of decisions quickly. Since I initiated the contact with Kanavin, I figured I might as well continue to push.

"Tom doesn't smoke, but I'll step out with you."

We got up from our table and walked toward the hotel entrance. Just as we reached the door, Tom mumbled, "Be careful" to me and then loud enough for both of us to hear, "I'll be in the room."

Kanavin and I stepped out onto the sidewalk. I offered him a Marlboro. Most Soviets preferred American cigarettes to Soviet *papirosy*, those half-cigarette-half-cardboard tubes. Kanavin gladly took the Marlboro. I remembered how in East Germany, Kanavin always smoked English cigarettes. He probably bought the old hair dryer he was talking about in our U.S. military store—the Berlin PX. Soviet officers assigned to Berlin had post-exchange privileges with us. Kanavin always seemed to enjoy living in close contact with the West. His wife, I remembered, dressed very stylishly for a Soviet. She seemed to have clothes none of the other Soviet officers' wives had.

"How's your wife?"

"Fine. It took her a little time to readjust to living in Lvov after the life of privilege in Potsdam and Wünsdorf. But she's settled in now. And yours?"

"Fine. She enjoys Moscow. Of course, now it's our turn to live the life of privilege, being diplomats and all that."

"But you Americans always live the life of privilege, don't you? And besides, Moscow is a lot different than Lvov. You'll see when you get there."

"That may be."

I wondered if Kanavin had caught the part about our returning to Moscow because Tom was ill.

"Let's go for a short walk and talk," the Soviet colonel suggested.

I hesitated for a moment, but then thought *"what the hell."* I was in their control anyway. I wasn't able to communicate with Moscow. Besides, maybe Kanavin would play the Soviet hand now.

"Sure. Why not?"

We walked for a few minutes without speaking. I wasn't sure whether Kanavin was waiting for me to say something, or whether he himself didn't know what to say. We began to discuss the pros and cons of Capitalism and Communism. I made a point that the Soviet system was a poor example of Communism. The Party seemed to have forgotten all the Communist ideals articulated by Karl Marx and Friedrich Engels. I recounted how once on Marx's birthday (5 May), I asked a Soviet officer if he knew what the day was. When he said no, I enlightened him. I told Kanavin I believed the only practical ideology of the Soviet Communist Party was based more on Lenin's and Stalin's techniques for maintaining absolute control over the population. Kanavin didn't argue with me, but insisted that Communism was still a vital ideology in the USSR.

Then out of nowhere, he stopped and turned to me.

"So, how's it really going? Are you having any problems on your trip?" he began.

So here it comes, I thought.

"No, everything's going fine. We had a little incident last evening in the hotel, but it's really nothing."

"What happened?"

I decided to give him a rough sketch of what went on. No sense pretending Kanavin didn't already know. "But it's nothing to be alarmed about."

"You may think that. But couldn't you get in trouble if your people found out what you did?

"Oh, I suppose I might."

"I have good contacts in Moscow. I could make sure your people never find out about your indiscretion. Would you like me to do that?"

I knew my next response would propel him in one direction or another. I was sure the KGB or GRU would be able to cover up the incident. But the day would come when they would want their payback.

"No, that's not necessary."

"It would be very simple for me. And then you could repay me by picking up a hair dryer for my wife when you get back to Moscow and sending it to me. I'll give you my mailing address. That's all there would be to it."

"I appreciate your wanting to help, but I think it was just a minor incident anyway. No need to make more out of it than that. I'd still be happy to get you the hair dryer. Just give me your address."

"When we get back to the hotel. I'll bring it down for breakfast tomorrow."

We turned around and started back for the hotel. There was no more talk of the incident or Kanavin's offer. Instead, we talked about the weather in the Ukraine compared to that in Moscow. Just as we parted, Kanavin volunteered that his room number was 335.

I found Tom in our room, watching TV.

"You were gone for some time."

"Kanavin and I went for a walk."

Tom's eyes lit up in anticipation of learning what transpired. I simply nodded my head and took out a piece of paper, where I wrote: "He promised to have the incident covered up. Said I could repay him by sending him a new hair dryer. A way too obvious first step toward recruiting me, don't you think?" We both chuckled.

"I think we can give up on the car," Tom said. "How long are we going to have to stay here? I tried to call the embassy again, but couldn't get through."

"I think we'll find that tomorrow things will go smoother."

The next morning Kanavin was not to be found in the restaurant. We had gone down early and sat drinking coffee for over an hour. I felt like things were being left up in the air. I was itching to take the next step, if for no other reason than to get on with our return to Moscow.

"Tom, I'm going by Kanavin's room. To see if he's still here and to ask for his address in Lvov."

As we walked up to our room, I stopped on the second floor landing. I told Tom to go on, that I would be back to the room in about ten minutes. On the third floor, the *dezhurnaya* eyed me suspiciously. When I tried to walk past her, she stopped me.

"Is your room on this floor?"

"No, I'm one floor down. I'm going to Colonel Kanavin's room for a minute. He asked me to come by."

"Oh. It's 335."

"Yes, I know."

I walked down the hallway and knocked on the door. When the door opened, it was the other man whom I had seen with Kanavin. His "brother-in-law."

"Is Colonel Kanavin here?"

"Is that you, Major Holbrook?" A voice called out from inside the room. "Come on in."

I saw a half-empty bottle of vodka, some bread and an empty sardine can on the coffee table.

"We decided to eat breakfast in our room," Kanavin said.

"Well, we're hoping to leave today and I wanted to stop by for your address so I could send you the dryer."

"Oh, yes. I forgot. Better yet, let me write my phone number down for you. If I'm at home when you're in Lvov, give me a call."

I took the slip of paper. "It was good running into you," I said.

Kanavin got up and walked to the door with me. He stepped out into the hall with me and spoke quietly.

"Don't forget my offer."

"Thanks again, but I doubt anything like that will be necessary."

As I walked back to my room, I looked at the paper and noticed the telephone number was a Moscow exchange. When I got back to the room, Tom told me that Intourist had called and said there had been a cancellation and now we could get two tickets on a plane to Moscow that left in the afternoon. He told the Intourist agent he would get back to them within the hour.

"I think we should try the car again."

I shook my head and spoke quietly to Tom.

"No, that would be a waste of time. I think they want us back in Moscow as fast as we can get there to see what our next move is."

As much as I wanted to get out of Rovno, I wasn't looking forward to what awaited me in my office. It was beginning to dawn on me that

I was in for some trouble with my own people. How would they react to Kanavin trying to pitch me?

And how would I explain to my wife, to my boss and to embassy security what I had done? How would they react? Would they relieve me from my assignment and send me home? Would they want me to string Kanavin along? I knew that if I remained in Moscow, the GRU or KGB would be approaching me again. I was also sure they were on their toes in Moscow to try to determine what I would do when I arrived back. I decided the longer I could keep the Soviet intelligence agencies guessing, the better it would be and the more options would be available for me. Despite the fact that I had always expected a pitch and had promised myself I would not fold under any pressure, I never realized how much was at stake when it actually happened.

We would be back in Moscow by early evening and I would soon find out what awaited an American military intelligence officer who had used poor judgment that led to being pitched by Soviet intelligence.

RETURN TO MOSCOW

We arrived back in Moscow in the evening and went straight to the embassy. Tom went up to our office. I went into the cafeteria and ordered a pizza and beer. In a few minutes the cafeteria telephone rang. One of the waitresses answered.

"Is Major Holbrook here?"

"Yes, over here."

It was Tom.

"You need to come up to the office as soon as possible."

"Let me get my pizza and I'll be right up."

When I got to the office, Tom was holding a telegram. As he handed it to me he rolled his eyes. The cable was from the Army Deputy Chief of Staff for Personnel. (Since the print on my copy of the cable has faded too much to be scanned and inserted here, I've copied it verbatim.)

141700Z JAN 81
FM CDR MILPERCEN ALEX VA // DAPC-OPD-J //
TO RUEHMY/USDAO MOSCOW USSR
INFO RUEADWD/DA WASHINGTON DC // DACS-DSZ-A //
BT
UNCLAS
SUBJECT: INTERVIEW FOR POSSIBLE ASGMT AS
AIDE TO THE VICE PRESIDENT OF THE UNITED
STATES
1.   MAJOR JAMES R. HOLBROOK HAS BEEN
SELECTED TO BE INTERVIEWED FOR POSSIBLE

ASSIGNMENT AS AIDE TO THE VICE PRESIDENT OF THE UNITED STATES.

2   INTERVIEWS WILL BE CONDUCTED IN WASHINGTON DC ON 21 JAN 81 AND PERHAPS ON 22 JAN. UNIFORM WILL BE GREENS. ANTICIPATE INTERVIEWS WITH PERSONNEL WITHIN THE OFFICE OF THE SECRETARY OF DEFENSE AND WITH THE OFFICE OF THE VICE PRESIDENT.

3.   ON MORNING OF 21 JANUARY, REPORT TO COL. C. MULLEN, OFFICE, CHIEF OF STAFF ARMY (OCSA), ROOM 3E669, THE PENTAGON. FOLLOW ON INTERVIEW SCHEDULE WILL BE AVAILABLE AT THAT TIME. UPON ARRIVAL IN WASHINGTON DC, CONTACT LTC GOODBARY (HOME 703-976 9546 / OFFICE 202-325 8127 / AUTOVON 221 8127) FOR REPORT TIME TO OCSA.

4.   FUND CITE: 212020 13-4000 P951212.9000-2112, 2130, 2119, 2199 S49092, APC IP9A CIC; 2 01 2020 013 49092

5.   PLEASE ACKNOWLEDGE RECEIPT OF THIS MESSAGE TO CDRMILPERCEN ALEX VA//DAPC-OPD-J //

I looked at the message again. "This must be some kind of joke?"

"Nope. That's an authentic message from Washington. So how do you like them apples?"

"I can't believe this."

I noticed that it was neither classified nor encrypted for transmittal. I wondered whether the Soviets knew about my possible appointment ahead of time. The message might as well have been sent in the clear, if in fact it wasn't. I looked at the date of the cable: 14 January 1981—the day after our incident in Rovno. There was no indication of precedence so it must have been routine. The Soviets might have read it before it even reached Moscow. Before the cable was finally sent on the 14th, I'm sure Army and the Transition Team personnel discussed my nomination for such a high position for several days in Washington, probably on unsecure phones. With the new Reagan-Bush administration about to take over the reins of our government, I was sure the Soviet intelligence was focused on the transition. Soviet paranoia about the Reagan Administration was exemplified by their "Operation Ryan." Soon after Reagan became President a joint KGB/GRU effort was launched— "Operation Ryan"—to determine the new administration's plans for a nuclear first strike. (See Christopher Andrew and Vasili Mitrokhin's *The World was Going Our Way.*)

None of this mattered anymore. I would have to respond to the message with a request that my name be taken out of consideration for the Vice-Presidential position.

Tom and I went home after about an hour at the embassy. If there were any Soviet employees watching to see how we behaved when we returned from Rovno, they would have to report that we spent little time at the embassy.

I spent an uncomfortable night at home. My wife Elaine asked me why we had come home early. I told her there had been some trouble on the trip and we decided to return to Moscow. I promised her details later.

What baffled me the most was why the KGB had sprung this on me at this time. Their conduct toward me these last few months in Moscow had given the impression they were handling me with kid gloves. I had transgressed against both Soviet and U.S. rules several times during my activities in Moscow. Why had the Soviets said nothing about my deliberate passing as a Soviet at Domodedovo Airport during troop rotation? They could have expelled me for that alone. Why hadn't they confronted me during or after my affair with Natasha? Their failure to do that suggested I wouldn't have to worry about any "honey trap." Why didn't they detain me or complain later to our DAO when I accidentally stumbled into the GRU complex at Khodinka? And what about the Soviet major's offer to personally introduce me to Army General Pavlovsky? The timing of Kanavin's recruitment attempt could have been related to my pending Vice-Presidential appointment.

I had banked on the KGB realizing I was, in fact, a fair, more or less objective observer of the Soviet scene. I made it a point to show some understanding for certain USSR policies when I talked to Soviet officers at receptions. Although I complained about Soviet behavior during our Iran hostage crisis, I told them I could see some basis for their concern and intervention in Afghanistan. That country on their border threatened to become anti-Soviet.

I also wondered whether the Rovno attempt to recruit me was a KGB or GRU operation. Kanavin was believed to be a GRU officer, but the GRU would never attempt recruitment of an American in the USSR without at least getting a go-ahead from the KGB. I never considered the GRU would be actively targeting Americans in Moscow. It seemed clear I still had a few things to learn. In any case, I believed Soviet intelligence had committed an egregious error. They needed people like me on the American side who tried to be objective about the USSR. How many intelligence officers genuinely tried to understand the other side?

In the end I decided that if it was ever in their plans to make a recruitment pass at me, their knowing I was probably leaving for the Washington assignment could have meant they had to act fast. They probably decided having a mole in the White House was worth scrapping any other plans they might have had for me. Colonel Kanavin was the clincher. In all the expanse of the Soviet Union, what were the odds we would meet in Rovno? And that just after the compromising incident the night before?

In the meantime, I discovered that in December our office received a report that a Soviet military attaché had left Washington abruptly. Supposedly, he had been the target of an FBI recruitment attempt. He apparently reported this to his embassy and was recalled. Was this another possible reason for the timing of the Rovno recruitment incident? The Soviets were notorious for their insistence on reciprocity. Our two countries often engaged in tit-for-tats. Or maybe they saw the circumstances provided them with a chance to kill two birds with one stone? Either recruit me or reduce my effectiveness as an intelligence officer.

I dreaded going to work in the morning. I was going to have to report the incident and didn't know how embassy officials would react. I didn't even know how I would react to whatever ideas came up. This incident didn't really fit into circumstances that obligated me to report to the CIA office. Or did it? No decision had yet been made about what we would do. My boss, the Army Attaché had seen the cable from Washington so it was natural to report first to him.

When I met with my colonel, I recommended he bring in the CIA. We sent a message to the Army respectfully requesting they withdraw my name from consideration for the Vice-Presidential job. The colonel commended me for reporting the incident and was generally very supportive. We were now using secure CIA channels for transmission of messages.

We then sent a message to DIA outlining the incident and requesting guidance on how to proceed. Within hours we received a cable from the Deputy Director of DIA, Major General Larkin (formerly our Defense Attaché). The message was simple. "Get Major Holbrook out ASAP. We'll work things out here in Washington."

There was some concern about whether the Soviets would actually let me out of the country. Regardless of my diplomatic status, we all knew the Soviets would do whatever they wanted, diplomatic niceties be damned. I needed a viable pretext for a sudden departure.

"I believe we can get some leverage from the cable in which I was nominated to be aide to the Vice-President," I said. "If they *did* read it, they might even be happy to see me go back."

"That's true," said the CIA representative. "Put in a request for a trip to DC and then tell the Soviet gals who work in the Admin office that you're leaving to interview for a job with the Vice- President. If they believe you, or already know about this, all the skids will be greased for your quick exit."

"What about Colonel Spencer?" asked my boss.

"General Larkin didn't say anything about Spencer being called back. Besides, the Vice-President job is more credible if Jim leaves by himself."

We began to make arrangements for me to leave on the first available flight. American attachés didn't require permission to travel back to the States, but as a courtesy we always informed the MOD when such trips were to take place. I prepared the necessary paperwork and personally took it down to the administrative office, where the Soviet secretaries made all travel and accommodation arrangements for embassy travel.

I went over to Tanya, whom several writers referred to as a possible "KGB colonel." She definitely was the boss of the administrative office.

"Tanya, I need an immediate flight to Washington, DC."

"What's up? Why so urgent?"

I leaned over and whispered in her ear, "I'm going back for a possible job as military aide to the new Vice-President. Please keep this as quiet as possible."

"OK, I'll see what I can do."

When I returned home late in the afternoon, I told Elaine we needed to go for a walk. That's what we always did when we wanted to discuss something privately. We assumed the Soviets' listening devices wouldn't be good enough to pick up our whispered conversation on the sidewalk, what with all the traffic. When we got out on the street, I explained that I had been set up in Rovno by the KGB and caught with a woman in my hotel room.

"What the hell did you think you were doing?"

"I don't know. Things just got out of hand."

"That's an understatement."

"I'm sure they were gunning for me. Colonel Kanavin... you remember him from Potsdam? Well, he showed up the morning after and made a thinly veiled attempt to recruit me. They had some kind of plan, but I didn't go for it. I'm surprised this didn't happen earlier."

"What do you mean?"

"I may have been causing the KGB some discomfort with my running about town and meeting with all types of Soviets."

"Well, you're causing me a little discomfort right now."

"I'm sorry, dear. But just stick with me for a little here. I need your support. I don't know what's going to happen when I get back to DC."

"And I don't know what I'll do when I get back."

I explained that I was to leave in a couple of days. I would be flying Lufthansa to Frankfurt and the next day on to Washington, DC. I planned to stay with our friends in the DC area when I arrived. I assured my wife DAO promised to take care of her and the children and to make arrangements for them to return to Washington at the end of the month.

EXILE
FAREWELL, RUSSIA!

17 January 1981. My suitcase was packed. I was about to go into exile from Moscow and the Soviet Union. A melodramatic way of putting it, perhaps, but that's how it felt to me. I would never be able to return to Russia.

I was sorry to be leaving, but at the same time something deep down was saying "Get out as soon as you can." I was focused on the next few hours and was still a little concerned whether the Soviets would let me out of Moscow. They had no idea what had transpired during the meetings at the embassy, but if somehow they had intercepted and read the cables going back and forth between the embassy and Washington, they might not want me to leave.

I wasn't actually thinking too much about the future. I was still stunned by the events of the past few days. My blood pressure was up. The embassy doctor gave me some Benadryl, which he said would calm my nerves. I decided to wait until I reached the airport to take a pill because I knew it would make me drowsy. Very few people knew I was leaving. After the news broke in the world media they would find out.

The embassy driver was waiting when I stepped out into the apartment quadrangle.

"Hello, Sasha."

"Good morning, Mr. Holbrook. We're going to Sheremetyevo, right?"

"Right. But I have a special request. Could we go through the center of the city? Past the Kremlin?"

"Of course."

Generally, I liked to talk to the drivers, but this morning I wanted no small talk. I was deep in thought as we traveled down Leninsky Prospekt toward the center of the city. I made a mental photograph of the landmarks. One was the gigantic statue of Yuri Gagarin near my apartment, which I had watched the Soviets erect. Its size and location—on the route all visiting VIPs took from Vnukovo Airport—spoke of justifiable Soviet pride for the first man in space. I thought of General Leonov, the first man to *walk* in space.

We did some maneuvering through October Square and took Yankimanka Boulevard toward the Kremlin. As we crossed the Bolshoi Kamenny Bridge over the Moscow River, I looked out the right window and imagined this was probably the last time I would ever see the Kremlin. The Kremlin itself had to be one of the most interesting government complexes in the world.

I would never be allowed back into Russia once the KGB and GRU concluded that I had reported everything fully upon return from Rovno. For the time being, however, I was banking on the Soviets believing I was returning for the Vice-Presidential Aide interview. I would be well placed and they knew I would be vulnerable to their overtures if I hadn't reported the incident to my own people.

How ironic that this was one of those very rare days in January when the sun shone. It was like Moscow was saying farewell to me. Surprisingly, the sunshine had the effect of making me feel sadder. Perhaps Moscow was taunting me. I could now imagine what it felt like to be sent into exile. I deeply regretted that I hadn't had a chance to make a last visit to the Tretyakov Art Gallery and say goodbye to Masha Lopukhina. Despite all the bad things about the Soviet Union, and there were plenty, I had developed an attraction to the country and its people who lived with the oppression of Communist Party rule. In the current Cold War struggle, being an intelligence officer and a Russian specialist was one of the more rewarding pursuits anyone could ask for.

Just past the Lenin library, as we drove along the back of the Kremlin, I saw a wedding party at the Tomb of the Unknown Soldier. Strange. Weddings usually occurred only on weekends. We turned onto

Gorky Street, past City Hall and Belorussky Railway Station, where I had spent many hours counting shave-headed conscripts during the semiannual Troop Rotations. North up Leningradsky Prospekt, past the Soviet Army sports complex Dynamo. The traffic had thinned out some and Sasha sped up. We turned onto Leningradskoye Shosse, which led to the airport.

I had arrived at Sheremetyevo I in 1979. Today I was departing from Sheremetyevo II. Designed and completed only a year earlier by West Germans for the 1980 Moscow Summer Olympics, the new Sheremetyevo II gave the appearance on the outside of being a modern western-style airport. When we pulled up at the passenger drop-off point, my thoughts quickly turned from the melancholy of my being exiled from Russia to those of wanting to get out of the Soviet Union quickly. I took the Benadryl.

Large numbers of travelers were bunched up at the regular customs gates, which made me appreciate the fact that I was carrying a diplomatic passport. As I approached the diplomatic customs gate, I began to wonder whether the KGB had given airport officials advance warning of my departure. Customs officials were usually brusque, even to diplomats, but I could put up with that because my diplomatic status allowed me to clear without luggage inspection. Still, I was uneasy because my experience in the USSR told me to expect anything from Soviet officials. I began to worry again about whether I would actually get out of the USSR today. What if the KGB didn't find out about my trip until after the tickets were issued? What if they didn't want me to leave? Would they concoct some incident here at the airport?

The customs inspector carefully looked at my ticket, but asked no questions. The check-in line at Lufthansa was short. I soon found myself in front of the passport control booth. No matter how many times we traveled in and out of the Soviet Union, this was always a tense moment, or sometimes a tense few minutes. I couldn't see what the young border guard was doing with my passport and visa. It was not until I heard the "clack, clack, clack" sound of his stamps on the documents that I could relax and assume detention was unlikely. Leaving a passport control booth and passing through the swinging gate into the waiting area usually felt like escaping from the Soviet Union. Today, however, I realized I was still on Soviet turf and anything could yet go wrong.

The sign on the waiting room window said Lufthansa flight No. 55 departed from Gate 10. I started down the corridor, but stopped at a small kiosk and bought an ice cream cone. This gave me time to casually look around again to see if there was anyone suspicious nearby. This didn't really help, however, as in my current state of mind, everyone looked suspicious. Finally I entered the lounge, laid my shoulder bag on a seat and placed my suitcase next to it. *One more ticket check, down the ramp, and onto the freedom bird. Only 15 minutes more to go.* I continued to scan the waiting area. There was only one couple with a small child beside me in the waiting lounge. Apparently, the flight was going to be far from full. Maybe that partly explained why I was able to get a ticket so quickly. Lufthansa flights were usually fully booked far in advance.

Movement on one of the overhead balconies caught my eye, but whoever it was quickly disappeared. I began to walk back and forth in the lounge. The loudspeakers blared announcements of arriving and departing flights, but I paid no attention. The minutes passed slowly. By now there should have been someone at the ticket gate, preparing to let passengers board the plane. But no one appeared. According to the clock in the lounge, half an hour had passed. Still no activity at the ticket gate.

Glancing back up at the balcony, I saw two men leaning over the rail. They were looking off in another direction and I couldn't see their faces. They were above Lounge 8, further down the corridor. I moved to the end of the lounge to get a closer look. Suddenly I realized I had just heard an airport announcement that had something to do with Lufthansa. I listened carefully. In a few moments the announcement was repeated, first in Russian and then in German and English: "Lufthansa flight No. 55 has switched gates. It is scheduled to depart at Gate 1. All passengers should now be on board."

Damn! That's on the other end of the passenger area!

I grabbed my suitcase and shoulder bag and ran out of the lounge into the corridor. I saw the two men turn to leave as I ran past Lounge 8.

When I reached Gate 1, there were no passengers in the lounge. A ticket taker still stood at the entrance to the ramp. When I approached the x-ray machine, the two women checking baggage waved me through. I ran over to the ramp.

"Mr. Holbrook, where have you been? The plane has been waiting for you."

"I was in Lounge No. 10, where the signs in the corridor said to go for this flight."

"Hurry up. Everyone is waiting just for you."

The woman taking tickets quickly collected my boarding pass and smiled at I began to run down the ramp.

"Have a nice flight, Mr. Holbrook."

A uniformed woman with Border Guard shoulder boards waited at the entrance to the plane.

"Mr. Holbrook, please hurry. They've been waiting for you."

The flight attendant said nothing. She simply took a quick look at my ticket and pointed to the row where I would find my seat. I entered the cabin of the Boeing 707. Everyone looked up at me. It was clear they had been seated for some time and were perturbed by the fact that the plane had been held up just for me. I felt a mixture of relief and embarrassment and addressed the passengers in German.

"Please forgive me. I was in the wrong lounge and didn't hear the gate change announcement in time."

Some passengers smiled; others maintained their disapproving expressions. I placed the suitcase above my seat and sat down. I realized I was breathing hard, but not just from exertion. I was breathing a long sigh of relief. Almost immediately I heard the pilot's announcement.

"Flight attendants, prepare for departure."

As I had witnessed several times before, as soon as the aircraft left Soviet ground and went wheels up, most of the passengers cheered and applauded. I couldn't bring myself to join in.

PHOTOS AND DOCUMENTS III

Sergei Vishnevsky with author at Spaso House picnic

Soviet jazz expert Georgii Bakhchiev

Book jacket from Frederick Starr's *Red and Hot*

**Marshal of the Soviet Union Nikolai Ogarkov,
Chief of Soviet General Staff**

Mishka Bear, Moscow Olympic mascot logo

24 января 80 г.

Многоуважаемый генерал Одом!

Пару слов с целью подтвердить «с места происходящего» уже Вам известный факт: Олимпиада 80 играет чрезвычайно важную роль в советской мировой пропаганде. Следовательно, предлагаемый бойкот со стороны США и других стран нанес бы чрезвычайно сильный удар авторитету и престижу правительства СССР.

История не часто дает такие возможности влиять на международные события без применения военной силы.

Теплый привет Анне и Марку.

Искренне,

Яша Холбрук, Москва

Author's 24 January 1980 letter to Brigadier General Odom

Farewell party flyer

**Soviet Order of Victory, one of which was
awarded to General Eisenhower**

The author, Admiral Foley and official Soviet guide

Author and Elaine with Rumanian Defense Attaché

CIA-produced *Moscow* Guide, 1980

Communist Party "Iconostasis" at Domodedovo Airport

Pass to Red Square Parade on 7 November, 1979

Author with other military attachés on Red Square, May 1979

**Photo of Leonid Brezhnev atop Lenin
Mausoleum taken by author**

Author (left) on Gorky Street with Soviet tank, 7 November 1980

Photographing halted tank at choke point, 7 November 1980

Colonel Kanavin (holding box) at a Potsdam meeting of
the American and Soviet CINCs. Behind Kanavin is U.S.
Major Rich Kosevich; left to right in front of Kanavin
are: U.S. General Blanchard, Soviet Senior Lieutenant
Yegorov and Soviet General of the Army Ivanovsky

Kanavin's drawing of his "Dog"

AFTERWORD

So what happened next? In the first place, my exile lasted only a little over nine years. In the spring of 1990, now a civilian, I joined a Pan Am tour group for a two-week trip to the Soviet Union. I had no difficulty getting a visa. In 1991, as a senior research analyst at the Science Applications International Corporation (SAIC) think tank in Denver, I attended a NATO conference in Moscow. In 1992, after the collapse of the USSR, I spent a two-week vacation in Moscow as a normal foreign tourist. In 1994, Dr. John Battilega, one of the SAIC directors of the office where I worked, and I traveled to Russia on business. During all those visits I encountered no overt or obvious surveillance. Such was the case also in 1994-96, when I returned to work in Moscow as a civilian contractor.

Immediately upon my return from Moscow to Washington in January 1981, Defense and Army counterintelligence personnel subjected me to an intensive interrogation. Counterintelligence personnel seemed to hope that perhaps they had a real Soviet spy on their hands. Despite providing full disclosure of my activities in Moscow and passing a polygraph test, later that year I lost my top secret and special compartmented intelligence access.

On 16 February 1981, *The Washington Post* published a front-page story on my incident in Rovno. Although not entirely accurate, the story was near enough to the truth to suggest someone at the U.S. Embassy had leaked it to *Washington Post's* Kevin Klose. This was followed by stories in other U.S. and world newspapers. That same evening, on the CBS Evening News, Walter Cronkite reported:

> The U.S. Assistant Military Attaché, Army Major
> James Holbrook, was said to have been set up in what
> was described as a crude attempt to compromise him.
> But he reported it to his superiors and was immediately

sent home to Virginia. What makes the story interesting is that Holbrook was under consideration as a possible military assistant to Vice President Bush. The question on which American authorities refuse to speculate: Did Soviet intelligence know that, and were they trying to plant a spy right in the White House?

Four days later, the Soviet news agency TASS published a scurrilous item about our incident in Rovno. Very little of what they reported was true. TASS even misspelled my name, although the Soviets had the correct spelling on record in Moscow.

The *Washington Post* article and Walter Cronkite's report were followed on 2 March by an article in *Time* magazine, including a picture of me. People began to recognize me on the street. Obviously, my family and I felt the stress of this increased and unwelcome notoriety. Elaine and I soon separated and later divorced.

Without my top clearances, I could no longer work directly in intelligence. My friends and colleagues at NSA came to my aid by taking me on as a Senior Research Linguist at the National Cryptologic School, a position that required only a secret clearance., As a staff sergeant, I had taught Russian at NSA in 1964-65.

While at NSA, I began to fight to have my top secret clearances returned. In the process, I obtained a copy of the Army's memorandum nominating me as "Junior Aide to the President of the United States." (See Appendix A) The memorandum was dated 16 December, a full month before my incident in Rovno.

That my efforts to regain all my clearances finally paid off is due in part to the efforts of an FBI agent. Word had come to me, I don't remember from where, that an FBI expert on counterintelligence, David Major, was using my case in his lectures and had stated I should have been decorated, rather than have my clearances pulled. My lawyer and I visited and deposed him. I then used his statement as part of my application for a reversal of the Army's decision. (A copy of the deposition report is at Appendix B.)

While at NSA (1981-86), I was promoted to lieutenant colonel, taught Russian and did research on Colloquial Russian—the topic of my doctoral dissertation. From NSA the Army assigned me in 1986 to the faculty of the U.S. Army Command and General Staff College (CGSC) at Fort Leavenworth, Kansas. There I was Chief of the Historical Research Committee and taught American and Soviet military history.

In the late 1980s, the "joint was jumpin" in the Soviet Union as a result of Mikhail Gorbachyov's reforms, especially *glasnost*. Reading about all this in Soviet magazines and newspapers at CGSC, I felt I was missing out on the action. I wanted to resume my work as an analyst of what was happening in Moscow.

In 1988, during a vacation in Colorado, I visited a think tank in Denver and became convinced it was time to retire from the Army. Upon return to Fort Leavenworth, I put in my retirement papers. I left the Army on 1 August 1989 and went to work immediately for the think tank—the Foreign Systems Research Center (FSRC), a unit of SAIC. This organization attracted me because of its efforts to analyze various Soviet political and military issues on the basis of how and why the Soviets arrived at their technical and policy decisions. Working there gave me the opportunity to work with two of the top experts in this field—Directors Dr. John Battilega and Judy Grange. Doing research and writing papers at FSRC brought me back into the Soviet studies fold. In early 1994, I went on that business trip to Russia with Dr. Battilega.

As relations between the USSR/Russia relaxed in the early 1990s, FSRC hosted various Soviet/Russian scientists and military officers. For example, the editors-in-chief of the Soviet *Military History Journal* and the Soviet General Staff journal *Military Thought* visited FSRC in Denver. A retired Soviet colonel, who had been an operations analyst on the Soviet General Staff, visited us and provided insights into several projects we were working on. I briefed them all in Russian and, together with my son, Yasha, who at the time was also working at FSRC, coordinated all the interpreting.

At the Soviet Army Studies Office at Fort Leavenworth, I met former KGB Colonel Vladimir Rubanov. He became a leader in the reforms the new KGB Chairman, Vadim Bakatin, was trying to put into effect after the demise of the Soviet Union. I later visited Rubanov and his family in Moscow.

A unique opportunity arose in mid-1994. SAIC sent me to Moscow as chief of an American-Russian translator team tasked with producing a glossary to be used in the joint U.S.-Russian chemical demilitarization project.

I found Moscow to be almost an entirely different world under the new Russian regime. My office was in a formerly top-secret research institute. The Central Airfield, which the Soviets used to assemble equipment for the 7 November parades, was now a public museum and a park where Americans held a Fourth of July celebration in 1995. I was able to visit the grave of General Ivanovsky (former CINC, Soviet Forces in East Germany) at Novodevichy Cemetery.

In 1995, I stood on the overlook at Sparrow Hills and watched and videotaped the breathtaking fireworks all across the city as the Russians celebrated the 50th anniversary of the defeat of Nazi Germany during the "Great Patriotic War."

I finally was able to meet and thank Professor Elena Zemskaya at the Academy of Sciences Russian Language Institute for the help she and other scholars had given me many years earlier when I was writing my doctoral dissertation. *Red Star*, the central Russian military newspaper, interviewed me and later published one of my short stories. One sad note during this final sojourn in Moscow was that my jazz friend, Georgii Bakhchiev, died in 1995. I participated in his New Orleans-style funeral that was organized by Moscow jazz musicians.

Upon completion of my work on the chemical weapons glossary in 1996, I returned to Colorado and retired from SAIC. I've been reading and writing since then.

Research for this memoir and reflections on my life in Moscow and, in particular, the incident in Rovno, Ukraine, convinced me that Soviet SIGINT played a role in the Soviet attempt to recruit me. They were capable either at their old embassy on 16th Street in Washington, DC, or the new embassy at Mount Alto, or perhaps from several other collection sites in the city, of becoming aware of my impending nomination to be an aide to the President or Vice President. On the roof of the 16th Street embassy (not far from the White House) were 12 antennas, many more than were necessary for communications with Moscow or their consulates in the U.S. or for local TV reception. Some distance away, the new embassy being built at Mount Alto was at an altitude of 350 feet—third highest point in Washington. It had a direct intercept line to the Capitol, the White House, the Pentagon and the State Department. Although not fully occupied until 1991, some of the new embassy apartments were being used as early as 1979. Given the strategic location of the new embassy for electronic warfare, it takes little imagination to speculate who and what occupied those apartments.

It is probable, if or when the Soviets found out about my nomination, they realized I would be leaving Moscow and it was either now or never to approach me. Although Colonel Kanavin was likely GRU, the KGB decided to use him for the approach because he and I had known each other in East Germany. My own behavior in Moscow may have given them reason to believe they could trap me.

Although the KGB failed to recruit me, they still came out on top. For them it was a win-win situation. If I accepted their offer of help, they had me, perhaps for later use. If I turned them down, which I did, they knew they would have successfully neutralized me. The KGB was well aware of the fate of any intelligence officers around the world who are pitched by the opposition. General Victor Cherkashin and Gregory Feifer wrote in their *Spy Handler: Memoir of a KGB Officer*:

> The KGB wasn't unique in returning intelligence officers targeted in recruitment attempts by the other side. It meant, first of all, that they were known to the adversary. There was also the possibility that they'd accepted an offer, no matter how convincingly they denied it. Even in cases where they clearly turned "pitches" down, they nonetheless remained tainted.

In my case, the KGB calculated correctly. Although eventually I had my top clearances restored and was able to work on top secret matters again, both in the Army and as a civilian, it was unlikely I would ever work in high-level intelligence again.

Russian Leaders

Due to the current (2018) cooling of U.S.-Russian relations, I leave the reader with the following quotes to ponder when assessing the "new" Russia and its leadership:

> Today I am able to conclude that the deification of Stalin, or the "cult of the personality," as it is now called, was at least as much the work of Stalin's circle and the bureaucracy, who required such a leader, as it was his own doing.

Milovan Djilas, *Conversations with Stalin*

> Stalin paced the room [in 1926] and said, "Yes, this is true—the party, the CC, the politburo. But consider, the people understand little of this. For centuries the people in Russia were under a tsar. The Russian people are tsarist. For many centuries the Russian people, especially the Russian peasants, have been accustomed to one person being at the head. And now there should be one."

Stephen Kotkin, *Stalin*

> Our country has a tsarist mentality, it's subconsciously tsarist. Geneticall.y. Everyone needs a Tsar. Ivan the Terrible…is remembered with fear and awe. The same goes for Peter the Great and Stalin. While Alexander II, the Liberator…who abolished serfdom…he was murdered. [We] need a Tsar. The Tsar, the Father of the Russian people! Whether it's a general secretary or a president, it has to be a Tsar.

A former Kremlin insider, quoted by
Svetlana Alexievich in *Second Hand Time*

APPENDIX A
U.S. ARMY RECOMMENDATION AS AIDE TO THE PRESIDENT
(Copy)

SPECIAL JUSTIFICATION
MAJOR JAMES ROGER HOLBROOK

1. Major Holbrook is a natural selection for the position of Junior Aide to the President. He has specialized in international security affairs for the past six years at Headquarters, U.S. Army Europe, Office of the Chief of Staff Army, and currently as Assistant Military Attaché, Moscow. Major Holbrook has consistently proven himself capable of assuming greater responsibility.

2. Major Holbrook has undergraduate, graduate, and PhD degrees in foreign languages and taught Russian for three years at West Point. The Assistant Director of Instruction at the Military Academy's Department of Foreign Languages described Major Holbrook as the most outstanding instructor in the Russian Group in his memory and as one of those very rare Americans who has mastered Russian to the point of near-native fluency. During his service at Headquarters, US Army Europe, Major Holbrook quickly became recognized as the authority on Warsaw Pact forces and is currently being acclaimed as an "absolute pace-setter" at the US Embassy in Moscow.

3. Regarded as without peer in his many intelligence duties, Major Holbrook has established himself as an outstanding academician as well. He has been lauded as a superior researcher, writer and orator. He possesses a wealth of knowledge and experience in military and international affairs, and is an absolutely outstanding representative of the US Army. Major Holbrook has received the highest acclaim from all those with whom he has been associated during his thirteen years of military service. Extremely intelligent, unusually versatile and resoundingly energetic, this officer stands far above his contemporaries as a soldier, leader and manager.

    US Army Military Personnel Center
    Justification for Appointment as
Junior Aide to the President of the
United States
    16 December 1980 (Attached as
Incl to DAPC-OPC-M Memo, 17 Feb 81)

Appendix B
Deposition of FBI Special Agent David Major
[Copy]

===

CPT SANDUL: Mr. Major, would you please tell us your full name and job title?

MR. MAJOR: My name is David Gregory Major. I am the Supervisory Special Agent Foreign Counterintelligence Program Manager and the International Terrorism Program Manager of the Baltimore Division.

CPT SANDUL: What is your background and experience in dealing with intelligence measures?

MR. MAJOR: Since joining the FBI in 1970, I have been assigned to the following field offices: Tampa and Sarasota, Florida; Newark, New Jersey; Washington, DC; and Baltimore, Maryland. Since 1971 I have been working in Foreign Counterintelligence. I conducted foreign counterintelligence investigations in the Newark, New Jersey and New York areas and the Washington Field Office. The majority of those investigations were directed against Soviet intelligence. In 1980, I was assigned to the Federal Bureau of Investigation Headquarters as SCI Control Officer. From 1981 to 1984, I was assigned to the Intelligence Division in the FBI Training Unit. I was responsible for training FBI Agents and others in the intelligence community how to conduct Foreign Counterintelligence investigations. Since May of 1984, I have been the Foreign Intelligence Program Manager at the Baltimore Division for the states of Maryland and Delaware.

CPT SANDUL: If an individual is granted an SCI access, are there any assurances that that individual will not become a security risk?

MR. MAJOR: There are never any such assurances. What has been determined when such access is granted is that the individual is not a sociopath, in other words, that he is not in conflict with society. Anyone with a security clearance is a potential target for recruitment by foreign intelligence.

CPT SANDUL: Is there a distinction between compromise and recruitment, and, if so, what is the distinction?

MR. MAJOR: Anyone who works in the intelligence field is a potential target. When a person is identified as a potential target for recruitment, assessment data is gathered for a recruitment operation. Recruitment operations differ depending on where they occur. In the United States, hostile intelligence services do not generally employ compromise as a means of recruitment. People are not blackmailed. The reason is very simple, that is, it is the least productive way to go about recruiting in this country. Because the hostile intelligence services do not own the environment, they do not have control when they operate in the United States. It is a different situation in their own country. There, they have control. The Russian KGB, for example, has two different directorates for recruitment. One of the directorates runs operations abroad and the other, the internal service, runs the operations within their own country. The internal service may target anyone who has access to classified information. Because they own the environment, they can compromise anyone at anytime. Once someone has been compromised or gotten into trouble, they will offer to assist that person to solve the problem. At that time, the intelligence service will have two possible goals. The first goal is recruitment of the individual. The second goal, if recruitment fails, is to neutralize their effectiveness. Our intelligence services do the same thing within the United States. If the person who has been compromised agrees to work for the foreign intelligence service, that intelligence service has attained its first goal. If the person does not and reports the attempt to his own people, he generally will be taken out of the country. Therefore, he has been neutralized and the second goal has been attained. The Soviets know that the individual's own intelligence service will have a "knee jerk" reaction and treat him as a problem. If the intelligence service reacts in that way, however, it has failed to assess the situation and properly to realize that this was one of the results desired by the hostile intelligence service.

CPT SANDUL: What is the general policy within the United States intelligence community with regard to attempts at compromise or recruitment of an individual?

MR. MAJOR: The underlying premise is that the individual must immediately report the attempt. That is the foundation of all security programs. It is stressed by the FBI, the Department of Defense, National Security Agency, and the State Department.

CPT SANDUL: How can you ensure that an individual who has been approached will report it?

MR. MAJOR: He must be convinced that he has done the right thing and that he won't be punished for it. That's important, not only to the individual, but to everyone else who knows him or knows about his situation. It impacts on the entire security system. We try to stress that everyone is vulnerable because everyone is human. Experience has shown that if a person goes along with the hostile intelligence service himself, then we have got real trouble.

CPT SANDUL: What happens to an individual who reports a compromise or recruitment attempt?

MR. MAJOR: It can be misread if people are not familiar with the operations of intelligence services. Some people immediately think it is necessary to determine why a particular person became a target. It is my professional opinion that it is our own responsibility as a security service to break through that kind of thinking. Everyone is vulnerable.

CPT SANDUL: If a person reports a compromise or a recruitment attempt, what does that indicate about his future security reliability?

MR. MAJOR: It makes him a better security risk for three reasons. First, he has become a true believer. A person always feels that it will never happen to him. When it does, he becomes much more sensitive to security concerns. He'll ask himself "How did I let myself get into this situation?" And conclude, "I'll never do that again." Second, he has proved himself under fire. He used his best judgment in the worst situation and that's very important. Third, once he has reported himself to his own intelligence service, he will not be approached again. If he did not report himself, they'll take another run at him because he has already become a co-conspirator. At that point, the recruitment has already moved to the next phase. Recruitment is a complicated flow of interrelated events leading to a clandestine relationship. I know of no cases where an individual who has reported a recruitment attempt has ever committed espionage. The hostile intelligence service is looking for the person who did not report the attempt.

CPT SANDUL: In your experience, has LTC Holbrook's situation had any impact within the United States intelligence community?

MR. MAJOR: As I have traveled around the country in my capacity as an FBI trainer and briefer on foreign counterintelligence, I have been asked many times about the Holbrook case. I have described it as a classic recruitment operation, which failed precisely because LTC Holbrook reported it. A number of people have expressed concern about what would happen to them if they reacted as LTC Holbrook had, and reported themselves compromised, or were the targets of a recruitment attempt. LTC Holbrook is a very high profile figure and his situation is very familiar to the people who work against the Soviet intelligence services. The final disposition of his case will have a ripple effect on others. The significance of his situation goes beyond him as an individual. It will have a big effect on many security programs. It is amazing the number of people who know LTC Holbrook or know about his situation. Personally, I would like to use LTC Holbrook as a lecturer. I believe he should talk to everyone who will come into contact with the Soviet intelligence services. He would be able to give a first-hand account of what to expect from the Soviets.

I have read and fully understand the substance of this report. It is true and accurate to the best of my knowledge.

/s/
DAVID C. MAJOR
SPECIAL AGENT IN CHARGE
Foreign Counterintelligence
Baltimore Division

APPENDIX C
SOVIET GRU COLONEL
IGOR KANAVIN

Who was Soviet Colonel Igor Kanavin? Who was he working for in 1981 when he offered to help me out of a situation the KGB (and I) had created in Rovno?

As I've noted in this book, I knew Colonel Kanavin from our days together in East Germany. I say "together" because on several occasions we worked together at U.S.-Soviet social events. In fact, if I couldn't remember a word quickly enough when I was interpreting, Colonel Kanavin often quietly prompted me. At other times, I would be the interpreter when our USMLM Chief, Colonel Peter Thorsen, met with Kanavin to deliver an official protest. We were convinced Kanavin was a GRU officer, but he seemed always to be a gentleman. He appeared quite comfortable with Westerners. During social occasions, he and I were always on good terms, often quite casual with each other. At one point, I even suggested to our counterespionage personnel that Kavavin might be a good Prospekt for recruitment.

Over 25 years after I returned to the United States from Moscow, I began to hear rumors that Kanavin had been recruited by the CIA, found out and punished by being sent off to Central Asia. I had my doubts about that then and continue to have doubts about it today. In the first place, I believe if a GRU colonel is caught spying for the United States, he is executed. Such a death may not be as gruesome as Victor Suvorov portrays in his book, *Inside the Aquarium*. ("Aquarium" was the nickname of the GRU Headquarters building.) Suvorov describes the last minutes of a spy being placed alive into a furnace in the GRU Headquarters. That may be a GRU myth told to new officers, but I'm sure none of them ever doubted that a shot to the back of the head was a likely outcome for a Soviet traitor.

In 2007, an article, "The Secret War of General Ustinov," appeared in the Russian Army newspaper, *Red Star*. It was an excerpt from KGB General-Lieutenant Ivan Ustinov's memoirs. The general served in the "Military Counterintelligence Directorate" of the KGB. In his memoirs he stated that in 1978, a "certain Colonel Kanavin" came to Group of Soviet Forces, Germany (GSFG). Soviet counterintelligence apprehended the colonel when he received a package from a CIA officer during a Soviet officer excursion to West Berlin. Supposedly, the Americans had recruited him when he served in Thailand.

There were several discrepancies in this article if it referred to the Colonel Kanavin I knew. First of all, he had free movement in West Berlin and spent several evenings at events there. I remember one that was held at the West Berlin Officers' Club. Certainly, he didn't need to attach himself to a Soviet officer excursion group to go to West Berlin. Secondly, he didn't come to GSFG in 1978. I know for a fact he was there in 1976-1977.

Kanavin may have served in Thailand (I remember him saying he had spent some time in North Vietnam) and might have been recruited by the CIA. But if so, why was he attempting to recruit me? If he was working for the Americans at that time, was he just trying to see if I would take the bait and then report that back to U.S. counterintelligence? Or was he, as General Ustinov suggests in his memoirs, trying to get back into the good graces of the GRU/KGB?

I believe General Ustinov used bits and pieces from several cases to describe this Kanavin and his activities. This is a common tactic by intelligence agencies. By releasing some information and obscuring many details, enemy intelligence cannot discern the true nature or the source of the information.

Former Soviet officers from the unit Colonel Kanavin headed in East Germany have told former colleagues of mine from USMLM that Colonel Kanavin died. I will probably never know the answers to the questions I pose above. In any case, this story adds a possible new dimension to my incident in Rovno, Ukraine, in 1981.

APPENDIX D
AMERICANS FIGHTING IN
NORTHERN RUSSIA, 1918-1920

"On the morning of January 19, Mead was awakened by a heavy shelling. Over the crust of snow thirty inches deep, Mead saw a long skirmish line of gray-coated Bolsheviks emerge from the forest two thousand yards away. The Bolos were advancing with fixed bayonets. Mead rang Captain Odjard and told him the Bolos meant business. Odjard told him to delay the attackers as long as he could before pulling out.

"Mead got his small unit in a line and waited for the Bolos to draw closer for more telling fire. From immediately below the Yanks, suddenly materializing like ghosts on Walpurgis Night, white-clad Bolshevik infantrymen leaped from hiding places in the snow to charge upon Mead's startled platoon.

"One of the Yank machine guns raked the attackers and drove them back into the ravine. But the Bolos took a toll. Many of them bypassed the point itself and charged into Nijni Gora, where they killed unsuspecting Yanks who were rousing themselves from sleep.

"Mead signaled his men to get out. They dashed down the slope, darting to the right of the main street, which they discovered was covered by a Bolo machine gun. Yanks struggled through the back streets, hard movement because the snow reached their waists. Dashing from one peasant hut to another, they paused to gasp for breath in the rarefied air. They kept on until they came to the open space between Nijni Gora and Ust Pedenga. Here there was no cover and no path, nor was there helping fire, for the Cossacks had deserted at the first sound of battle. The temperature was forty-five degrees below."

Richard Goldhurst,
The Midnight War

"At noon a Bolshevik shell landed squarely on the blockhouse. 'It crumpled like paper,' as Lieutenant John Cudahy of the American infantry company described it. Two of the men inside were killed instantly; the others were badly wounded. Except for Private Charles Bell, who elected to stick by his machine gun in the shattered remains of the blockhouse despite an ugly face gash that left him scarred for life. The injured crawled out of the wreckage and across to the house of the Toulgas parish priest, twenty yards away. The bridge was now in danger of being taken by the Soviet infantry, who had been crouching at the edge of the forest waiting for the knockout blow on the blockhouse. As they charged for the bridge, however, three Americans, carrying a Lewis gun and panniers of ammunition, rushed from a peasant dwelling across the road from the ruined blockhouse, heading for a ditch alongside the house of the priest. Falling flat every few yards, and proceeding by zigzag rushes in between, they made the cover of the ditch, set up the machine gun, and turned back the Soviet charge on the bridge with lethally accurate fire. They were happy to find themselves assisted in this crisis by crossfire from a second American machine gun, which other doughboys had thoughtfully installed in the village church directly across the road from the priest's house. So it was that the Bolshevik infantry found themselves repulsed in their rush on the bridge, despite the fact that the American blockhouse had been reduced to splinters."

E. M. Halliday,
The Ignorant Armies

"The enemy, reported to have 2,700 men in Kodish, were supported by five pieces of artillery and a reserve force of 500. From every door and window they fired rifles or machineguns. Most bullets passed overhead...

"Responding to the repeated call: 'Medical man! Medical man!' I came upon a Lewis gun crew, including corporals Baker and Benson, and Pvt. Walter Franklin, on the edge of a wooded crest. Franklin, terribly wounded in the small of the back by a number of machine gun bullets, lay groaning in a slight hollow. He had been hit while loading pans.

"I concluded Franklin's wounds were mortal and had no heart to talk to him. He told the corporals that he was in too much pain to be carried except in a litter. In my condition I could not have carried him anyway. Sad that this fine Tennessee lad should meet such a fate so far from wife and home… Franklin died the next day after being removed from the rear…

"Just after leaving the forest I tripped on some hard object and went down just as a bullet whistled over me… It sounded as if the bullet passed exactly where my head had been. Regardless of flying bullets and being so physically weary that death would have been a delightful end, I stumbled on, often falling, until finally reaching the village and reporting to Sergeant Comstock…

"Thus ended the longest day of my life."

Private First Class Donald E. Carey,
Fighting the Bolsheviks

NOTE ON SOURCES

Since starting to work on this memoir in 1999, I've used many sources. First of all, faulty as it may be, is my own memory. So far as living conditions in Moscow were concerned, members of my family, including our nanny Holly, filled me in on some aspects.

At my request, the Defense Intelligence Agency declassified and sent me most of the Information Reports (IR) I had written in Moscow. These reports were crucial in: 1) providing an approximate timeline of my activities; 2) allowing me to discuss certain items that had been earlier classified; and 3) stimulating my memory regarding certain events. In some cases—for example, the evening with *Pravda* correspondent Sergei Vishnevsky—I was able to extract from my IR all the details that I had reported in 1980.

The many books and articles I've consulted over the years since my return from the USSR allowed me to elaborate, corroborate and add depth to certain little-known, but important historical topics and to shed more light on the contemporary scene in the Soviet Union in 1979-1980. I've identified these sources in my narrative, which I believe obviates the need for footnotes and makes the story go smoother.

KGB General-Major Rem Krasilnikov's book on counterintelligence against Americans in Moscow during my tour was helpful in establishing some background for the operations that went on there.

Acknowledgements

Many people helped me with this memoir by reading and making comments on various drafts. I am indebted to retired Army Brigadier General Randall Greenwalt, a former Defense Attaché in Moscow, retired Colonel Bernard McDaniel, a former Defense Attaché in Bonn, Germany, and Lonnie Knickmeier for reading and commenting on early versions. David Baker and Judy Myers contributed especially valuable comments, as they commented on each part of the near-final draft manuscript, chapter-by-chapter, page-by-page.

In addition to the help provided by my Moscow family, a special debt of gratitude is due to my daughter, Tarisa, who spent several days with me at the kitchen table, working on the final draft.

It's impossible to thank Colonel McDaniel enough for his advice on several topics and his relentless efforts in helping me cut through some of the red tape that came with getting the book reviewed and approved by Washington, DC intelligence agencies. He hand-carried (actually drove through horrendous Washington, DC traffic) several versions of the book to DIA.

I'm indebted to Mary McDaniel and my son, Yasha, for their diligent proofing as I prepared this second edition.

I owe special thanks to former FBI Special Agent David Major for his help during my turbulent years immediately after I returned from Moscow and for permission to reprint the deposition in Appendix B.

During the last four years, members of my writers' workshop at Happy Trails Resort in Surprise, Arizona, made significant contributions. They included: Beverly Anderson, Karen Cameron, Fran Daley, Duane Davis, Jim Ladd, Aina McCormick, Laura Perkins, Mary Ann Stohlman, Louise Watkins, Dee Weeder and Joanne Williams.

And last, as one would expect in this day and age, I frequently used Google and Wikipedia for some dates and other details.

Any mistakes in this final version, of course, are mine.

CREDITS

Cover Photo. Boris Sobolev (by permission)
All Maps. Dion Good, Cartographer (by permission)

PHOTOS AND DOCUMENTS I

Spaso House. U.S. Government (Public Domain)
Soviet Cosmonaut Alexei Leonov. (Public Domain, Wikipedia Commons)
American Embassy, Moscow. (NVO Google Earth)
SALT II Signing. Bill Fitz-Patrick (Public Domain)
Maria Lopukhina Portrait. (Public Domain, Wikimedia Commons)
Moscow Pool. Fmaschek (Wikimedia Commons)

PHOTOS AND DOCUMENTS II

"Bolshevik Prisoners." Ray Mentzer (Great War Primary Document Archive: Photos of the Great War)
"Babi Yar." Yash Holbrook (by permission)
"Brest Fortress Wall." Sergei Semyonov (Wikimedia Commons)
"Minox Camera." (Central Intelligence Agency, Public Domain)
"Mount Ararat." Serouj Ourishian (Wikimedia Commons)

PHOTOS AND DOCUMENTS III

Cover of "Red and Hot." Frederick Starr (by permission)
Marshal Nikolai Ogarkov. Central Intelligence Agency (Wikimedia Commons)
Olympic Mishka Bear. Boris Babanov (Wikimedia Commons);
Order of Victory. (Wikimedia Commons);
"Iconostasis" at Domodedovo Airport. Galina Kmit (Wikimedia Commons).

All remaining photos and document images are owned by the author.

BIBLIOGRAPHY

In English

Alexievich, Svetlana. *Secondhand Time: The Last of the Soviets* (Translated by Bela Shayevich). New York: Random House, 2016

Andrew, Christopher and Oleg Gordievsky. *KGB: The Inside Story*. New York: Harper Perennial, 1990

Andrew, Christopher and Vasili Mitrokhin. *The Sword and the Shield: The Mitrokhin Archive and the Secret History of the KGB*. New York: Basics Books, 1999
_____. *The World Was Going Our Way*. Basic Books (AZ), 2005

Arutunyan, Anna. *The Putin Mystique*. Northhampton, Massachusetts: Olive Branch Press, 2015

Baclawski, Joseph A. "The Best Map of Moscow." Washington DC: *CIA Studies in Intelligence*, 1997

Bailey, Thomas A. *America Faces Russia*. Gloucester, Massachusetts: Cornell University Press, 1950 (Reprint 1964)

Baldacci, David. *Simple Genius*. New York, Boston: Warner Books, 2007

Barron, John. *KGB: The Secret Work of Soviet Secret Agents*. New York: Bantam Books, 1974
————————. *Operation Solo*, Chicago: Henry Regnery Company, 1996

Baxter, John and Thomas Atkins. *The Fire Came By*. New York: Doubleday & Company, 1976

Bearden, Milt and James Risen. *The Main Enemy*. New York: Random House, 2003

Berlin, Isaiah. *The Soviet Mind*. Washington DC: Brookings Institution Press, 2004

—————-—. *Russian Thinkers* (Second Edition). London: Penguin Books, 1994

Bidwell, Bruce W. *History of the Military Intelligence Division, Department of the Army General Staff: 1775-1941*. University Publications of America, Inc, 1986

Billington, James R. *The Icon and the Axe: An Interpretive History of Russian Culture*. New York: Vintage Books, 1970

Borman, Donald A., William T. Kvetkas, Charles V. Brown, Michael J. Flatley and Robert Hunt. *The History of Traffic Analysis: World War I – Vietnam*. Fort Meade, Maryland: Center for Cryptologic History, National Security Agency, 2013

Braithwaite, Rodric. *Across the Moscow River*. New Haven and London: Yale University Press, 2002

Brinkley, George. *The Volunteer Army and Allied Intervention in South Russia, 1917-1921*. South Bend, Indiana: University of Notre Dame Press, 1966

Carey, Neil G. *Fighting the Bolsheviks: The Russian War Memoir of Private First Class Donald E. Carey, U.S. Army, 1918-1919*. Novato, California: Presidio Press, 1997

Cherkashin, Victor and Gregory Feifer. *Spy Handler: Memoir of a KGB Officer.* New York: Basic Books, 2005

Conquest, Robert. *The Great Terror: A Reassessment.* Oxford: Oxford University Press, 2008

Crumpton, Henry A. *The Art of Intelligence: Lessons from a Life in the CIA's Clandestine Service.* New York: The Penguin Press, 2012

Davidson-Houston, J.V. *Armed Diplomat: A Military Attaché in Russia.* Suffolk, UK: Robert Hale Limited, 1959

Davies, Joseph E. *Mission to Moscow.* New York: Simon and Schuster, 1941

Deacon, Richard. *The Israeli Secret Service.* London: Sphere Books Limited, 1977/1979.

Deane, John R. *The Strange Alliance.* Bloomington, Indiana and London: Indiana University Press, 1946

De Custine, Marquis Astolphe. *Journey for Our Time.* London: Phoenix Press, 2001

DeMille, Nelson. *The Charm School.* New York: Warner Books, 1988

Devine, Jack. *Good Hunting.* New York: Sarah Crichton Books, Farrar, Straus and Giroux, 2014

Djilas, Milovan. *The New Class.* New York: Praeger, 1957
—————————-. *Conversations with Stalin.* New York: Penguin Classics, 2014

Dobson, Christopher and John Miller. *The Day They Almost Bombed Moscow: The Allied War in Russia 1918-1920*. New York: Atheneum, 1986

Doder, Dusko. *Shadows and Whispers*. New York: Penguin Books, 1986

Dumas, Alexandre. *Adventures in Czarist Russia* (Translated and edited by Alma Elizabeth Murch). New York and Philadelphia: Chilton Company, 1961

Earley, Pete. *Confessions of a Spy: The Real Story of Aldrich Ames*. New York: G.P. Putnam's Sons, 1997

Fischer, John. *Why They Behave Like Russians*. New York and London: Harpers and Brothers, 1946

Freemantle, Brian. *KGB: Inside the World's Largest Intelligence Network*. New York: Holt, Rinehart and Winston, 1982

Garrels, Anne. *Putin Country: A Journey into the Real Russia*. New York: Farrar, Strauss and Giroux, 2016

Goldhurst, Richard. *The Midnight War: The American Intervention in Russia, 1918-1920*. New York: McGraw-Hill Book Company, 1978

Gorokhova, Elena. *A Mountain of Crumbs*. New York, London, Toronto, Sydney: Simon & Schuster, 2009

Gup, Ted. *Book of Honor*. New York: Doubleday, 2000

Halliday, E. M. *The Ignorant Armies*. New York: Bantam Books, 1990 (Original Harpers Bros edition published 1960)

Haslam, Jonathon. *Near and Distant Neighbors: A New History of Soviet Intelligence*. New York: Farrar, Straus and Giroux, 2015

Haynes, John Earl and Harvey Klehr. *Spies: The Rise and Fall of the KGB in America.* New Haven: Yale University Press, 2010

Hilton, Richard. *Military Attaché in Moscow.* London: World Affairs Book Club, 1949

Hingley, Ronald. *The Russian Mind.* New York: Charles Scribner's Sons, 1977

Hoffman, David E. *The Billion Dollar Spy.* New York: Doubleday, 2015

Holbrook, James R. *Potsdam Mission: Memoir of a U.S. Army Intelligence Officer in Communist East Germany.* Bloomington, Indiana: AuthorHouse, 2013

Hood, William. *Mole: The True Story of the First Russian Spy to Become an American Counterspy.* Washington DC: Brasseys (US), 1993

Hope, Bob. *I Owe Russia $1200.* New York: Doubleday & Company, 1963

Infield, Glenn B. *The Poltava Affair.* New York: Macmillon Publishing Co., 1973

Kaiser, Robert. *Russia.* New York: Atheneum, 1976

Kalugin, Oleg (With Fen Montaigne). *The First Directorate.* New York: St. Martin's Press, 1994

Kelly, Laurence. *Diplomacy and Murder in Tehran.* London: Tauris Parke Paperbacks, 2002

Kennan, George F. *The Decision to Intervene.* New York: Atheneum, 1967

Kessler, Ronald. *Spy vs. Spy: Stalking Soviet Spies in America*. New York: Charles Scribner's Sons, 1988

—————————-. *Moscow Station: How the KGB Penetrated the American Embassy*. New York: Charles Scribner's Sons, 1989

Klose, Kevin. *Russia and the Russians: Inside the Closed Society*. New York and London: W.W. Norton & Co., 1984

Knight, Amy. *Spies Without Cloaks: The KGB's Successors*. Princeton, New Jersey: Princeton University Press, 1996

Knightley, Phillip. *The Second Oldest Profession*. New York and London: W. W. Norton and Company, 1986

Lewis, S.J. *"American Military Attachés* in Russia 1914-1917." *War, Revolution, and Peace. Essays in Honor of Charles B. Burdick*. Lanham, Maryland: University Press of America, 1987

Lowenthal, Mark M. *Intelligence: From Secrets to Policy*. Washington, DC: CQ Press, 2000

Ludlum, Robert. *The Moscow Vector*. New York: St. Martin's Paperbacks, 2005

Lyakhovsky, Alexander. *The Tragedy and Valor of Afghan*. Moscow: Iskon, 1995 (Excerpted from the Internet)

Maneki, Sharon. *Learning from the Enemy: The Gunman Project*. Fort Meade, Maryland: NSA Center for Cryptologic History, 2012

McDaniel, Tim. *The Agony of the Russian Idea*. Princeton: Princeton University Press, 1996

Message from Moscow, An Observer [George Feifer]. New York: Vintage Books, NY, 1971

Nagorski, Andrew. *Reluctant Farewell*. New York: Holt, Rinehart and Winston, 1985

O'Toole, G.J.A. *Honorable Treachery: A History of U.S. Intelligence, Espionage, and Covert Action from the American Revolution to the CIA*. New York: The Atlantic Monthly Press, 1993

Pasternak, Boris. *Safe Conduct*. New York: A Signet Book, New American Library, 1959

Perrault, Gilles. *The Red Orchestra*. Reprint ed., New York: Schocken Books, 1989

Peterson, Martha D. *The Widow Spy*, Wilmington, North Carolina: Red Canary Press, 2012

Peterson, Roy. *American Attaché in the Moscow Maelstrom*, Bloomington, Indiana: AuthorHouse, 2005

Powers, Thomas. *Intelligence Wars*. New York: New York Review of Books, 2002

Richardson, Paul E. *Moscow Rules*. Montpelier, Vermont: Edward & Dee, 2011

Richelson, Jeffrey T. *Sword and Shield: Soviet Intelligence and Security Apparatus*. Cambridge, Massachusetts: Ballinger Publishing Company, 1986

Rositzke, Harry. *The KGB: The Eyes of Russia*, New York: Doubleday and Company, 1981

Salisbury, Harrison E. *The 900 Days: The Siege of Leningrad*. New York: Avon Books, 1969

Scanlon, Charles Francis. *In Defense of the Nation: DIA at Forty Year*s. [No publisher or date. Probably DIA, 2001]
————————————. *The Attachés*. Fairfax Station, Virginia: IM Press, Inc., 1997
—————————————. *Attachés* II: Retribution. Fairfax Station, Virginia: IM Press, Inc., 1999

Sheymov, Victor. *Tower of Secrets*. Annapolis, Maryland: Naval Institute Press, 1993

Shipler, David. *Russia: Broken Idols, Solemn Dreams*. New York: Penguin Books, 1984

Silva, Daniel. *Moscow Rules*. New York: A Signet Book, 2009

Silverlight, John. *The Victors' Dilemma*. New York: Weybright and Talley, 1970

Smith, Hedrick. *The Russians*. New York: Ballantine Books, 1976

Smith, Walter Bedell. *My Three Years in Moscow*. Philadelphia and New York: J.B. Lippincott Company, 1950

Standley, William H. and Arthur A. Ageton, *Admiral Ambassador to Russia*. Chicago: Henry Regnery Company, 1955

Starr, S. Frederick. *Red and Hot: Jazz in the Soviet Union*. New York, Oxford: Oxford University Press, 1983

Steinbeck, John. *A Russian Journal*. New York: Penguin Books, 1948

Stevens, Leslie C. *Russian Assignment.* Boston: Little, Brown and Co., 1953

Suvorov, Viktor. *Inside Soviet Military Intelligence.* New York: Macmillan, 1984
————————-. Inside the Soviet Army. New York: Berkeley Books, 1984
————————-. *Inside the Aquarium.* New York: Macmillan, 1986
————————-. *Spetsnaz: The Inside Story of Soviet Special Forces.* New York: Pocketbooks, 1990

Thayer, Charles W. *Bears in the Caviar.* Montpelier, Vermont: Russian Life Books, 1950, 2015

Tolley, Kemp. *Caviar and Commissars: The Experiences of a U.S. Naval Officer in Stalin's Russia.* Annapolis, Maryland: Naval Institute Press, 2003 (Originally published in 1983)

Vagts, Alfred. *The Military Attaché.* Princeton, New Jersey: Princeton University Press, 1967

Voinovich, Vladimir. *Moscow 2042.* New York and London: Harcourt Brace Jovanovich Publishers, 1987

Voyce, Arthur. *Moscow and the Roots of Russian Culture.* Norman, Oklahoma: University of Oklahoma Press, 1964

Waters, W. H. H. *"Secret and Confidential": The Experiences of a Military Attaché.* New York: Frederick A. Stokes Company Publishers, 1926

Westerfield, H. Bradford. *Inside CIA's Private World.* New Haven and London: Yale University Press, 1995

Wise, David. *Cassidy's Run.* New York: Random House, 2000

Woodward, Bob. *VEIL: The Secret Wars of the CIA.* New York: Simon and Schuster, 1987

Zacharias, Ellis. *Secret Missions.* Annapolis, Maryland: Naval Institute Press, 1946

In Russian

Баташев, Алексей. *Советский джаз* (Soviet Jazz). Москва: Музыка, 1972

Holbrook, James R. "Золотой век России еще впереди» (Russia's Golden Age is Still Ahead), Interview in *Red Star,* 10 March 1994

Красильников, Рэм. *Призраки с улицы Чайковского: шпионские акции ЦРУ США в Советском Союзе и Российской Федерации в 1979-1992 годах* (Ghosts From Chaikovsky Street: Spy Files of the CIA in the Soviet Union and Russia in 1979-1992). ГЕЯ ИТЭРУМ, Москва, 1999

Медведев, Александр и Ольга Медведева (Редакторы и составители). *Советский джаз: проблемы, события, мастера* (Soviet Jazz: Problems, Events, Masters). Москва: Советский композитер, 1987

Москва в цифрах 1990 (Moscow in Numbers, 1990). Moscow City Directorate of Statistics, 1990

INDEX

S

Sakharov, Andrei 194
Salisbury, Harrison 109, 362
SALT II 57, 73, 108, 215, 258,
    265, 266, 353
Samovar 124
Sandul, Michael L. 335
Santa Claus 54, 55
Saratov University 63
Sardelka 173
Savicheva, Tanya 109
Scali, John 177
Science Applications
    International Corporation
    (SAIC) 325, 327, 328
Second Main Directorate 88
Second World War (WWII) 17,
    52, 186, 194, 240
Sergiev Posad 134, 135, 136
Sergius of Radonezh 135
Seventh Main Directorate 88
Sheremetyevo Airport 7, 28, 57
Shipler, David 275, 362
Shostakovich, Dmitri 186
Shuttle Bombing 130
Siberia 11, 18, 83, 85, 94, 95,
    115, 116, 138
"Siberian Seven" 15
SIGINT (Signals Intelligence)
    xiv, 24, 328
Sizemore, William 22
Skinheads 232, 235
Smith, Walter Bedell 17, 362

Smolensk 102, 104, 105,
    121, 241
Snegurochka 54, 55
Sochi 150
Sokolniki 173, 174
Sokolov, Sergei 32
Solidarity 216, 220, 258, 260,
    265, 272
Solzhenitsyn, Alexander 33
Soviet Army 9, 21, 24, 27, 28,
    50, 59, 96, 123, 184,
    216, 225, 232, 295, 312,
    327, 363
Soviet Civil War 93
Soviet Employees 15, 16, 54,
    199, 305
Soviet Ministry of Defense
    (MOD) 22, 89, 157, 206
Soviet Republics 81, 122, 123,
    138, 145, 149, 205, 227
Spaso House 3, 5, 6, 16, 19, 61,
    66, 141, 189, 190, 200,
    212, 213, 259, 315, 353
Spassky Gate 243
Spy Dust 11, 12, 13
Standley, William 17, 362
Starr, Frederick 185, 316, 353
Steinbeck, John 32, 39, 362
Storyville 185
Subbotnik 40, 71
Sudarmardi, Colonel 204
Sukhodrev, Viktor 212
Sukhumi 149, 150, 151
Surveillance 14, 21, 22, 30, 38,
    39, 88, 97, 106, 111, 117,